D1257983

THE DYNAMICS
OF SOCIAL MOVEMENTS

Previous *Frontiers of Sociology* Symposia

Date of Conference	Title and Publisher	Director-Editor	Publication Year
1969	*Power in Organizations,* Vanderbilt University Press	M. N. Zald	1970
1970	*Racial Tensions and National Identity,* Vanderbilt University Press	Ernest Campbell	1972
1974	*The Labelling of Deviance: Evaluating a Perspective,* Halsted Publications	Walter Gove	1975
1975	*The Production of Culture,* American Behavioral Scientist and Sage Publications	Richard Peterson	1976

THE DYNAMICS
OF SOCIAL MOVEMENTS

Resource Mobilization, Social Control,
and Tactics

Edited by

Mayer N. Zald
University of Michigan

John D. McCarthy
Catholic University of America, and
Boys Town Center for Youth Development

Winthrop Publishers, Inc.
Cambridge, Massachusetts

Library of Congress Cataloging in Publication Data

Main entry under title:

The dynamics of social movements.

  Bibliography: p.
  Includes index.
  1. Social movements—Addresses, essays, lectures.
2. Infrastructure (Economics)—Addresses, essays,
lectures. 3. Social control—Addresses, essays,
lectures. I. Zald, Mayer N II. McCarthy,
John David,   date
HN16.D96   301.24′2   79-1393
ISBN 0-87626-200-0

Cover design by Katy Homans

© *1979 by Winthrop Publishers, Inc.*
  17 Dunster Street, Cambridge, Massachusetts 02138

10   9   8   7   6   5   4   3   2   1

Contents

Preface vii

INTRODUCTION 1

I COLLECTIVE ACTION AND THE RESPONSE
  OF AUTHORITIES 6

Utilitarian Logic in the Resource Mobilization
Perspective
  Bruce Fireman and William A. Gamson 8

Protracted Conflict
  Anthony Oberschall 45

Media and Movements
  Harvey Molotch 71

External Efforts to Damage or Facilitate Social
Movements: Some Patterns, Explanations,
Outcomes, and Complications
  Gary T. Marx 94

Repertoires of Contention in America and
Britain, 1750–1830
  Charles Tilly 126

II   MOBILIZATION AND TACTICS
       IN CONTEMPORARY MOVEMENTS   156

White-Hot Mobilization: Strategies of a
Millenarian Movement
     John Lofland   157

Resource Mobilization and Strategy: A Model for
Analyzing Social Movement Organization Actions
     Jo Freeman   167

III   THE COURSE AND OUTCOMES
       OF SOCIAL MOVEMENTS   190

The Sixties Observed
     Charles Perrow   192

Strategies for Investigating Violence and Social Change:
Illustrations from Analyses of Racial Disorders and
Implications for Mobilization Research
     David Snyder and William R. Kelly   212

EPILOGUE: AN AGENDA FOR RESEARCH   238

Bibliography   247

Notes on Contributing Authors   259

Index   261

Preface

This volume contains revisions of papers delivered at the fifth *Frontiers of Sociology* symposium held on the Vanderbilt University campus, March 17–18, 1977. It had become apparent to us that in the last several years a number of scholars had become disenchanted with the collective behavior conceptualization in the study of social movements. They were moving toward a resource mobilization approach that nested the study of social movements more closely in the central political processes of the society. The resource mobilization approach deemphasizes grievances and focuses upon societal supports and constraints of movements, tactical dilemmas, social control, media usage, and the interplay of external supports and elites.

Although there were a number of scholars considering roughly parallel problems, there had been relatively little direct communication among them. The conference was organized to facilitate such an interchange. We wanted to discover the limits of the approach: What areas of social movement analysis needed more attention? What methodological issues were posed by the approach?

In organizing the conference, we attempted to include a number of different emphases. We expected the resource mobilization perspective to be useful to scholars studying specific social movements. So, we commissioned papers from scholars studying the women's movement and a modern millenarian movement. It seemed desirable to include theoretical papers that both criticized and synthesized the resource mobilization perspective and extended it into new areas. The theoretical papers range from a critique and extension of Olson's *Logic of Collective Action* to a use of a rational choice model to examine protracted and intensive conflict. Finally, we were aware of some of the large gaps in the literature on social movements that had been previously highlighted by the resource mobilization perspective. Although it was impossible to commission papers that addressed all of these topics (see the Epilogue), several papers were commissioned that begin to fill some of these gaps. The papers on the mechanics of external social control and on measuring the outcomes and effects of social movements are examples.

We asked several scholars to critique the papers. These included Myra Marx Feree, John Howard, Joan Lind, Mancur Olson, Anthony Orum, Amos Perlmutter, Richard Peterson, and Gary Wamsley. After the conference the authors revised their papers, in many cases taking into account the criticisms of the discussants. Resources for the conference came from several sources—a grant from the Vanderbilt University Research Council, a grant from the Shell Foundation to the Department of Sociology, and, primarily, a grant from the National Science Foundation (NSF: 76–16819). We are especially indebted to Patsy Doherty, Susan Hershey, and Cindy Miller for their help in organizing the conference and bringing this manuscript to light.

THE DYNAMICS
OF SOCIAL MOVEMENTS

INTRODUCTION

For quite some time a hiatus existed in the study of social movements in the United States. Leaders of activist movements (here and abroad) attempted to enunciate general principles of movement tactics, strategy, and movement dilemmas in overcoming hostile environments. Such leaders as Mao, Lenin, Saul Alinsky, and Martin Luther King have each in turn attempted to develop principles and guidelines for action. These theories stress problems of mobilization, the manufacture of discontent, tactical choices and the infrastructure of society, and movements necessary for success. At the same time, sociologists, with their emphasis upon structural strain, generalized belief, and deprivation, have largely ignored the ongoing problems and strategic dilemmas of social movements.

Recently a number of social scientists have begun to articulate an approach to social movements, the *resource mobilization approach*, which begins to take seriously many of the questions that have concerned social movement leaders and practical theorists. Without attempting to write handbooks for social change (or for the suppression of social change), the new approach deals in general terms with the dynamics and tactics of social movement growth, decline, and change. Accordingly, it provides a corrective to the practical theorists, who naturally are most concerned with justifying their own tactical choices; and it also adds realism, power, and depth to the truncated research on and analysis of social movements offered by many social scientists.

The resource mobilization approach emphasizes both societal support and constraint of social movement phenomena. It examines the variety of resources that must be mobilized, the linkages of social movements to other groups, the dependence of movements upon third parties for success, and the tactics used by authorities to control or incorporate movements. The shift in emphasis is evident in much of the work that has been published recently in this area (John Wilson, 1973; Tilly, 1973, 1975; Gamson, 1975; Oberschall, 1973; Lipsky, 1968; Downs, 1972; McCarthy and Zald, 1973*b*). The new approach depends more upon political, sociological, and economic theories than upon the social psychology of collective behavior. Let us highlight some of the issues that need to be explored as the resource mobilization approach is developed.

GRIEVANCE, COSTS AND INCENTIVES

Social movement theory has shared with interest group theory the assumption that people will act upon their interests (or deprivations). Mancur Olson (1965), examining interest groups, has seriously questioned this assumption. Essentially he argues that successful interest groups provide collective goods alike to both their members and those who share certain categorical characteristics with members. All members of the social category will receive benefits if the movement succeeds. Therefore, all social movements have free rider problems; it makes little sense for any one individual to incur the costs of participation when his own personal benefits are likely to be small and when, in any case, he will receive the benefits of success from the activities of others.

Anthony Oberschall (1973) builds on Olson's work as he argues that risk-reward considerations are central to understanding mobilization. Not only apathy and false consciousness explain the failure of extremely deprived individuals to be mobilized. Instead, the absence of expendable resources and fear of incurring costs lead extremely deprived groups to be dependent upon external supports for their mobilization. At each stage of analysis, the balance of costs-rewards for members and leaders is crucial to explaining the degree and types of mobilization.

RESOURCE CUMULATION

When resources are considered at all in classical approaches they are thought to come from the group incurring strain. But historical examples lead us to argue that crucial and extensive resources may be obtained from sources external to the group undergoing strain. The modern civil rights movement in the United States, the Russian revolution of 1917, and the American abolitionist movement of the nineteenth century each depended upon external supports at crucial points and for long duration (Marx and Useem, 1971). External support may be based upon altruistic or malicious motives; but the important point is that social movement theory must be prepared to look outside the confrontation of movement beneficiaries and opponents.

Leites and Wolf (1970) use straightforward economic analysis to examine the support bases of guerrilla movements. They argue that a "hearts and minds" approach to guerrilla movements predicts that reducing the frustration and deprivation of peasants by raising their income will reduce their support of guerrilla movements. Leites and Wolf treat the guerrilla movement as an economic producer and the peasant as a buyer of services. As the peasant's income rises, income effects occur; he can now buy a more diversified basket of goods. No matter whether he identifies with the movement or is afraid of it, more income allows him to supply some of it (because he likes the movement or to buy protection for himself and his family) to the movement.

ORGANIZATIONAL COMPETITION AND PRODUCTION DILEMMAS

Many analyses of social movements (including Oberschall's) make little distinction between the social movement and the social movement organizations that form to mobilize and combine resources for social change. Yet both revolutionary and reform movements are often characterized by a host of competing-cooperating organizations. (See Zald and Ash, 1966; Killian, 1972). At the same time each organization must combine resources (men, money, and machines) to produce programs and tactics that mobilize more support and effect organizational goals.

There are, as well as a division of labor amongst social movement organizations, competition and battles for a symbolic hegemony over the movement. Extremism in one part of the movement helps leaders in another part.

LEGITIMACY BARGAINING AND MEDIA USAGE

If support is mobilized from outside the group that experiences deprivation, communication processes and the mobilization of third-party support must become a central focus. In modern society the mass media are a major forum for this communication. Movement leaders and organizations seek to use the media to portray grievances and to engage in legitimacy and credibility bargaining with their opponents. Hubbard (1968) has analyzed the competition for legitimacy in the eyes of the nation that occurred between Martin Luther King and southern sheriffs. Media portrayal played a central role in the competition.

Lipsky's (1968) analysis of protest as a political resource in mobilizing diverse audiences and reference elites and Turner's (1969) analysis of the public perception of protest also contribute a key component of resource mobilization analysis. Authorities respond to protest not alone through fear of the direct political and violence potential of the movement, but also because of the activation of a reference public and elites who in turn control resources relevant to the authorities. Though this is recognized in some analyses of revolutionary situations (where the neutrality of major groups is seen as crucial), it rarely is considered as an analytic issue in the study of reform social movement organizations.

ISSUE ELASTICITIES AND CYCLES

What activates reference publics and elites? Why does an atrocity in one decade receive bland acceptance and in another crystalize movement activity? What are the mechanisms of selection amongst issues, and why do some issues remain prominent longer than others? Classical analyses focus upon one movement at a time; only when movements coalesce in a revolutionary situation or in a major period of turmoil are pan-movement activities treated. The concepts of issue elasticity and issue cycles are relevant to these concerns.

Strickland and Johnson (1970) present an abstract analysis of the elasticity and inelasticity of political issues. Issue elasticity parallels the economic concept of price elasticity: in their analysis elasticity is the amount of change in political commitment (behavior) as issues change. One can conceive of perfect inelasticity and perfect elasticity for individuals or groups. Furthermore, one can begin to think of the complementarity and substitutability of issues, satiation effects, and the like. Families of issues and overlap of issue commitment can be treated.

Issue elasticity is related to media arousal, and social movement organizations have a stake in this arousal. Anthony Downs (1972) has analyzed "issue-attention" cycles. A problem is discovered, audience attention is attracted, euphoric solutions are suggested, some change is attempted, the stubborn and extensive costs of change are encountered, and the problem moves to the background. Social movements exist and may be maintained even when the media do not focus upon them. Yet in a society where movement success in mobilizing resources and in affecting authorities depends to some extent upon arousing constituencies through the media, issue-attention cycles become predictors of movement and organizational success. The greater the competition from other issues, the greater the likelihood that the movement must allocate resources to maintain audiences, and the less ability it has to sustain continuing support.

REGIME STRUCTURE AND THE CONTROL OF MOVEMENTS

It should be apparent that authorities do not just respond to social movements, but shape the direction or very existence of movements. They can repress, partially incorporate, give symbolic reassurance to, and even use the apparatus of the state to foster movements or the direction of movements. Yet an examination of social movement textbooks will find little mention of this topic. Whether we examine the suppression of liberty in totalitarian regimes or the fostering of the War on Poverty by the Johnson administration, it is apparent that this is an important topic, too important to be ignored. Gamson's book *Power and Discontent* (1968) brought the relation of authorities and partisans to center stage. Even more relevant to us are works such as that of Tilly (1978) which see the structure and response of the regime and the institutions surrounding it as central to the social movement life of society.

MOVEMENT OUTCOMES

Finally, the outcomes and effects of social movements must be dealt with. Social movements may mobilize great energies, yet the energy may be dissipated. On the other hand, social movements may catalyze wide-scale social change. Including authorities and societal response as central issues in the task of movement analysis suggests that much more systematic attention be given to direct and indirect outcomes of social movements both on the participants and upon the society and governance of societies.

The papers in this volume touch upon many of the issues raised above. However, the papers are loosely organized into three sections. The first section includes essays on collective action and the response of authorities. The second section includes two papers that apply a resource mobilization approach to contemporary social movements. The third section includes papers dealing with the course and outcomes of social movements.

I

COLLECTIVE ACTION AND THE RESPONSE OF AUTHORITIES

OVERVIEW

The agenda for theory and conceptual development in the area of social movements includes the development of formal models of social movement process and the elaboration of concepts and theory to treat specific aspects of social movements. The papers in this section are of both kinds.

The first two papers, those of Fireman and Gamson and of Oberschall, deal directly with the collective choice and collective goods aspect of social movements. Fireman and Gamson critique and extend Olson's model of collective action. In doing so they develop a model of collective action that gives a more prominent weight to solidary incentives. They also argue that the collective goods provided by social movements vary in the extent to which they are provided to large groups, many of whom may not participate in the pursuit of those goods, or to only those who are part of the movement or movement organization. Treating the issues of collective goods, joint supply, and free riders as variables permits one to make predictions about the kinds of mobilization problems that different movements will confront.

Oberschall's discussion of protracted conflict suggests the utility of a formal, rational choice model to analyze some of the most deadly conflicts of recent years. The issue he raises is whether a formal model can illuminate such enduring crises as Northern Ireland, Lebanon, and Israel. Oberschall exposes a hidden logic in what often seems an irrational social process. He examines the individual and collective costs and benefits of options for both insurgents and authorities (in his terms, challengers and target).

Gary Marx and Harvey Molotch focus upon two key aspects of the facilitation and control of movements. Marx pays detailed attention to the techniques used by government agents to suppress and control social movements in the sixties. Drawing upon revelations of CIA, FBI, and police activities, he catalogues the myriad ways in which agents attempted to disrupt the civil rights and antiwar movements. Yet because in many ways these movements were successful, the effectiveness of these tactics is called into question. Marx concludes with a speculative discussion of the conditions under which attempts to control movements may be more or less successful.

Harvey Molotch discusses the extent to which the media can shape the images of movements. Reasoning from a class perspective that sees the media as in the hands of a ruling (though not unified) elite, Molotch argues that the agenda and images of movement activists are shaped less by the activities of the movement than by the media's decisions of "newsworthiness." They are complex mixes of political and social values and competitive desires to reach and hold audiences.

The final paper in the section, by Charles Tilly, develops the notion of a repertoire of contention. Drawing upon content analyses of newspapers in Britain and the United States, Tilly argues three fundamental points. First, the forms of contention, whether movements march, petition, assemble, or boycott, differ over time. Second, movement participants use standard forms and innovate not only *what* they will contend about, the substantive issues, but *how* they will contend, the methods of contention. Third, the selection of a repertoire is shaped and channeled by the response of authorities. Whether one boycotts or assembles is partially dictated by the costs imposed by authorities upon boycotts and assemblies. Over time the courts and authorities shape the modes of contentious alternatives.

Utilitarian Logic in the Resource Mobilization Perspective

Bruce Fireman and William A. Gamson

INTRODUCTION

Beware of economists bearing gifts. Their models are catching the fancy of a number of sociologists interested in social movements (e.g., Oberschall, 1973; McCarthy and Zald, 1973b, 1977; Tilly, 1978). We welcome the focus on resources, organization, and strategic interaction; and it is refreshing to get away from the concern with irrationality that blinded sociologists to problems of resource mobilization. But the economists' models carry their own set of blinders.

In the study of collective action, utilitarian assumptions and the conceptual imagery of economics are most useful when relevant interests are given, concrete, and selfish. Perhaps resource mobilization by business firms proceeds under roughly these conditions, but the mobilization of social movements often hinges on changing interests, changing opportunities and threats to interests, and changing inclinations to act on group interests rather than individual ones. Such matters tend to be obscured by utilitarian models, if not ignored altogether.

We try to unravel several problems with utilitarian approaches to social movements, by considering Mancur Olson's influential *Logic of Collective Action*. In fairness to Olson, we should note that he meant to account for the mobilization of long-standing unions, lobbies, and interest groups; he did not mean to account for the mobilization of collective action that is more drastic or short-lived. However, the thrust

We are grateful for comments on an earlier draft of this paper from Ronald Aminzade, Carol Conell, Myra Marx Feree, Anne Locksley, M. J. Maynes, John McCarthy, Mancur Olson, Michael Polen, Steven Rytine, Jan Smith, and Charles Tilly.

of the field in recent years has been to abandon sharp distinctions between dramatic social movements and other political organizations. Now, it may be worth considering the circumstances in which Olson's utilitarian logic does not fit social movements, or for that matter, collective action in general.

Olson was helpful in demonstrating that rational people with common interests do not automatically pursue them collectively. It is often difficult for people to get together and pool resources. Mobilization requires enterprise and effort. But when we investigate the strategy and tactics of organizers, we find Olson's logic misleading. We find that only in special circumstances is it both possible and worthwhile to use "selective incentives" to get people to struggle for common interests. More often, when events and organizers mobilize people, it is because they build solidarity, raise consciousness of common interests, and create opportunities for collective action.

So, we begin this essay with a critical look at how utilitarian logic has been applied to the mobilization of collective action. We go on to suggest that an alternative approach offers more promising ground for advancing research within the resource mobilization perspective.

RESOURCE MOBILIZATION AND
UTILITARIAN LOGIC

Research from the resource mobilization perspective finds people's shared grievances, interests, and aspirations considerably less problematic than their capacity to act on them collectively. From this perspective, the key question asked of a social movement is no longer, "Why do these people want social change so badly and believe that it is possible?" but rather, "How can these people organize, pool resources, and wield them effectively?"

It might seem that for a good part of our answer to the latter question, we would soon return to the former one. After all, isn't it easier to bring people into a social movement when they find the movement's goals and strategies worthwhile? Surely, the less concerned are potential constituents about the social change the movement is demanding, the more difficult it is for the movement to organize them. So, shouldn't students and organizers of mobilization focus their concern on the substance and intensity of shared grievances, interests, and aspirations?

Perhaps not—at least not if we accept the implications of Olson's *Logic of Collective Action* (1965). Oberschall (1973) and McCarthy and Zald (1977) apply Olson's logic specifically to social movements. They suggest that a theory of mobilization should focus on the costs and benefits selectively meted out to potential constituents, contingent upon whether or not they contribute to collective action. Shared grievances and interests may warrant less attention for one of several possible reasons.

First, people look out for their personal self-interest. They act collectively only if they are provided with selective incentives. Or, second, everywhere there is an abundance of interests to be realized and injustices to be protested. They may help us delimit the groups "at risk" to mobilization, but they do not help us select which potential groups we expect to mobilize a great deal, a little, or not at all. Or, third, perhaps changes in the substance and intensity of shared interests affect the propensity of potential groups to mobilize, but not in decisive ways. "Objective" interests change only with long-run historical processes; their impact upon the rapid dynamics of mobilization is mediated by processes that are more proximate and variable. "Subjective" interests may vary in the short run, but they are less problematic than the various forces that shape them. In other words, collective interests are either not proximate enough or not problematic enough to occupy center stage in the study of social movements.

We find these arguments dubious.[1] We don't deny that mobilization is heavily influenced by a number of factors slighted in traditional social movement research: the amount of resources at the discretion of potential constituents, the degree of previously existing organization among potential constituents, the configuration of allies and enemies, the social control policies of authorities, the strategy and tactics of organizers, and —overall—the structure of the political economy constraining the mobilization and wielding of resources.

But the impact of these factors upon mobilization for collective action is often mediated more by changes in group interests than by changes in the provision of "selective incentives," more by assessments of collective efficacy than by assessments of individual efficacy, more by solidarity and principle than by individual self-interest.

Before going into the argument, we should indicate what we mean by some key terms: "collective good," "selective incentive," "actor," and "collective action." Any good or service or state of affairs is a *collective good* insofar as all those in any given group can benefit from it (or enjoy it), regardless of whether they help to pay the cost of providing it. For example, a change in government policy, or a change in working conditions, is a collective good for everyone who wants it to happen. In this paper the redress of shared grievances, the realization of shared interests, the achievement of whatever is justified by shared beliefs—these matters are considered collective goods for all who share the grievances, interests, or beliefs.

Selective incentives are constraints or inducements that an individual actor may gain or lose contingent upon whether the actor contributes to collective action. *Actors* are persons, as well as organizations with tight decision-making and social control mechanisms. We assume here (for the sake of argument) that actors may be interested in the realization of various states of affairs much as they may be interested in the possession of various commodities. We assume further that the degree to which they are interested in each of a variety of relevant collective goods and selective incentives can be measured in comparable units. *Collective action* is struggle to bring about collective goods, struggle that involves organizing actors and mobilizing resources. *Collective actors* are organizers and formal organizations whose primary purpose is to carry on such struggles.

Consider the first and strongest of the three arguments cited above to explain why grievances and interests may be removed from center stage in the study of collective action. Olson argues that people act collectively only when there are "selective incentives" for them to do so (1965). He takes a utilitarian model of behavior in a market economy and applies it to collective action in general:

> The rational individual in the economic system does not curtail his spending to prevent inflation . . . because he knows, first, that his own efforts would not have a noticeable effect, and second, that he would get the benefits of any price stability that others achieved in any case. For the same two reasons, the rational individual in a socio-political context will not be willing to make any sacrifices to achieve the objectives he shares with others. [P. 166]

> Only a *separate and "selective"* incentive will stimulate a rational individual in a (large) group to act in a group-oriented way . . . group action can be obtained only through an incentive that operates, not indiscriminately, like the collective good, upon the group as a whole, but rather *selectively* toward the individuals in the group. [P. 151]

Olson concludes both that common interest in collective goods is not sufficient to bring a large group of actors together for collective action and that the provision of selective incentives is necessary. So mild a conclusion may be surprising. Much stronger conclusions are there to be derived from the utilitarian assumption on which he relies. If individuals are thoroughly self-interested and rational, common interests are *unnecessary* to collective action as well as insufficient—in fact, they are irrelevant. Furthermore, the provision of selective incentives not only is necessary to produce collective action but is *sufficient*.

What implications could social movement organizers draw from the utilitarian logic of collective action? Evidently it is a waste of time for organizers to demonstrate to potential constituents that their goals are worthwhile and their strategy is viable. Consciousness-raising cannot move actors whose pursuit of self-interest is unflagging. It seems that movement propaganda should advertise selective incentives rather than justify program and strategy.

Furthermore, when organizers target potential constituents for organizing drives, they need not be concerned with who may be most interested in the collective goods they are trying to bring about. They need only be concerned with who may be most interested in the selective incentives they can offer. Social movement organizations should often find themselves competing with other organizations for the resources of their potential constituents. There is no reason to expect this competition to come only from other collective actors. Social movement organizations are actually at a competitive disadvantage in providing selective incentives, compared to businesses, social clubs, and the Mafia, for example. None of these organizations is saddled with the burden of diverting resources for the provision of collective goods; they can offer better deals in the selective incentives market.

In fact, much of the collective action cited by Olson as evidence for his argument was mobilized by organizers who were at a competitive disadvantage in the selective incentives market, compared to their own antagonists. Consider the struggles that established the first big unions. Employers could hire, promote, or fire workers according to their stances toward the union. If union organizers could try to coerce wavering workers to honor picket lines, employers could hire scabs and thugs to disrupt them. Employers could often call on the government for help. And when employers chose to wield the "carrot" in addition to the "stick," they had the resources to provide more "social incentives" (e.g., status symbols and sociable occasions) and fringe benefits than those a struggling union could offer.

Olson does not explicitly portray the actors who join in collective action as though they scramble for individual benefits in a wide open market where collective actors would be well advised to advertise selective incentives rather than programs. But the assumptions underlying his conclusions do imply so crude a picture. If it is hard to believe that collective actors do their mobilizing in a selective incentives market, and if it is hard to believe that an actor's interest in collective goods is irrelevant to his propensity to join in collective action, then we must question Olson's conclusion that selective incentives are necessary for collective action.

Perhaps the appeal of the *Logic of Collective Action* to those who study social movements lies not in the plausibility of its assumptions or conclusions, but rather in the questions it suggests for our research agenda:

1. Of the many groups that could possibly mobilize to struggle for collective goods, how is it that some are able to mobilize a great deal, others much less, and many not at all?
2. How do actors assess what may be gained and lost through collective action, and how do such assessments shape their decisions to join in it?
3. How can mobilization be facilitated by "resourceful actors"— often previously established organizations and experienced organizers who control crucial resources?

These are good questions. But Olson's delimitation of groups at risk to mobilization, his handling of the free rider problem, and his treatment of resourceful actors present serious difficulties. We discuss these difficulties as a prelude to later discussion of an alternative approach.

Who Is at Risk to Mobilization

Take as a problem the investigation of a population at time t 1 in order to predict for time t what groups will be engaged in collective action. If the time interval is long enough (say a year or five years), it may be that a number of organizations engaged in collective action at time t did not even exist at time t 1, and it may be that some interests pursued fervently at t weren't articulated or even sensed at t 1. Until we specify the purpose and the theory underlying the investigation, it is not clear what combinations of people, organizations, roles, statuses, objective interests, and/or subjective interests extant in the population at time t 1 we should investigate to see if they give rise to collective action at t.

In *Logic of Collective Action* the entities at risk to mobilization are "groups"—defined as aggregates of individuals sharing common interests. More precisely, Olson considers an aggregate of actors to be at risk to mobilization when some collective good is worth more to each "group" member than his share of what it would cost to bring about the good were all "group" members to contribute their shares. He also suggests that already mobilized organizations tend to demobilize— perish, even—if they fail to serve the common interests of their members. So according to Olson, a group has the potential to mobilize or to survive as a viable collective actor when the total worth (to group members) of the collective goods exceeds the total cost (to group members) of the collective action it takes to bring them about.

But then Olson goes on to argue that the group will not realize this potential unless its members are provided with selective incentives. He states that in order to facilitate mobilization, the value of the selective incentives (in terms of each individual's preferences) must be greater than the individual's share of the cost of collective action. This is a bold assertion. Evidently Olson believes that until the worth of the collective good exceeds the cost of collective action, mobilization is out of the question; but once that threshold is exceeded, further increase in the worth of the collective good is irrelevant. From then on, mobilization hinges only on the worth of the selective incentives.

Olson's utilitarian assumptions are so heavy that they vitiate his initial method of selecting groups to investigate. After all, if the value of the selective incentives must exceed the cost of joining in collective action, then why be concerned with common interest in collective goods when selecting groups to investigate? Even actors who are thoroughly indifferent to the collective good would be apt to participate in collective action if offered selective incentives worth more than the cost of participation. (We don't doubt that social movement organizers provide such valuable selective incentives when they have the capacity to gain by doing so; we do doubt that they generally have this capacity, and we doubt that they generally need it to succeed.) It is possible that many social processes may be best understood with a theory positing that one variable only limits the outcomes while another variable only selects within the limits. But we can think of no good reason why actors' common interest in collective goods should preclude their mobilization when it is below a threshold level, yet be irrelevant above that level.

It would not help matters to abandon common interests altogether and move to a thoroughly utilitarian analysis of the limits that determine who is at risk to mobilization. It might make sense to do so were we studying the "mobilization" of labor by business firms. The unemployed, for example, are especially at risk to mobilization by a business offering pay for work, regardless of how much they are interested in the goods that business is trying to produce. But does it make sense to assume that people in need of the selective incentives that a social movement can offer are especially at risk to mobilization, regardless of what social change the movement is trying to produce? Whether one's taste for chocolate affects one's propensity to take a job in a chocolate factory, surely one's taste for civil rights affects one's propensity to join in a civil rights movement.

Later we argue that a number of factors, including interest in individual goods, interest in collective goods, and solidarity with others interested in collective goods, may all move actors to mobilize for collective action. Our discussion of how this is so centers on solidary groups —each a network of actors linked by relations to be described below, each with broad interests that conflict at key points with those of other groups, and each with members who may be more or less "resourceful." Long run predictions about who will mobilize what kind of collective action can only emerge from historical analysis of how economic and geopolitical forces (often themselves the outcome of past collective action) structure and interrelate these solidary groups. Short-run predictions about mobilization can rest on analysis of how particular events confront solidary groups with concrete threats and opportunities, how they raise group members' consciousness of common interests, and how they raise group members' loyalty to the collective actors who defend common interests.

One could assume a set of actors to be at risk to mobilization to the degree that they are a solidary group, to the degree that they face concrete opportunities and threats to their interests, and to the degree that some resourceful actors (inside or outside the group) are interested in having them mobilize. There is no marked threshold level with any of these factors below which groups are incapable of mobilizing. The same factors that delimit the potential mobilizers also select the actual mobilizers.

Although Olson chose potential mobilizers differently, our objection is less to his choice of groups to consider than to his claim that want of selective incentives is what keeps most of them from mobilizing. He concludes the book by commenting that "large unorganized groups not only provide evidence for the basic argument of this study: they also suffer if it is true." They do suffer. But their silence cannot tell us why they fail to mobilize. Unmobilized groups are a problem for investigation, but their continued existence cannot be evidence for any explanation of itself.

The Free Rider Problem

We are persuaded that calculations of what may be gained and lost through collective action are very important to actors' decisions to join in collective action. But contrary to utilitarian logic, we think that actors assess what their *group* may gain or lose as well as what they may gain or lose as individuals.

At the heart of the utilitarian approach to collective action is the "free rider" problem. The idea is that it makes little sense for an actor to join in collective action when he can "ride free" on the efforts of others. The free rider argument is developed, in large part, by the pursuit of two analogies. First and foremost, actors with common interests are compared to firms in a competitive market. Second, groups that do successfully mobilize are compared to governments. Despite strong common interests, firms in the competitive market do not act collectively. And despite much legitimacy, patriotism, and loyalty, governments rely on coercion to raise revenues and armies. Olson draws the wrong lesson from each of these analogies.

There is a concise statement of the first analogy in the argument of Olson's quoted above: "The rational individual in the economic system does not curtail his spending to prevent inflation because he knows, first, that his own efforts would not have a noticeable effect, and second, that he would get the benefits of any price stability that others achieved in any case. For the same two reasons, the rational individual in the large group in a socio-political context will not be willing to make any sacrifices to achieve the objectives he shares with others" (p. 166).

We submit that it makes little sense to attribute the failure of this rational individual to curtail spending to the two reasons that Olson gives. The individual is likely to have the quite plausible expectation that there will not be enough other people curtailing spending to produce any effect. Olson's reasons become relevant only if the individual is faced with collective action that stands a chance of success. By and large, it is reasonable for the individual to expect that the actors who share his interests will not mobilize effectively when they lack the organization to communicate and coordinate commitments.

When it does seem that collective action will actually take place and may succeed, would-be free riders may present problems for organizers and students of collective action. How should they be dealt with? Olson's answer is selective incentives, but what of ideology, class consciousness, and solidarity? Olson presents the analogy of the state: "despite the force of patriotism, the appeal of national ideology, the bond of a common culture . . . no major state in modern history has been able to support itself through voluntary dues or contributions . . ." (p. 13).

If any lesson is to be drawn from this unfortunate fact, it is not that selective incentives are necessary for collective action; it is rather that organizations powerful enough to force contributions from constituents will do so. However, most social movement organizations are poor in the resources necessary to impose taxes or a draft. And unlike governments, social movements vary considerably in their capacity to tolerate free riders. When three hundred thousand antiwar demonstrators turned out for a march on Washington during the sixties, they were not hamstrung by the existence of millions of free riders—people who wanted the demonstration to be big and effective but didn't show up. On the other hand, the Tobacco Night Riders had much to lose and little to gain unless they could control their free riders—the farmers who sold tobacco directly to the tobacco trust instead of marketing it through the Planters' Protective Association (see Gamson, 1975). Free riders pose different kinds of problems in different kinds of struggles.

Some of the factors that affect a collective action's tolerance for free riders include the cost to participants if collective action fails, the fraction of the constituency necessary for success, the visibility of the constituency's boundaries and common interests, the amount of middle ground between active support for collective action and direct aid to its target, the degree to which the collective good sought by the movement is "exclusive," [2] and the degree to which free riding violates specific commitments and norms.

Free riders are least tolerable in a struggle, when failure would be costly to participants and the chances of success do not amount to much until a large fraction of a readily identifiable constituency is mobilized. For example, free riders are generally less tolerable in a strike than in a demonstration. This is the case whether the mobilizing agent is a union, a political committee, or the leaders of a solidary group. The capacity of participants to make up for what free riders withhold varies more with the structure of the struggle than with the group involved. When the outcome of a struggle depends upon the money organizers can raise —perhaps to pay for professional lobbyists and campaign contributions —participants can often increase their contributions to make up for what is withheld by free riders. But when free riders plague a strike or a boycott, it is less feasible for participants to strike or boycott harder than for them to switch tactics.

It makes a difference to participants whether free riders are violating commitments to contribute, and whether they are violating norms against free riding. We suggested above that expectations about whether others will contribute are often important to assessments of the chances that collective action may accomplish something worthwhile. Actors communicate their commitment to act in order to provide the basis for each other's assessments of what kind of collective action is possible. Group norms specifying appropriate conduct for a strike, or a food riot, or any collective action in a group's repertoire may also provide a basis for expectations that other group members will do their shares. When free riders go back on prior commitments and violate norms, they undermine the grounds for others' participation and thereby threaten to set off a reverse bandwagon effect.

Like governments, the collective actors that are least tolerant of constituents who would ride for free are often those who must deal with constituents who would rather not ride at all. The more the bounds of the constituency are fixed by "objective" criteria—rather than including just those actors in sympathy with the social movement—the more possible it is that what is a collective good to some constituents is a collective bad to others, and that what seems like a viable strategy to some constituents seems immoral or impractical to others. A revolutionary movement raises such problems when it extends its constituency from its sympathizers to the population of some territory, by claiming to be a government. We have already suggested that it makes little sense to invoke utilitarian logic to account for nonparticipation when the collective action stands little chance of success; it makes just as little sense when there is not much reason to assume that nonparticipants want the collective good. The assumption that each actor pursues only his own interests tends to obscure differences among free riding, inefficacy, and indifference, as well as differences in how these separate problems may be handled by organizers. It implies that all three problems can be solved only when prior organizations or political "entrepreneurs" offer selective incentives.

All in all, utilitarian logic constitutes a bad basis for investigating variance in how extensive free riding is, how tolerable it is, and how social movement organizations handle it in different types of struggles and with different types of constituencies. Utilitarian logic steers us away from studying how collective action is constrained by ordinary actors' assessments of what their *groups* may gain and lose through alternative courses of action.

Resourceful Actors

Be they politicians, prophets, business firms, or voluntary associations, we call them "resourceful actors" insofar as each of them has the capacity to contribute a significant part of what it takes to bring about the collective good. By and large, we share Olson's conviction that the mobilization of a large group happens only when it is facilitated by contributions from resourceful actors. But we differ with utilitarian accounts of how resourceful actors facilitate mobilization and when they decide to do so.

Olson focuses on long-standing organizations with a surplus of resources that they are ready and willing to contribute for the provision of a collective good. The surplus is a "by-product" of past mobilization maintained by the ongoing provision of selective incentives. Other utilitarians model the efforts of individual organizers, as well as the efforts of long-standing organizations. Organizers may offer selective incentives even though they lack the resources to provide them right away. Like entrepreneurs, organizers try to create or pool resources by using their skills and connections to convince constituents that they will be able to deliver selective incentives in the future (see Frohlich, Oppenheimer, and Young, 1971).

But resourceful actors often facilitate mobilization without promising or providing selective incentives. Particularly in the early stages of mobilization, organizers try to convince ordinary constituents *not* that joining in collective action will bring about benefits only for those who join, but rather that collective action will bring about a collective good. Compared to the former kind of influence, this latter kind may be produced with different and perhaps fewer resources. There are important differences between persuading constituents to make an exchange and persuading them to make a contribution. Some resources—money, weapons, and printing presses—may be used in both endeavors, and these resources are often available only if contributed by long-standing organizations. But resources must be wielded differently if they are being used to back up selective incentives than if they are being used for a number of alternative tasks—to help constituents understand their common stake in a collective good, to alert constituents to threats and opportunities, to propose a course of action, to gather and communicate commitments, to organize decision making, and to coordinate action. In the latter half of this paper, we suggest that if these tasks are done well, then in some situations many ordinary actors mobilize without selective incentives.

When do resourceful actors decide to contribute to collective action? In Olson's account, they do so when it is likely to get them collective goods worth more than the cost of participating, collective goods that would not be forthcoming without their participation. In the complementary account by Frohlich, Oppenheimer, and Young (1971), "entrepreneurs" organize collective action when they can expect to get for themselves some of what is to be mobilized and won through collective action, something worth more than the cost of mobilizing. In our account, on the other hand, resourceful actors, as well as ordinary actors, may participate on the basis of solidarity and principle.

Two final points on resourceful actors are worth stressing. When we call an organization a "resourceful actor" we assume that the internal mobilization and social control of the organization over its members are not problematic, at least not for the purpose of the given investigation. When an army, a corporation, or an already mobilized political party fights for collective goods, the group is of interest here only insofar as it is centrally concerned with the mobilization of ordinary actors for the struggle. Much of Olson's discussion is not relevant to theories of mobilization because it focuses on actors for whom mobilization has become a routine matter of organizational maintenance.

Note also that much social organization crucial to mobilization is informal rather than formal. It isn't easy to see how the effects of informal organization upon mobilization can be understood from the utilitarian perspective. An informal organization—such as a community or a network of people—cannot be treated as an actor that sanctions people according to whether or not they join in collective action. If a community or network lacks a tight internal-control structure, each member of the community or network must be taken as a decision maker with an individual self-interest. When informally organized individuals sanction would-be free riders, the sanctioning is itself a problematic form of collective action that needs to be explained.

Soft Selective Incentives

We have pointed out a number of difficulties with Olson's *Logic of Collective Action*. Utilitarians may be tempted to escape the difficulties by softening the concept of selective incentives rather than by diminishing its role in the explanation of collective action. Assume that we are all agreed that in some situations people act because it would be disloyal and irresponsible not to act. The problem for students of mobilization then becomes how to predict when solidarity and principle will impel people to collective action.

Does the concept of selective incentives facilitate this endeavor? After all, if people experience satisfaction, guilt, or shame depending on whether they join in a worthwhile collective action or ride free, then it is simple enough to designate satisfaction, guilt, and shame as potent selective incentives. Why not allow moral satisfaction and money to count simply as different types of selective incentives?

To follow this route is to destroy the raison d'être of the selective incentive argument by reducing it to a useless tautology.[3] One begins by making it a matter of assumption that people do not participate in collective action unless they get something of value for participation. Therefore, if one finds no specific good or service that a participant receives, one postulates some "soft" selective incentive, such as moral satisfaction, friendship, alleviation of guilt, and the like.

Under such an approach, any explanation can easily enough be recast into a utilitarian framework. Take, for example, the frustration-aggression argument. An individual is upset and frustrated about his slow advancement in his career and turns to collective action that enables him to express his pent-up aggression toward some handy scapegoat. The pleasure of releasing frustration becomes the selective incentive that the person receives for participation.

To follow this tautological route is to remove the cutting edge from the selective incentive argument. If one blurs together such diverse incentives as satisfaction with participating in a worthwhile cause and some specific material inducement, the statement that people participate because of selective incentives loses interest. Immediately, one must ask whether material incentives or some other kind of incentives are involved. Any apparent parsimony in explanation is lost, and the idea of selective incentives becomes so much excess baggage, as the weight of explanation is carried by the subsequent distinctions among incentives.

There is an additional danger in broadening the concept of selective incentives in this fashion. Although soft selective incentives are allowed into the definition, their inclusion is often ignored in subsequent argument, where examples focus on clear-cut, material incentives. Arguments that may well hold for a specific material incentive are frequently problematic for nonmaterial incentives, but this difficulty is never faced in a forthright fashion.

We believe that the utilitarian argument for the value of selective incentives in promoting collective action has some usefulness, but only if it is defined narrowly. We suggest that it be limited to inducements or constraints, that is, some positive or negative sanction that is added to the situation of the actor.[4] When participation works through something other than sanctions, other concepts are more useful than selective incentives. If an actor participates because he feels that some solidarity group with which he identifies is threatened or because he feels responsibility to contribute his share to getting some collective good, no useful purpose is served and something of value is lost by forcing such considerations into a utilitarian mold. The second part of this essay and the Appendix suggest an alternative model in which selective incentives, narrowly defined, are given their due.

AN ALTERNATIVE APPROACH
TO MOBILIZATION

So far we have criticized the utilitarian approach to collective action for exaggerating the role of self-interest in mobilization while obscuring the role of solidarity and principle. What do we mean by solidarity and principle? How are they developed, changed, strengthened? How and when do they facilitate mobilization? In the remainder of the essay we discuss these issues, and the Appendix presents the same argument more formally.

Our starting point is some constituency—a solidary group that may be more or less solidary. Perhaps some collective actor has called upon this solidary group to mobilize for collective action. Or perhaps some social analyst has identified the group as a population whose propensity to mobilize is of interest. Either way, we discuss the contribution of solidarity and principle to the group's propensity to mobilize.

Solidarity

Solidarity is rooted in the configuration of relationships linking the members of a group to one another. People may be linked together in a number of ways that generate a sense of common identity, shared fate, and general commitment to defend the group. Drawing on Stinchcombe (1975) and Gamson (1968), we suggest five factors that constitute the basis for a person's solidarity with a group:

1. *Friends and relatives.* To the extent that a person has friends and relatives within the group, and to the extent that he is indirectly related to others in the group through their friendship and kinship with his friends and kin, he has a basis for solidarity with the group.
2. *Participation in organizations.* To the extent that a person acts collectively with other members of the group in productive organizations, voluntary associations, clubs, and other associations, he has a basis for solidarity with the group.
3. *Design for living.* Groups frequently offer members a set of techniques for handling the problems they encounter in their daily lives—problems like finding and keeping good jobs and good spouses, making friends, raising children, staying out of trouble, and getting treated with dignity and respect. In trying to implement some design for going through life, a person may rely to a greater or lesser degree on support from other people and organizations in the solidary group. To the extent that a person's design for living is shared and supported by other group members more than by outsiders, he has a basis for solidarity with the group.
4. *Subordinate and superordinate relations.* To the extent that a person shares with other group members the same set of subordinate and superordinate relations with outsiders, he has a basis for solidarity with the group.
5. *No exit.* To the extent that a person is readily identified and often treated as a member of the group, so that exit from the group is difficult, he has a basis for solidarity with the group.

A person whose life is intertwined with the group in these ways has a big stake in the group's fate. When collective action is urgent, the person is likely to contribute his or her share even if the impact of that share is not noticeable. Our argument, then, is that the relationships characterized above generate solidarity and that this solidarity becomes an important basis for mobilization.

Can an organizer create or strengthen a network of solidary relations within a constituency? The solidarity of a constituency must often be taken by organizers as the enduring result of long-run historical forces. In the short run it is hard to create solidary relations within an aggregate of unconnected individuals; it is even hard to intensify solidarity where it already exists. So experienced organizers pay attention to the density and quality of solidary relations within a constituency when assessing its potential for mobilization. When a constituency lacks solidarity, mobilization efforts are likely to fail.

A recent article by Burlingham (1977) describes the efforts of the Rhode Island Workers Association (RIWA) to organize the unemployed.

He quotes at length from one of RIWA's professional organizers, George Nee:

> You have to think of the glue that holds a group together. We were organizing people around being unemployed. Well, being unemployed is not part of a person's identity—like being on welfare, or being a worker, or being a member of an ethnic group. They didn't think of themselves as unemployed. They didn't really identify with other people who were unemployed. The only local chapters that took hold had other factors going for them. The East Bay group was mainly made up of Portuguese immigrants. West Warwick is an old, white working-class area, a cohesive community with high unemployment. And in both cases organizers emerged from the local communities. That didn't happen elsewhere. [Pp. 20–21]

When working within a low-solidarity constituency, organizers tend to focus their efforts on the actors who are most central to whatever solidary networks do exist. Sometimes people who are central to different networks within a constituency can be brought together to share experiences and develop a basis for cooperation. Kahn (1970, p. 35) suggests that "The organizer will use . . . [techniques] to bring together those people he feels need to know each other in the sense of sharing together the experiences and conversations they have shared with him."

If organizers are building for a long struggle, they have much to gain by undertaking the difficult process of strengthening solidary relations within the constituency. Clubs and voluntary associations may be formed, encouraged, and linked to one another. Cultural events can promote the group's "design for living," whereas collective goods may be provided that make the "design" work for constituents in their daily lives. Some collective actions may be organized less because of their potential for winning collective goods directly and more for the solidarity they are likely to produce. Social events, even rituals, can be useful in strengthening the solidary relations that help to sustain collective actors during quiescent times and then facilitate rapid mobilization when collective action is urgent. It should be one of the empirical tasks of research from the resource mobilization perspective to identify what strategies are most useful under what conditions for increasing solidarity.

Group Interests

Solidary groups have interests, some intense and others less so. In any given collective action, there may be more or less at stake for a constituent solidary group. Strengthening a person's ties to a solidary group boosts his propensity to join in collective action only insofar as the group has much at stake in the fate of collective action. So how do we determine a group's interests?

When assessing a group's short-run prospects for mobilizing, we look at the group's subjective interests.[5] The group has a subjective interest in whatever collective goods are believed by group members to affect their chances of having what they most ardently try to get, say they want, and claim they deserve. So we infer subjective interests from the primary pursuits of the group's leading actors, the goals they articulate, and the principles embedded in the group's design for living.

When assessing a group's long-run prospects for mobilizing, we must consider both the group's current subjective interests and its objective interests. The group can be assumed to have an objective interest in a collective good to the extent that the good promotes the long-run wealth and power of the group and the viability of its design for living (whether or not these consequences are known to group members). Objective interests exert an important influence on subjective ones. The former are more enduring; the latter affect mobilization more directly. Objective interests are most difficult to take into account. But the longer the time frame in question, the more necessary it is to consider them.

How do the interests of a solidary group get linked to a program of collective action? There are several ways that a collective actor may identify its program with constituents' group interests and thereby harness constituents' solidarity for collective action. Sometimes a social movement emerges through the actions of the leaders of a long-standing solidary group. Social movement structure is then coextensive with the structure of the constituency. If such a movement produces a formal organization with a concrete program, constituents are apt to support the program and be loyal to the organization right away. The counterrevolution in the Vendée appears to have been such a movement: it spread quickly and dramatically as solidary groups in the region identified with it and felt that the viability of their design for living hinged on its fate (see Tilly, 1964). In such a case, the movement organization appears to be the arm of its constituents, fighting for their common interests.

But what do social movement organizers do when they are not the long-standing leaders of their constituent solidary group and when their goals do not jibe with the group's subjective interests? Then they may acquire solidary group support more deliberately, by one of two paths. First, they can woo the solidary group. They can shelve their ultimate goals and develop a program that is closer to the group's subjective interests (or they can appear to do so); they can bargain for support with the group's leaders, and they can try to raise the consciousness of key actors within the group so as to move it in line with the movement.

But this path is not always feasible. Perhaps the constituency's pursuits and principles are incompatible with those of the organizers.

Perhaps the leaders of the constituency oppose collective action outright. Constituents who join in collective action may face loss of support from their solidary group. In this kind of situation, the organizers may try to make the movement itself the locus of a network of solidary relations. There may be deliberate efforts to promote a design for living with supporting institutions more compatible with the organizers' program.

On this second path, organizers sidestep the core leaders of the old solidary group along with their close affiliates, while wooing more sympathetic subgroups. By and large, the solidarity of a constituency is uneven; and there may well be subgroups in some conflict with, or isolation from, its dominant actors. Organizers may appeal to a subgroup by accommodating their program to subgroup interests. Perhaps they can formulate and advance demands on issues of particular concern to the subgroup. If subgroup members can be attracted to the movement on the basis of principle or common interest, they may develop loyalty to the movement as they develop solidary relations among its supporters.

This second path to social movement mobilization—that of forging new solidary relations rather than harnessing old ones—bears some resemblance to that posited by mass society theory. Though many of the social movements that concern us emerge from long-standing solidary groups whose interests clash with those of authorities, here we consider movements that must await (or bring about) the weakening of certain solidary relations that block collective action. We recognize, then, that some configurations of solidary relations crosscut and interlock classes, races, and religions; and we recognize that some cohesive solidary groups encourage their members to accept certain ongoing forms of oppression. Historical forces that weaken such solidarities may increase a population's propensity to collective action. We also recognize that a social movement may offer a refuge for people who abandon or are abandoned by their prior solidary groups.

Nevertheless, there is a crucial difference between our argument here and various "breakdown" theories of collective action, including mass society theory. We assume that people who drift without solidary relations, without firm principles, anxious, atomized, anomic—such people are unlikely to mobilize for collective action. Even the social movements least rooted in prior solidary groups are less likely to attract drifters than principled actors who have stable interests in the collective goods sought by the movement.

To align a program of collective action with the interests of constituents, organizers need to understand constituents. To mobilize through networks of solidary relations among constituents, organizers need to earn constituents' trust. Therefore, it helps if organizers can fit in with their solidary networks and understand their experiences. Alinsky (1971, p. 84) advises us that "Since people understand only in terms of their own experience, an organizer must have at least a cursory familiarity with their experience. It not only serves communication, but it strengthens the personal identification of the organizer with the others." Or, to quote Kahn (1970, pp. 5, 26):

> In some ways, the organizer's main job in the community in the early stages of organizing is simply to make friends with the people there. . . . Generally, an effective organizer will have a good deal in common with the people he is working among. In the mountains of North Carolina, for example, it helps to know a lot about fishing, hunting, pulpwooding, farming, trucks, country music, raising tobacco, shotguns, dogs, and religion. . . . If an organizer does not share knowledge and experiences with the people he is working among, he will have a hard time communicating with them.

For similar reasons, the O. M. Collective (1971, p. 38) suggests that organizers gain advantages in working with their own "age, class, and occupational group." It should be one of the empirical tasks of resource mobilization theory to identify what strategies in what situations work best to align the program of a social movement with the interests of a solidary consituency.

Personal Interest in Collective Goods

Not only solidary groups but also individuals have interests in the preservation or achievement of various collective goods. They may have various reasons for valuing these collective goods—some of them selfish and some quite altruistic. These valuations may be identical to those of their most important solidary groups, or, in some cases, they may disagree.

There is a particularly relevant subset of collective goods for the mobilization process. Certain collective goods may be perceived as an entitlement, as something deserved as a matter of justice, equity, or right. We propose to use the term "principles" to refer to this subset.

Collective actors frequently attempt to appeal to the principles of their constituents as a way of mobilizing support. They approach them with some vision of justice or equity with which they hope to raise some righteous anger. Discontent needs to be focused and channeled; the connections between proximate events and more abstract states of the system must be developed. Political education, ideological discussion, study groups, consciousness-raising sessions, newsletters, and political tracts frequently are intended to raise personal interest in the collective goods being promoted.

People's allegiance to the goals of a collective actor cannot be taken for granted as arising spontaneously from their social conditions. Alinsky

(1971, p. xxi) advises us that "Men don't like to step abruptly out of the security of familiar experience; they need a bridge across from their own experience to a new way. A revolutionary organizer must shake up the prevailing pattern of their lives—agitate, create disenchantment and discontent with the current values, to produce, if not a passion for change, at least a passive, affirmative non-challenging climate."

Other professional organizers offer similar advice against assuming support for the purpose of collective action. The O. M. Collective (1971, p. 40) points out that "Few people see themselves as abstractly 'oppressed' although they are acutely aware of the daily struggle to eat, make a happy home, educate their kids, keep their draft age boys alive, hold some hope for the future—in short, to live like human beings."

Wernette (1976, p. 11) suggests that "There are a number of ways in which the value of a collective good can be increased for the individual. One such way entails linking the collective good to other collective goods by means of an ideological analysis. . . . In addition, the individual, by seeing the sacrifices made by others in contributing to the provisions of the collective good, notes the value of the good to them."

There is no magic formula for raising the value of the collective good, but imaginative mobilizing agents are constantly looking for opportunities to enhance its value. Sometimes events occur that present mobilizing agents with consciousness-raising opportunities. Sometimes they can stage their own events or actions. Yippie activities, such as throwing dollar bills on members of the New York Stock Exchange, or guerrilla theater have such a purpose. The aim of guerrilla theater, the O. M. Collective argues, "is to create a metaphor or symbolic revelation of reality that will force people to see and to think about the world in new ways. The metaphor seizes upon the *essence* of everyday events and, through exaggeration, distortion, and change of context, strips them of their familiar aspects—'blows them up' to expose the shocking truths within" (p. 73). It should be one of the empirical tasks of resource mobilization theory to identify what strategies and tactics are most useful under what conditions for raising personal interest in collective goods.

The Urgency of Collective Action

Mobilization is more likely when collective action is more urgent. Urgency is a straightforward function of necessity and opportunity. Whatever events lower the chances that constituents can realize their interests without collective action thereby increase the *necessity* for collective action. Whatever events raise the chances that collective action can successfully promote or protect constituents' interests thereby increase the *opportunity* for collective action.

Collective action, then, is most urgent when there is no reason to believe that collective goods will be preserved without collective action, and every reason to believe that they can be preserved through collective action. We say "preserved" without adding "or brought about" only to suggest that many constituencies, especially ones that are poor and poorly organized, have a stronger subjective interest in protecting existing collective goods than in winning new ones. But once the strength of a group's interest in a collective good is given, we mean "urgency" to be *not* a matter of whether the group already has the good, but rather a matter of the difference collective action will make to constituents' chances of having it in the future. (See the Appendix for a more formal treatment of these issues.)

Here we mention some ways in which various events can affect the necessity and opportunity for collective action. Sometimes organizers can only prepare for such events and await them. Other times it is possible to precipitate them.

NECESSITY.   What kinds of events lower the chances that constituents can realize their interests without collective action? Unfortunately for those who want to predict mobilization, new threats to group interests can come from almost anywhere (within broad limits set by the nature of the group and the political economy of its environment). Authorities can break commitments to the group, reverse policies that were beneficial, and form alliances with the group's enemies. Authorities can repress the group's organizations and leaders. The collective action of outsiders can threaten to damage some state of affairs that the group has a stake in conserving. Employers can speed up the work process, tighten discipline, cut wages, fire militants. When ongoing processes erode constituents' access to jobs, markets, land, or whatever else they need to secure a livelihood, particular events epitomizing the deteriorating situation can be especially threatening.

If events can increase the necessity of collective action by posing direct threats to specific group interests, events can also increase the necessity of collective action more diffusely by reducing constituents' trust in authorities. Authorities often pretend to be above conflicts of interest among various groups under their rule. They claim to have the intention of providing and the capacity to provide collective goods that benefit everyone by benefiting the whole country. The extent to which people believe such claims varies considerably, over time and among constituencies. Sometimes when agents of authority support the group's enemies, restrict the group's access to government protection and welfare services, and otherwise violate the group's principles of justice, group members still trust that higher authorities will rectify the situation. No matter how seriously their interests are threatened, the actors in a constituency may fail to mobilize until they lose the trust that authorities will take care of things sooner or later. So the necessity of collective action can be increased by events that display authorities' bad faith and highlight their conflicts of interest with constituents.

It is just such reasoning that leads Lenin to call strikes "a school of war": "A strike . . . opens the eyes of the workers to the nature, not only of the capitalists, but of the government and laws as well. . . . Soldiers are even ordered to fire on the workers and when they kill unarmed workers by shooting the fleeing crowd in the back, the tsar himself sends the troops an expression of gratitude. . . . It becomes clear to every worker that the tsarist government is his worst enemy, since it defends the capitalists and binds the workers hand and foot" (1967, 4:316–17).

A collective action under consideration may be only one of several alternative courses of action, each advocated by a rival collective actor within the constituency. The necessity for supporting some social movement organization may be small if an established interest group can be relied upon to protect group interests, or if a rival social movement organization is more viable. NAACP, CORE, SNCC, SCLC, as well as a number of others, offered various alternative courses of action to American blacks during the 1960s. Each tried to mobilize support from somewhat different subgroups within the black community and from somewhat different sources outside the black community; and they sometimes coordinated their activities. Still, to a substantial degree these collective actors were rivals. The necessity of joining with any particular collective actor is reduced by whatever elements increase the prospects of rival collective actors.

In sum, the necessity of some collective action is increased by events that threaten the interests of its constituents, undermine their trust in authorities, and discredit rival possibilities of collective action. Organizers try to predict when such events will happen in order to get constituents ready for them. Organizers may also try to precipitate these events, but they must act discreetly in order not to discredit themselves. Constituents are unlikely to appreciate the organizer who deliberately creates threats to their interests to get them to mobilize. Discrediting rivals may undermine the chances of forming a useful coalition; and destroying trust in authorities can have delicate consequences for bargaining with them. Regardless of who precipitates these events, organizers react to them by trying to point out the necessity for collective action. It should be one of the empirical tasks of research from the resource mobilization perspective to identify what strategies in what situations best increase constituents' consciousness of the necessity for collective action, if not the collective action itself.

OPPORTUNITY. What kinds of events increase the chances that constituents can realize their interests through collective action? As with necessity, there are multiple sources of opportunity. First, a collective actor may create its own opportunities by establishing its credibility and effectiveness in the eyes of the constituency. Opportunity is created when a given collective actor convinces members of its constituency that its proposed collective action is viable and can produce some results. Potential participants want to know whether the actor who proposes collective action should be taken seriously as an instrument, whether it is a potentially efficacious organization. The calculation the person makes is whether the collective actor is serious, honorable, dedicated, tough, determined, wise, or whatever else is deemed necessary for success in producing the collective good.

Low collective efficacy is a central problem in efforts to organize the oppressed, and those in the business of doing this organizing have many suggestions to offer on dealing with it. The basic strategy is to demonstrate influence by picking a target that offers promise of a quick success, thus showing potential constituents that the social movement actor is one to be reckoned with and that opportunities exist for collective action. "The organizer knows," Alinsky (1971, p. 113) writes, "that his biggest job is to give the people the feeling they can do something."

How does one accomplish this? The O. M. Collective (1971, pp. 4, 15, 16) says: "It is desirable to make the first organized project of the group a short term one that has a high probability of success"; "Your first issue should be an attainable goal which will provide you with your first victory"; and "Try to keep tangible, though perhaps small, victories coming as well as continuous action and progress on longer-term work." Ross (1973, p. 215), advising us how to conduct Naderite citizen action groups, remarks that "The initial projects should be small, specific, and achievable." Kopkind (1977, p. 28) describes the strategy of the Fair Share organization in Massachusetts: "Following good neighborhood organizing strategy, Fair Share concentrated on small victories at the local level: tax abasements in Dorchester, bridge repairs in East Boston, a dump relocation in Worcester. Those issues did what organizing is supposed to do: engage people in work that teaches them something about power, about struggle, about leadership. . . . The actions were picked to be winnable 'by the most powerless people, . . . in the most militant fashion,' one Fair Share worker said."

Building the credibility of the collective actor is only one aspect of increasing opportunity. Disarray in the target of collective action can dramatically increase chances for successful collective action. Sometimes external events—a war or economic crisis—will leave a target of collective action in an especially vulnerable state. Sometimes internal conflict will become so acute that the possibilities of effective counteraction against the collective actor become greatly diminished.

Trotsky (1959, p. 311) describes such a situation as one of the "political premises of a revolution": "The ruling classes, as a result of their practically manifested incapacity to get the country out of its blind alley, lose faith in themselves; the old parties fall to pieces, a bitter struggle of groups and cliques prevails; hopes are placed in miracles or miracle workers."

Finally, opportunity may be increased by the actions of coalition partners and third-party supporters. When others plan actions or lend support to a collective actor, new possibilities for collective action may become available through the aggregation of resources involved. Lipsky (1970) and Schattschneider (1960) have been particularly attentive to this aspect of opportunity.

In sum, the opportunity for collective action is increased by events that raise the credibility of the collective actor, throw its antagonists into disarray, and make available coalition partners and third-party support. As with necessity, organizers attempt to anticipate such events so that they are prepared to take advantage of them. They may also attempt to precipitate them, a less delicate matter than precipitating increases in necessity. Increasing opportunity does not require the same discretion. Regardless of who or what precipitates the events, organizers try to point out increased opportunities for collective action. It should be one of the empirical tasks of research from the resource mobilization perspective to identify what strategies in what situations increase constituents' consciousness of opportunities for collective action, as well as the opportunities themselves.

Loyalty and Responsibility

In the Appendix to this paper, we suggest how the variables discussed combine to produce mobilization for collective action. Two different mechanisms operate, one acting through people's loyalty to a group with which they experience solidarity, and the other acting through people's responsibility to personal principles that are at stake in collective action.

When group interest, solidarity, and urgency combine, we may talk about people as being activated by loyalty. When personal interest in collective goods, especially those we have called principles, combines with urgency, we may talk about people as being activated by responsibility. Note that urgency is a part of both combinations. We argue that the call on *either* loyalty or responsibility is greater when the urgency of collective action is increased.

It is useful to think of loyalty and responsibility not merely as attributes of individuals but as properties of cultural codes or belief systems. Individuals exist in a climate of cultural beliefs about their obligations to those groups with which they identify and their responsibilities for contributing their shares to just causes. Some individuals will have internalized these beliefs more than others, and the content and strength of these beliefs may differ by culture and subculture. Nevertheless, we expect considerations of loyalty and responsibility to be important, because there are certain central components in loyalty and responsibility codes that are widely shared, regardless of the political principles, ethical beliefs, or religion on which they are based. These include an expectation that people will contribute some share when groups with whose fate they are linked have a big stake in collective action and that they will contribute some share to see that the principles they hold dear are realized.

The demands of loyalty and the demands of responsibility happily coincide much of the time. However, they may on occasion diverge. The hallmark of loyalist behavior, as Hirschman (1970) notes, is the commitment to participate in a group in spite of disagreement with it. Loyalty becomes manifest and distinguishable from responsibility when the two promote opposite tugs—when people feel that their principles conflict with the group's interest as the group defines it. Such principled opposition may, of course, claim to represent the group's "true" interest in resisting the call to honor the group's discipline.

SELF-INTEREST REVISITED

Here we return to a consideration of the individual costs and benefits that affect constituents' propensity to join in collective action. We do not suggest that actors ignore what they have to gain and lose individually when deciding whether to support collective action. Such considerations are important, sometimes decisive, but in ways that tend to be obscured by utilitarian logic and the conceptual imagery of economics. Some of these ways are even awkward to discuss in the language of "goods" and "costs," but we try to do so in order to confront the utilitarian argument more directly.

In any constituency, the cost of collective action per actor may be reduced over time by a number of historical forces. If, for example, the constituency is a social class and the collective good is control of the state, the cost per constituent of the good goes down as the number of actors in the class increases, their control of strategic resources increases, their access to support from outside parties increases, the repressive power of authorities declines, and so forth. McCarthy and Zald (1973b) point out how the mobilization of social movement organizations in the United States has been facilitated by increases in the income and discretionary time of people in many constituencies, and by increases in the size of a liberal conscience constituency with particularly high levels of income and discretionary time. Clearly, the cost to a constituent of giving fifty dollars and fifty hours is more when he or she earns five thousand dollars a year working forty fixed hours each week than when he or she earns twenty-five thousand dollars a year with much discretion on when and how much to work.

Regardless of changes in the income and occupational structure of the constituency, and the political economy of its environment, joining in collective action still involves significant costs. Good organizers do their best to reduce them. Sanctioning potential constituents—providing selective incentives—is only one way to reduce or offset costs. First, we consider some of the other ways of reducing costs. Next, we consider how the effectiveness of many selective incentives provided by social movement organizers is primarily dependent upon constituents' solidarity, their principles, and the viability of collective action. And, finally, we delimit the situation in which the concept "selective incentives" seems most appropriate to characterize important determinants of social movement mobilization.

Reducing Costs Without Selective Incentives

1. Entrepreneurs, inventors, and engineers strive, often successfully, to reduce the costs of producing various economic goods and services. Likewise, a foremost task of organizers is to search for more efficient ways of bringing about the collective good. If they succeed, they reduce the amount that constituents must contribute. By distilling their own experiences, learning from others' experiences, and developing theoretical understanding of their historical situation, organizers can assess opportunities and perhaps discover ways of creating opportunities. Many activists spend much time planning and arranging so that it will be less costly for constituents to pool resources, attend meetings, demonstrate, petition, and otherwise participate.

2. When organizers provide constituents with goods and services, these are often collective goods rather than selective incentives. A number of antiwar groups, for example, provided draft counseling. Feminist organizations have provided free medical services, crisis centers, and community centers. When carried far enough, the more collective goods an organization provides, the fewer individual goods constituents need. An expensive strategy of providing individuals with some specific benefit in exchange for their participation may be supplanted by a cheaper strategy of providing goods that all can enjoy. If some potential

constituents ride free, others get acquainted and linked with the movement.

3. Through struggle, social movements may succeed in forcing authorities to bring about collective goods that reduce the costs of participation. When a protest movement succeeds in forcing the repeal of repressive legislation, it reduces future costs to participants. When unions succeeded in reducing the work week, they increased the discretionary time of their constituents; when unions succeeded in raising wages, they increased the discretionary income of their constituents. These struggles reduced the subsequent costs of contributing time and money to the union.

Selective Incentives Dependent upon Consciousness and Solidarity

1. When a potential constituent views a social movement and sees something in it for him, it is often something he expects to receive (or avoid) in the future only if the movement succeeds. A peasant gives his support to revolutionaries in the hope of being rewarded after the revolution, only if he expects there to be a revolution. If bringing about the collective good will put the movement in a position to reward its friends, then consciousness raising inevitably provides selective incentives, and the latter are an uninteresting explanation of mobilization. But the convictions that "History is on our side" and "Victory is inevitable" rarely attract opportunists until the opposition is visibly crumbling. During the early stages of many social movements, when mobilization is most problematic and interesting, distant promises of selective incentives are easily discounted. Some theorists have suggested that the anticipated gain of future individual goods is what motivates many organizers of collective-good-providing outfits (see Frolich, Oppenheimer, and Young, 1971). Though there may be quite a few such political Elmer Gantrys, it is hard to believe that they play a decisive role in most social movements.

2. Whereas some selective incentives depend on a consciousness of the movement's opportunities, others depend on a consciousness of the movement's worth. If social movements provide constituents with valued friends, esteem, status, insignia, posters, red books, or brown shirts, they facilitate mobilization primarily to the extent that constituents share principles that the movement defends. As we have already noted, social clubs and fraternal orders can generally provide "social incentives" at less cost, as they do not bear the burden of providing collective goods. And even when a social movement organization is the best fraternal order on the market (or when a fraternal order becomes a social movement organization), the problematic aspect of mobilization is raising the

consciousness that the continued value of the "social incentives" ultimately depends upon. It is relatively easy for a social movement to provide opportunities for people to make friends or display insignia. If this were what it takes to mobilize, mobilization would be less difficult an enterprise.

3. In some communities, scab workers would run the risk of being ostracized, despised, and spat upon. These are very real social incentives. Perhaps they would also run the risk of losing access to various informal mutual aid services that carry material benefits. And maybe they would run the risk of getting beaten up. By utilitarian logic, they wouldn't scab. But, insofar as these selective incentives are dished out spontaneously by informally organized members of the community, the interesting question for students of mobilization is why community members negatively sanction scabs. If the community is large, each sanction has an imperceptible effect on the outcome of the struggle. Sanctioning is less costly than the struggle, but it is part of the collective action nonetheless.

We would look for an answer to this problem along the lines suggested in the "solidarity" section of this essay. When a person's fate is bound to the fate of the group, he feels threatened when the group is threatened; and he expects others in the group to feel the same way. He is likely to support the goals of group action, but he is obliged to support the group anyway. Inspired by loyalty in other group members and offended by disloyalty, he may sanction them accordingly. And, depending on his own response to the group's call to action, he feels self-respect or shame.

Solidarity blurs the distinction between individual and collective goods. When a person's self-concept and way of life are tightly bound to a group, especially when the group is democratically organized and when the group is powerful, participants experience a control over their fate that they lack as individuals. The logic of their action is unlikely to be utilitarian.

When Does Mobilization Best Fit the Utilitarian Account?

1. When social movement organizations have the armed force it takes to tax and draft soldiers, or when they control access to crucial goods and services (e.g., jobs, patronage), they may have the capacity to maintain or extend their levels of mobilization primarily by means of selective incentives. If the past enterprise that produced such power to induce or constrain is not of interest to the investigation at hand, it may be assumed.

2. Some social movement organizations mobilize enough resources from one constituency on the basis of solidarity and responsibility so that they can mobilize another constituency on the basis of self-interest. Sometimes it is worthwhile to do so because the mobilization of the latter constituency is vital to success. Even in such cases, as in (1) immediately above, the amount of inducement or constraint necessary to mobilize the problem constituency should vary with its solidarity and strength of principle: it is easier to govern a sympathetic population than a hostile one.

CONCLUSION

The problem we adress in this essay is akin to the classic problem of social order. Sociologists have long recognized that the existence of social order cannot be taken for granted, that an explanation is required to account for large numbers of people going about their daily lives in coordinated fashion and, in the process, producing certain collective goods (and bads) that hold society together.

The problem of the mobilization of a potential constituency by social movement actors addresses similar issues with reference to a group. By posing the production of social movements as the production of social order (rather than a symptom of disorder), the resource mobilization perspective breaks sharply with much past research. Yet within the resource mobilization perspective there are differing approaches to social movement mobilization that parallel differences in the approaches of past research to the origins of social order. We are not suggesting that the mixture of coercion, shared values, and voluntary exchange that glues together any particular society is similar to the mixture that glues together any social movement, only that many of the issues raised in this essay have long been discussed outside the social movement literature.

Without evaluating utilitarian approaches to the problem of order in a society, we consider problems with utilitarian accounts of social movement mobilization. We suggest that research focus on how organizers raise consciousness of common interests, develop opportunities for collective action, and tap constituents' solidarity and principles. Systematic investigation of what works for organizers should offer promising ground for theoretical advance.

APPENDIX

Here we summarize some of our argument more formally. Let us assume that we know the interests of an actor (A). A has an interest in getting, bringing about, or keeping each of a number of goods, services, and specific states of affairs. We array them so that the first m are the individual goods and the last n are the collective goods. Let "i" represent any of the individual goods and "j" represent any of the collective goods.

$V_a(i)$ and $V_a(j)$ represent the values to A of the ith and the jth goods, respectively. These values may be thought of as dollars, utiles, or any unit of worth that lets us compare A's interests in different goods.

Let $P_1(i)$ and $P_1(j)$ be the probabilities that A will get the ith and the jth goods, respectively, if A organizes or joins in the collective action that we are considering. $P_2(i)$ and $P_2(j)$ represent the probabilities that A will get the ith and the jth goods if A takes the best alternative course of action. The alternative may mean joining in an alternative collective action, or it may mean doing nothing in particular.

Now, insofar as utilitarian assumptions are valid, A will join in collective action if and only if

$$\sum_{i=1}^{m} V_a(i)[P_1(i) - P_2(i)] + \sum_{j=m+1}^{m+n} V_a(j)[P_1(j) - P_2(j)] > 0.$$

Unless A is especially resourceful or any of the collective goods are especially easy to come by, it should be clear that for each j:

$$P_1(j) \approx P_2(j).$$

Therefore:

$$\sum_{j} V_a(j)[P_1(j) - P_2(j)] \approx 0.$$

And A will join in collective action if and only if

$$\sum_{i} V_a(i)[P_1(i) - P_2(i)] > 0.$$

So if A is any ordinary actor (resourceful actors are treated separately below), A's interests in collective goods drop out of the model. For any j, neither $V_a(j)$ nor $P_1(j)$ nor $P_2(j)$ nor any relations among them is relevant to A's propensity to join in collective action—except insofar as these factors affect

$$\sum_{i} V_a(i)[P_1(i) - P_2(i)].$$

We may also drop from consideration all individual goods for which $P_1(i) = P_2(i)$, namely, all individual goods that A is just as likely to get whether or not he joins in collective action. The remaining individual goods include the contribution to collective action,[6] any inducements, any constraints, and any opportunity costs.

We argue that most social movements would never get off the ground if their constituents' decisions to participate were based exclusively, or even primarily, upon individual self-interest. Social movements are often facilitated by the solidarity of a group of actors sharing common interests. Rapid mobilization of social movements is often precipitated by conspicuous threats to common interests and by conspicuous opportunities for common interests to be defended by collective action. Self-interest is only one basis for mobilization. To state this formally we introduce several terms that were not needed in presenting the utilitarian model.

Let S stand for how much A is linked to a solidary group at risk to mobilization. (In the section on solidarity we note the kinds of relations we would count to determine A's linkage to a solidary group.) Solidary groups have interests; they have stakes in preserving some states of affairs and in changing others. Let $V_g(j)$ be the interest the group has in the jth collective good. For the sake of the discussion here, the strengths of a group's various interests may be treated as though they are measurable in comparable units.

Let $P_3(j)$ stand for the probability that the group will get (or preserve) the jth collective good even if the collective action under consideration does not take place. Perhaps authorities will bring about the collective good anyway, or perhaps it will be brought about by some alternative collective action. Recall that for each ordinary actor $P_1(j) = P_2(j)$, and they amount to the probability that the jth good will somehow be brought about. Subtracting $P_3(j)$ from this probability, we can let $P_2(j) - P_3(j)$ represent the "urgency" of the collective action—the difference that the collective action makes to the chances of getting the collective good. (Some of the factors that affect the urgency of collective action are discussed in the text above.) Now the group's stake in collective action can be represented by

$$\sum_j V_g(j)[P_2(j) - P_3(j)].$$

Combining the group's stake in collective action with the actor's stake in the group, we suggest that

$$\sum_j V_g(j)[P_2(j) - P_3(j)]S$$

represents an important basis for collective action. The higher the value of this expression for the actors in a group at risk to mobilization, the more solidarity and loyalty impel them to join in collective action. This is so even if free riding could reap for them all the benefits of collective action without risking penalties.

Until now we have assumed that only one group is the locus of solidarity for any actor. But sometimes actors have various important ties to several groups that may differ in their interests. Let g stand for any of G relevant groups, and let S_g stand for A's linkage to g. Now we can let

$$\sum_{g=1}^{G} \sum_{j} V_g(j)[P_2(j) - P_3(j)]S_g$$

represent the combined effects upon A's propensity to join in collective action of A's stakes in these groups and these groups' stakes in collective action. The more the different groups to which A is vitally linked share common interests in threatened collective goods, the more loyalty impels A to join in collective action. But if the groups have conflicting interests in the collective goods, A's propensity to join in collective action is attenuated.

So far we have presented two bases for mobilization among ordinary actors: first, pursuit of individual self-interest, and second, solidarity with a group in the pursuit of group interests. Now we present a third basis. The general idea is that actors may feel a responsibility to contribute their shares to collective action insofar as that action stands a chance of bringing about something they value. The terms needed to express this idea more formally have already been introduced. $V_a(j)$ represents A's interest in the jth collective good. $P_2(j) - P_3(j)$ represents the difference that collective action makes to the chances the jth good will come about. We suggest that the higher is

$$\sum_{j} V_a(j)[P_2(j) - P_3(j)]$$

for A, an ordinary actor, the greater is A's propensity to join in collective action.

This expression represents the expected value of what A would gain from free riding. We are simply suggesting that the more worthwhile the ride is to A, the more likely A is to contribute a share of the costs.

For the most part, a person's interest in a collective good ($V_a(j)$) is broadly constrained by his interests in individual goods ($\sum_{i} V_a(i)$) and by the interest of his solidary group(s) in the collective good ($V_g(j)$). So, in many struggles, this third basis of collective action reinforces the other two presented above. But in constituencies with strong ethical codes, there are actors who may join in collective action that breaks with all their past solidary groups and involves personal sacrifices. The two nonutilitarian bases for mobilization are especially likely to work in tandem in many situations, because both depend in part upon $[P_2(j) - P_3(j)]$—that is, the difference collective action is likely to make to the provision of the collective good. Our point here is that this third basis for mobilization is distinct from the other two, although it may often supplement them.

Now we put together the terms discussed so far and model the propensity of the ordinary actors in a solidary group to join in collective action. (Resourceful actors will be added to the model later.) For the sake of argument, we assume that the terms in the model—the interests, the probabilities of realizing them, and the group affiliations—all may be estimated for the actors in a solidary group, at a time when some organizers or organizations are trying to mobilize the group for collective action. Initially, our dependent variable is whether or not an actor joins in collective action. The model is:

$$Y = b_0 + b_1 X_1 + b_2 X_2 + b_3 X_3,$$

where

$$X_1 = \sum_i V_a(i)[P_1(i) - P_2(i)]$$

$$X_2 = \sum_g \sum_j V_g(j)[P_2(j) - P_3(j)]S_g$$

$$X_3 = \sum_j V_a(j)[P_2(j) - P_3(j)].$$

All the terms have already been defined, but we define them again here for convenience:

$V_a(i)$ and $V_a(j)$ are the values to the actor of the ith and jth goods, respectively;

$V_g(j)$ is the value of the jth collective good to the gth group;

S_g is the actor's degree of linkage to the gth group;

$P_1(i)$ and $P_1(j)$ are the probabilities that the actor will receive the ith and jth goods, respectively, if he organizes or joins in collective action;

$P_2(i)$ and $P_2(j)$ are the probabilities that the actor will receive the ith and jth goods, respectively, if he takes some alternative course of action (for example, does nothing);

and $P_3(j)$ is the probability that the actor will receive the jth good if the collective action in question does not occur.

The model suggests some relationships among what we consider to be key determinants of actors' propensities to join in collective action. Such a model can help make sense of various strategies by which organizers try to mobilize various constituencies. And it enables us to state more precisely our disagreements with the utilitarian logic of collective action.

It makes sense to think of "self interest" when interpreting b_1, "loyalty" when interpreting b_2, and "responsibility" when interpreting b_3. By utilitarian logic, b_1 should be substantial, but the other parameters (and the error) should be trivial. In other words, only changes in X_1 should affect the actors' propensities to mobilize. In contrast, we think that b_2 and b_3 differ in interesting ways according to the constituency and the historical epoch, but they are often quite substantial. Our expectations about b_1 do not differ from utilitarian expectations; but we believe that it is often more difficult for organizers to raise X_1 than it is for them to raise the other variables. Even though b_2 may be much lower than b_1 in some constituency, organizers may find that they make the most efficient use of their resources if they work on the X_2 rather than the X_1 of their constituents.

The argument becomes stronger when we use an aggregated version of the model to consider mobilization over time. Let Y be the proportion of the constituency mobilized at each point, and let the Xs estimate average levels of the relevant interests, probabilities, and solidarities within the constituency at each point. We expect that when variance in X_1 is decisive to mobilization, it is usually brought about by historical forces, conjectures of events, or agents of repression; social movement organizers usually lack the kind of resources it takes to negatively sanction constituents with selective incentives.

Over time, the most volatile term in the model is $P_2(j) - P_3(j)$, a component of both X_2 and X_3. Recall that this term represents the "urgency" of collective action—the difference collective action is likely to make in the chances that the collective good will be gained (or protected). The collective action under consideration is not very urgent when authorities or rival collective actors are likely to provide the collective good anyway, when constituents are not mobilized enough for the collective action to seem possible, and when the target is relatively invulnerable to the collective action. But $P_2(j) - P_3(j)$ may rise suddenly with events bringing sharp changes in the availability of coalition partners, in the policies and capabilities of enemies and rivals, and in the number of constituents who are already mobilized.

The consequences of the latter are the key to mobilization's volatility. If constituents' propensities to mobilize are affected by the extent to which they are already mobilized, then mobilization and demobilization feed upon themselves. Not only does mobilization at one point affect mobilization at the next, but at each point actors' decisions depend upon their estimation of one another's current and future decisions. Constituents estimate one another's intentions through processes that are neither scheming nor irrational, neither "strategic interaction" nor "circular reaction." Among actors who share solidary relations, interaction can be cooperative, sensible, and principled, at least as much so as circumstances permit. Here is the point at which organizers can often intervene most efficiently. Even if they cannot provide selective incentives, organizers may be able to coordinate communication and decision making, pool the resources that constituents are ready to contribute, and offer a plan of action. Demonstrating to constituents that they share a readiness to mobilize and that they have a mobilizing agent increases their propensity to mobilize.

But when do organizers and prior organizations commit themselves to mobilizing other actors for collective action? So far our model only deals with ordinary actors. We now expand it to include "resourceful" ones as well.

"A resourceful actor" is defined as any actor (A) for whom $P_1(j) - P_2(j)$ is noticeably greater than zero, for some collective good (j) at stake in collective action. When they contribute, resourceful actors noticeably increase the expected value of what is to be gained by collective action. Unlike ordinary actors, they get a less worthwhile ride if they decide to ride for free.

We agree with utilitarian logic that it makes a difference to A whether A makes a difference to the outcome of collective action. We think this is so whether the basis for the given mobilization is self-interest, responsibility, or loyalty. So we expand the model to include X_4 and X_5, where

$$X_4 = \sum_g \sum_j V_g(j)[P_1(j) - P_2(j)]S_g$$

and

$$X_5 = \sum_j V_a(j)[P_1(j) - P_2(j)].$$

By definition, $X_4 = X_5 = 0$ for ordinary actors. The expanded model, thus, looks like this:

$$Y = b_0 + b_1X_1 + b_2X_2 + b_3X_3 + b_4X_4 + b_5X_5,$$

where all terms are as defined earlier.

How should the two new parameters be interpreted? If it makes sense to interpret b_1 as self-interest and b_3 as responsibility, then the interpretation of b_5 is inherently ambiguous. The higher X_5 is, the more A has to gain from contributing; and so self-interest impels A to contribute. At the same time, it is frequently included in responsibility codes that those who can make a difference have a special responsibility to contribute. So self-interest and responsibility may coincide, dictating the same response to any change in X_5.

To untangle this ambiguity in the interpretation of b_5 in any particular study, we would have to consider the nature of the resourceful actor's stake in the relevant collective goods. Following Olson and other utilitarians (in order to confront them more directly), we do not limit the worth of a collective good to its material worth. For the purposes of this discussion, we allow actors to have strong interests in a collective good (like the liberation of distant people) from which they may gain no concrete benefits. If "altruistic" interests are awkward in utilitarian analysis—and we think they are—it is particularly awkward to call "self-interest" those altruistic interests that are pursued by resourceful actors who may be sacrificing valuable individual goods. On the other hand, when we call those interests "responsibility," we should keep in mind that regardless of whether material interests are at stake, what is a collective good to one group is very often a collective bad to another; and it may be awkward to apply the term "responsible" to action we oppose. After all, social movements often find that most actors resourceful enough to contribute substantially to their mobilization are responsible to their antagonists.

The interpretation of b_4 as loyalty rather than self-interest makes sense insofar as $V_a(j)$ differs from $V_g(j)$ for the resourceful actors in the constituency, and insofar as S accounts for some of the variance in X_4. (Otherwise X_4 reduces to X_5, and there are more ambiguities.) Generally, b_5 should be smaller than b_3, and b_4 should be smaller than b_2. Though all free riding may be irresponsible and disloyal in some situations, free riding is worse on both counts when the withheld contribution noticeably damages the prospects of realizing common interests. (Depending upon the units of $V_g(j)$, b_2 and b_4 may shrink with group size. Loyalty dictates that an individual help the group, but the bigger the group, the less of the group's total needs must come from that individual.)

When the cases we consider are either actors in a solidary group or time points in the history of a solidary group, we take the bs as fixed for the solidary group (as assumed in the model). But if we consider a number of groups in several societies and epochs, we may assume the bs to be variables. Then it would be interesting to ask how and when self-interest, responsibility, and loyalty are institutionalized as bases of mobilization for collective action.

ENDNOTES

1. Others have expressed similar skepticism about the arguments that we question here. We found James Q. Wilson's *Political Organizations* (1973) especially helpful, although Wilson is less focused on social movement actors than we are. K. Wilson and Orum (1976) and Wernette (1977) more specifically address political mobilization by social movement actors with an argument similar to that of this paper. See also Gamson (1975, chap. 5) for a discussion of some of the arguments developed more completely here.

2. Free riders may be especially demoralizing when the goals of collective action are "exclusive collective goods." The latter, unlike "inclusive collective goods," are worth less to each constituent as the constituency is enlarged. When the actors in the construction industry pressure the government to encourage construction, they seek an exclusive collective good—the more actors in the industry, the less each actor gains from whatever collective action achieves. On the other hand, those who seek clean air or an end to war are not in this situation. When the goals of collective action are "exclusive" in this sense, free riders can be seen not only as failing to contribute their share but also as reducing the worth to participants of whatever collective action may gain.

3. White (1976) explores this version of the selective incentive argument and points out that, under such a definition of selective incentives, "Olson is correct in asserting that people do not act on their interests unless they gain a private benefit" (p. 271). But she correctly recognizes that such a tautological solution deprives the idea of any explanatory value. Heath (1976) also has a very helpful discussion of the tautology problem in more general social exchange theory.

4. We rely here on the distinction made in Gamson (1968) between, on the one hand, inducements and constraints, which operate on the situation of the actor, and, on the other, persuasion, which operates on the orientation of the actor. For a fuller discussion of the distinction, see Gamson (1968), pp. 73–81.

5. Our discussion of interests is quite similar to and influenced by that of Tilly (1978).

6. The contribution generally consists of time and effort, money, or perhaps some other source. Some readers may find this representation of the utilitarian model clearer if the contribution is taken out of the expression that sums the expected value of the individual goods, and added to the right side of the inequality. To do this, let the contribution be the last individual good in the array of A's goods—the mth good. Then we can assume the utilitarian actor (A) will contribute and continue to contribute as long as

$$\sum_i^{m-1} V_a(i)[P_1(i) - P_2(i)] > V_a(m).$$

Protracted Conflict

Anthony Oberschall

Much intellectual effort has been devoted to understanding the origins of social conflict, to explaining mobilization for collective action, and to describing leaders, participants, and their ideologies. Less attention has been paid to the dynamic aspects of group conflict: its course, duration, intensity, and outcome. In this essay I will present a useful way of analyzing some dynamic aspects by viewing them as the result of a sequence of interrelated choices made by the contesting parties: choices about means of confrontation, conciliation, escalation and repression, and withdrawal. The benefits and costs of these choices change over time as the parties in the conflict mobilize and use up resources, and as the balance of forces and the chances of success change. Conflict dynamics needs to be linked systematically to mobilization theory. I will link the two as a first step by analyzing the extent to which size of challenges, support from without, and degree of organization of the challenges constrain the choices of both contestants.

Assume that there are two groups, one positively privileged and the other negatively privileged. Some members of the negatively privileged group seek a collective good—equality, independence, religious freedom, political rights, full citizenship—which to members of the positively privileged group is undesirable, that is, a collective bad. The demand for change will therefore be resisted.

Negatively privileged groups, the "challengers" in Tilly's (1975) terminology, put forward collective goods demands because they cannot increase their well-being through individual effort. Such a situation is common when group membership and boundaries are defined along ascriptive criteria. If blacks cannot become white, Moslems cannot become Christians, and Catholics in Northern Ireland cannot become

I wish to thank Drs. Judi Lachman, Mancur Olson, Jr., Gary Wamsley, and Mayer Zald for helpful comments.

Protestants, then the only way that blacks, Moslems, and Catholics can obtain the rights, advantages, and goods enjoyed by the privileged groups is by obtaining a collective good. If you can't join them and if you want a better deal for yourself, you've got to obtain a better deal for your entire group. In Hirschman's (1970) terms, if the "exit" option is not available (through emigration, social mobility, changing group membership), the "voice" alternative alone remains. What forms will it take?

There are two principal ways of inducing others to give up or share something they consider valuable. The first, through exchange, is to provide them with something that is equally or more valuable to them. The second is to threaten, pressure, and coerce them into giving it up or sharing it. The challengers make life so unpleasant for the target group that the target's welfare is diminished. An entirely new situation has been created. The challenger now is in a position to offer the target something that will increase his welfare: he offers to desist from threats, disruption, and violence in return for the collective good he is seeking (J. Q. Wilson, 1961).

When a negatively privileged challenger faces a positively privileged target, exchange is not likely, because the challenger has no resources that would make the target better off. The initiative therefore rests with the challenger. His only option is to pressure, threaten, or coerce the target. The prospect of the cessation of disruption becomes the positive inducement for the target to negotiate, that is, to enter into exchange.

It is therefore inevitable that a negatively privileged challenger will resort partly to nonconventional means of conflict for obtaining his desired goals, and that these nonconventional means will have to include at least some elements of harassment, obstruction, coercion, and threatened or actual violence, which lower the welfare of the target. By nonconventional means of waging conflict I mean marches and demonstrations, picketing, strikes, boycotts, civil disobedience, civil disorders, riots, terrorist acts, kidnappings, sabotage, and guerrilla warfare. Nonconventional conflict lowers the welfare of the target group, if only through public embarrassment, such as may result from a demonstration, civil disobedience, or a hunger strike; much nonconventional conflict does create damage, injury, and disruption. Conventional means, by contrast, are the exercise of persuasion, influence, and bargaining in negotiations and routine political transactions. Conventional means of conflict are not intended to lower the welfare of the contestants but are undertaken for the purpose of increasing it. I do not mean to draw a sharp boundary between conventional and nonconventional means. In most real-world conflicts, both parties pursue their aims with a mixture of means, conventional and nonconventional, at least for a time.

In most situations of interest, the positively privileged target is either protected by the authorities or includes the authorities. Nonconventional means of challenge necessitate a response: demonstrations are tying up traffic, workers are on strike and prevent nonstriking workers from entering work places, students refuse induction into the army, a meeting has been disrupted, a bomb has caused injury and death, and so on. Authorities are under pressure to provide a safe, peaceful environment for the citizenry so that it can go about its daily business without fear of personal injury, property loss, and inconvenience. And if laws are violated in nonconventional confrontations, the machinery of law enforcement and justice is put into motion. Consequently, whether or not the target or the authorities are inclined to be conciliatory, social control measures will be taken to deal with the immediate problem of law violation and disruption.

Thus, in addition to the original issue at stake in the conflict—the collective good sought by the challenger—the challenger's nonconventional tactics and the authorities' social control response in the confrontation create new issues; that is, derivative issues are added to the original issue. Did the police use rough tactics and unnecessary force against peaceful demonstrators? Were the demonstrators responsible for broken windows? Did the prosecuted lawbreakers get fair trials? Was the speech made by a leader an incitement to violence? And so on. Derivative issues will create conflict over the apportionment of responsibility, blame, penalties, and compensation for wrongs, damage, injuries, and deaths resulting from nonconventional means of waging conflict. Conciliation between the antagonists may now be complicated by the derivative issues piled on top of the original issues.

The target's response of reestablishing law and order and of prosecuting lawbreakers is not the only social control option open to it. The challengers may well have resorted to nonconventional means in order to pressure the target group into negotiating over the original issue. But instead of making unilateral concessions or entering into negotiations, the target group may decide in turn to lower the welfare of the challenger in order to induce the challenger to abandon his challenge or lower his original demands: he may decide to repress the challenger. In return for ending the repression, and thus restoring the welfare of the challenger to its previous level, the target expects the challenger to give up nonconventional means of conflict. If the challenger, however, responds by stepping up nonconventional conflict, which lowers the target's welfare yet further, a spiral of destructive conflict is well on its way. The aim of the antagonists eventually is no longer to induce conciliation or establish a strong bargaining position, but to destroy or permanently weaken the opponent and unilaterally impose an outcome to the conflict. On top of the original issues and the derivative issues, a

Protracted Conflict

third and even more fundamental issue has been created by escalation: that of survival.

A simplified version of the sequence of moves and countermoves described here can be presented schematically as a decision tree in figure 1. The technique is similar to viewing a system in continuous motion by means of a sequence of still photographs. The sequences NE—ne, ne—NE, and uc—NE result in conflict resolution, whereas the TE choice results in a unilateral imposition of an outcome upon the challenger. These terminal points to the conflict are indicated by one symbol, $\odot$. The possibility of a unilateral win by the challenger resulting from a disintegration of the target is omitted from the scheme.

The choice of the amount, type, and mixture of conciliatory and coercive means of challenge and of response will depend on a calculation of expected gains and losses, of benefits and costs, by both groups. I assume that both antagonists will maximize net benefits, subject to constraints.[1] What are the benefits and costs of conciliation and of confrontation?

CONCILIATION

By conciliation I mean recognition of and negotiation with representatives of the opposition in order to reach an agreement that will lead to a cessation of nonconventional conflict. Conciliation implies abandoning the goal of weakening or crushing one's opponent, lowering his welfare, and imposing an outcome on him unilaterally. What, then, are the benefits and costs to both parties of conciliation during confrontation? How do they change with duration of the conflict?

The authorities, or target, seek to reestablish peaceful life, so that citizens and businesses can conduct their routine activities in complete security. At the same time, a termination of hostilities will reduce the cost of social control. Continued coercive social control may also be a source of international and domestic embarrassment for a target whose claim to legitimacy is based on the consent of the governed.

The costs the target will have to bear are those resulting from concessions on the collective goods demand of the challenger and those of settling the derivative issues. Low resistance to challengers' demands and lenient treatment may encourage other potential challengers, however, and may even undermine the legitimacy of the regime in the eyes of its supporters. In an extreme case, vigilante groups may form to protect members of the target and to settle scores with challengers if the authorities are unwilling or unable to do so. Protestant assaults on

Figure 1 *A Decision Tree for Moves and Countermoves*

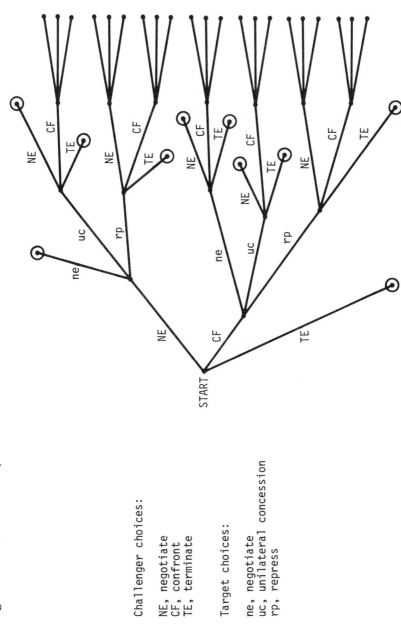

Challenger choices:

NE, negotiate
CF, confront
TE, terminate

Target choices:

ne, negotiate
uc, unilateral concession
rp, repress

49

Catholics revived the IRA, and IRA violence produced Protestant execution squads.

It is evident that, to the target, the principal immediate benefit of conciliation is the cessation of hostilities. But to the extent that challengers are not an organized entity, with a leadership capable of enforcing discipline among followers, negotiations do not guarantee the cessation of destructive conflict. The choice of conciliation by negotiations is thus not an attractive one to the target. Moreover, if the target is faced wih a factionalized challenger, as is so often the case, the same dilemma exists. It is the more violent and hard-line factions that most influence a target's calculations of benefits and costs from conciliation, because they hold the trump cards for stopping hostilities. If the target appears to yield to the hard-liners' threat of force, it invites the more conciliatory, moderate challengers to resort to coercive tactics, which would increase their bargaining power in an overall settlement. If, on the other hand, the target seeks to isolate the hard-liners by reaching a settlement with the moderates, the cessation of destructive conflict is not assured. There are indications that Ian Smith, the Rhodesian Prime Minister, boxed himself into just such a dilemma at the 1976 Geneva Conference on Rhodesia.

A dynamic view of conflict will have to incorporate some assessment of the impact of prolonged confrontation on the challengers as an entity. Paradoxically, then, if intransigence and repressive social control weaken, factionalize, or destroy the leaders and social movement organizations of the challenger, the likelihood of a subsequent enforceable agreement with the challenger will decrease, and thus also the target's incentive to negotiate a settlement to the conflict.

Unilateral concession made without a negotiated agreement is another possible conciliatory response in conflict. It corresponds to Schelling's (1963) notion of tacit bargaining. The target then faces the dilemma that loosened social control and reform (the conciliatory moves) decrease the challengers' costs of mobilization for collective action and increase their resources as well. Thus, the target may be faced with a more powerful challenger in the near future, should the challenger not reciprocate in turn by curbing coercive means of challenge and by demobilizing (Oberschall, 1973, pp. 137–38, 163–64).

Benefits from conciliation expected by challengers include gains on the original collective good issue; personal security; a lower cost of organization maintenance and mobilization, resulting from a greater freedom of action and a lower risk of prosecution; an image of moderation and restraint that will attract third-party support; and the establishing of a cooperative relationship with the authorities, leading to low-cost, conventional, institutionalized demand making. The principal cost of conciliation is settling for less of a collective good than originally sought and for paying some of the penalties from settling derivative issues.

The dilemma faced by a conciliatory challenger is very much the same as that of the target when it loosens social control. After personal security and collective goods benefits are promised and partly implemented, the challenger will demobilize in part. The target may then decide to renege on promises or on the terms of the settlement.

Insofar as destructive conflict increases suspicion and mistrust between antagonists, the mutual trust necessary for taking a gamble on conciliation may be lacking on both sides. Prolonged and destructive conflict often brings to prominence hard-liners within the target who will not be trusted by the challenger and extremists in the challenger who will not be trusted by the target. Conditions favorable to conciliation decrease as the duration of coercive conflict increases.

Even if conciliation is initiated by both sides, the chances of bringing it to a successful conclusion amidst a destructive conflict are low. Who to negotiate with is by no means a clear-cut question, for a loosely structured, factionalized challenger speaks with many voices, each claiming to represent the challenger. Thus, the authorities' recognition of some, but not other, leaders and factions as legitimate spokesmen of the challenger may itself become an additional issue in the conflict, and sometimes becomes *the* principal issue. This was the case with the seating of the National Liberation Front of South Vietnam with the North Vietnamese and inclusion of the South Vietnam government with the United States in the Paris peace negotiations, and it is still the principal issue in the inclusion of the Palestine Liberation Front on the Arab side in an overall Middle East peace settlement.

What issues to negotiate (i.e., what to do about nonnegotiable demands and other preconditions set by the two sides); in what sequence to take up issues; under what rules, where, and when to negotiate—these are all potentially divisive issues in nonconventional conflict resolution. Moreover, even if negotiations are undertaken, violence, provocations, arrests, and injuries may continue and keep calling into question the good faith of the parties for honoring future agreements and their capacity for abiding by a negotiated settlement.

Because protracted conflict keeps creating derivative issues, factionalizes opponents, destroys trust, invites outside intervention, and brings to power hard-liners and extremists, the conclusion from my analysis is that the chances of conciliation diminish with the duration of the conflict. Expected net benefits from conciliation tend to decrease for both sides as the conflict escalates and becomes more intense, destructive, and prolonged. Conciliation in destructive conflict will in many cases be undertaken only as a result of third-party interposition based on superior force: examples are Syrian intervention in Lebanon and NATO pressures and UN interposition in Cyprus.

BENEFITS AND COSTS OF NONCONVENTIONAL CHALLENGE

If a conflict is not terminated by conciliation, it can end only with the imposition of an outcome by one party upon the other: the target might cave in, or the challenger could unilaterally abandon nonconventional confrontation. What then determines the choice of confrontation by the challenger in the face of target resistance?

Costs and benefits of nonconventional challenge to a participant in the challenge can be broken down into the following component parts, which will be commented upon later:

$$NB = P(G_1 + G_1{}^*) + (1 - P)(G_2 + G_2{}^*) - C_1 - C_2 - G_3 - G_3{}^*,$$

where

NB is the net benefit from participation in the challenge;

P is the probability of obtaining the collective good;

G_1 is the gain (or loss) to the challenger from the collective state if the challenge is successful (i.e., if the collective good is obtained);

G_2 is the gain (or loss) to the challenger from the collective state if the challenge is not successful (i.e., if the collective good is not obtained);

G_3 is the gain (or loss) to the challenger from the collective state if the challenge is abandoned;

$G_1{}^*$ is the gain (or loss) to the challenger from his individual status if the challenge is successful;

$G_2{}^*$ is the gain (or loss) to the challenger from his individual status if the challenge is not successful;

$G_3{}^*$ is the gain (or loss) to the challenger from his individual status if the challenge is abandoned;

C_1 is the cost of collective action;

C_2 is the opportunity cost of challenge.

The G and G^* can be positive or negative quantities.[2] The assumption is that a rational challenger will participate or continue participating in a challenge if his net benefit is greater than zero, but that he will abandon the challenge if his net benefit is zero or negative.[3] I now turn to an expression for net benefit.

Benefits will first of all consist of the utility G_1 from the collective good itself, contingent on obtaining the collective good. At a particular point in time during the conflict, benefits of a collective kind will be the utility of the collective good G_1 multiplied by the probability P of obtaining it, plus the probability of not obtaining it $(1 - P)$ multiplied by the utility from another state of group welfare G_2 (what one expects if the challenge is not going to be "successful" from that point on). The utilities have to be assessed relative to the expected state of group welfare without continuing the challenge, G_3, which may be quite different from the preconflict state.[4]

For instance, during the antiwar movement, after U.S. ground troops were being withdrawn, net benefits from continued antiwar activity would be derived in this way. Multiply the probability P of immediate, total U.S. disengagement from Indochina (the goal of the movement) by the utility from disengagement G_1; add 1 minus this probability multiplied by the utility from some other state of troop withdrawal and Vietnamization of the war, G_2; subtract the utility, G_3, associated with some other level of American involvement in the Vietnam war that would occur without the antiwar movement.

Looking only at the collective good component of the net benefit, then,

$$NB = PG_1 + (1 - P)G_2 - G_3.$$

Costs of a collective kind do not have to be introduced separately in this expression because they are already included in this manner of defining net benefits. Should continued challenge give rise to a repressive regime (a collective bad for challengers), then G_2 in the above expression would be negative, and unless P is close to 1, net collective benefits are likely to be negative. Negative net collective benefits would deter continued challenge. This is a state of affairs in which active opposition is expected to make things worse, rather than better, for the challenger as a group.

In addition to collective goods and bads, individual incentives and disincentives also enter choice. Some utility G_1^* is expected from being part of a successful challenge, such as, for instance, being in a leadership position. Another utility, G_2^*, is expected if the challenge is not successful, such as spending time in prison or losing one's job. Still a third utility, G_3^*, is expected if the challenge is abandoned.

C_1 refers to the costs of collective action, that is, the time and effort of one's contribution to the challenge and the risk of injury, imprisonment, and even death to which one is exposed in confrontations. Costs will depend on the means of challenge chosen, as well as on the social control response. Another cost is opportunity cost, C_2: participation in a challenge uses up time, money, and effort that might have been put to other uses. When peasant bands melt away at harvest time, the opportunity cost of collective action for them has become too high: they know that even if the challenge is successful, they simply have got to provide themselves and their kinfolk with food. C_1 and C_2 are also expressed in utility units.

Net individual benefits depend on the sign and magnitudes of G_1^*, G_2^*, and G_3^*, as well as P. Consider the kinsmen or close associates of an active challenger who expect a regime to persecute them even if they are not themselves active challengers. For them, G_3^* may be less than either G_1^* and G_2^*; that is, there may be a positive incentive for joining the challenge regardless of the probability of success P. Marx argued along these lines when he told the proletariat that it had nothing to lose but its chains. Similarly, if a challenging group can make life miserable for fence sitters, and if the target cannot protect them from challenger coercion, they may have positive incentives for joining the challenger, whether or not they think they would benefit from the hoped-for collective good: $PG_1^* + (1 - P)G_2^*$ in that case would exceed $G_3^* + C_1 + C_2$.

Individual incentives and disincentives (G^*) are here viewed in terms of the future. If the challenge is continued and successful, an activist may look forward to high status, leadership position, and material rewards (G_1^*); if the challenge is not successful (G_2^*), or if it is terminated (G_3^*), he may look forward to a life in prison or perhaps to being blacklisted from decent jobs for a long time to come. This is particularly the case with conflict that has become violent, where an accounting for deaths, injuries, and law violation will follow its termination. To be on the losing side in these situations may involve costs greater than those from continued active opposition, C_1.[5]

Consider the case of a young IRA gunman. Assuming that the probability of British withdrawal from Northern Ireland is quite low, and because by 1979 many of the Catholic civil rights goals have been achieved, he would expect that the net collective benefits from continued terrorism are low: P is low; thus $P(G_1)$ is small. Though G_2 and G_3 do not differ by much, G_3 exceeds G_2 because the exercise of civil rights and the reestablishment of a normal peace-time economy are delayed by continued civil strife. Thus, net collective benefits are negative. Individual incentives and disincentives outweigh those benefits in his choice of continued terrorist activity. Whether or not he and the IRA quit, costs are going to be high: ten to twenty years in prison after he is tracked down, unless he can spend a life in exile, which is not likely, as the Republic of Ireland has also outlawed the IRA. If he does not quit, although he has a very low chance of success this low probability is multiplied by a very high utility term—being a free man, a hero, with good patronage prospects and influence. Individual incentives therefore keep him fighting.

One can express his dilemma, looking at the net personal benefit terms of the larger expression, as follows:

$NB = PG_1 + (1 - P)G_2 - G_3$, where P is probability of success and is very small; G_1 is positive and substantial; G_2 is negative and substantial (e.g., ten years prison), and G_3 is almost as negative (e.g., eight years prison) as G_2. As far as the cost terms (C) are concerned, they have become small. The IRA has been avoiding ambushes of British soldiers for some time, preferring to assassinate civilians and bomb nonmilitary targets. The British army in turn has avoided search and confrontation tactics that would lead to shootouts with the IRA. Thus, C_1 is low. Opportunity cost C_2 may even have become positive. The typical IRA activist has low skills and low earning potential in the labor force. For some time the IRA has been involved in economic crime, rackets, and extortion that have eluded law enforcement. Thus, the sum of C_1 and C_2 is probably close to zero or but slightly negative. For a wide range of realistic values, then, net benefits from choosing continued conflict will be greater than zero (because the $-G_3$ term will actually be positive and exceed the negative $(1 - PG_2$ term).

Indeed, net benefits from continued confrontation may grow larger. It may be more difficult to prosecute crimes as the time lapsed increases, which difficulty would offset the somewhat higher penalties to be expected (i.e., $d(G_2 - G_3)/dt = 0$). Opportunity costs decrease over time as IRA members become specialists in crime (i.e., $dC_2/dt = 0$). By the same token, their skill at escaping detection may also increase (i.e., $dC_1/dt = 0$). Thus, set personal benefits from continuing may even increase with time. Finally, the IRA believes that time is on its side (i.e., $dP/dt = 0$) because British public opinion will tire of the Northern Ireland mess and will force a withdrawal of the British army.

A move available to the British authorities is to declare (or negotiate) an amnesty or partial amnesty (an issue raised by the IRA in the past). G_3 would then be only slightly negative, perhaps even positive, making net benefits less than zero. Such an amnesty might well lead to unilateral termination of the conflict by the IRA. Whether the British government would negotiate an amnesty depends, however, on *its* calculation of benefits and costs from its various alternatives for ending the fighting.

The target's benefits and costs can be broken down into similar components, which, for the sake of simplicity, I do not present. The target, too, derives utility from its way of life and contributes to the costs of a social control apparatus which protects that way of life. The collective good demands of the challenger would lower that utility. The confrontations lower it, as well, because injury, damage, disruption, insecurity, and so on, create disutilities. If the target group shifts resources from normal institutional uses to social control in order to reduce the collective action of the challenger, the increased cost of social control also lowers the resources available for enjoying the chosen way of life. Members of the target group calculate costs and benefits of resisting the demands of the challenger by various means and of conciliating the challenger. Estimates of the chances of success also enter their calculations. They, too, choose the course of action with the highest expected net benefit.[6]

CONFLICT AS INTERACTION

The analysis that follows differs from the usual analysis of collective goods production insofar as I do not assume that a production curve for collective goods can be expressed as a function of the challengers' inputs, in the way that it is possible to state a production function for shoes or automobiles. In a conflict, the probability of obtaining the collective good depends not only on the amount and type of collective action mounted by the challenger, but on the social control response of the target. Although it is reasonable to expect probability of success P to be positively related to level of collective action A, that is, $\partial p / \partial A > o$, and P to be negatively related to the level of social control S, that is, $\partial p / \partial S < o$, there is an interrelation between A and S, because both parties may increase or decrease A and S depending on what the other does. The situation is similar to an arms race, which is a dynamic process (Boulding, 1963, chap. 2).

There is a further complication. The probability P of obtaining the collective good depends on the amount of collective action A and of social control S in the confrontation. The individual's net benefit depends on C_1, his personal cost from collective action. Increasing the amount of A will increase the total cost of A. What will be the individual's own contribution, C_1, to this total cost?

In many cases of group conflict there are substantial outside sources of support to defray the cost of A: the white, northern, liberal conscience constituency that bankrolled the civil rights movement; Col. Khadaffi's financial support of Palestinians; the contributions of U.S. citizens to the IRA. How to keep and increase such contributions may weigh heavily on the means of confrontation chosen by the challenger, and how to decrease them on the means of social control chosen by the target.

Despite support originating from outside the challenger, substantial costs borne by the challenger will usually remain and will have to be divided up among the challenger's members. I assume that the individual cost of collective action C_1 will be negatively related to the number of challengers, $\partial C_1 / \partial N < 0$, for two reasons: mobilization costs per capita will decrease for a given level A, and confrontation costs themselves will also be lower (there is safety in numbers). Thus, the net benefit from challenge will depend on the challenger's estimation of the total number of others who will assume the mobilization and confrontation costs of the challenge. Such an estimation gives rise to the problem of strategic interaction in collective action (Frohlich, Oppenheimer, and Young, 1971). Strategic interaction depends on communication among challengers, on a collective action repertoire, and on bandwagon and reverse bandwagon effects; it will be discussed below.

The target's choices also take into account strategic interaction and outside sources of support for challenger mobilization. An overreaction in social control may well create a negative public opinion reaction and increase conscience constituency contributions to the challenger. On the other hand, if confrontation costs C_1 are kept low as a result of lenient reactions to the challenger's actions, net benefits from challenge will be positive and anticipated net benefits even more positive, because positive benefits can be expected to increase the number of challengers, which further reduces C_1, and may set off a positive bandwagon.

Strategic interaction is important also within the target group. An assessment of low probability of success in resisting the challenger at a reasonable social control cost may well lead to low morale, factionalism, neutrality, defections, or outright emigration (as is happening among Rhodesian whites), which further lower the probability of target success and increase social control costs for those remaining in the target, and thus may set off a negative bandwagon effect.

The target has the option of manipulating G_3 and $G_3{}^*$ to insure that net benefits from challenge will not exceed those from abandoning the challenge. A firm social control response keeps C_1 high, deters an increase in N, and lowers P, and concessions on the collective good demands decrease the net benefits from challenge by raising G_3. Nevertheless, such a firm response has the build-in difficulty of lowering $G_3{}^*$ as well, which in turn increases net benefits from continued challenge. A firm social control response, as in the case of the British response to the IRA already discussed, may not leave the challenger an attractive individual exit mechanism, and it thus keeps net benefits from challenge positive, despite high C_1 and low P. That is why a political settlement in group conflict is important. The challenger may then have a chance to negotiate his own future $G_3{}^*$ level as part of the settlement, that is, to negotiate on derivative issues concerning penalties for injuries and law violations that resulted from confrontation.

CONSTRAINTS ON SOCIAL CONTROL

So far, I have examined the benefits and costs of various means of confrontation for both antagonists in the conflict. Choice of means of confrontation is constrained by the resources the challenger and the target have for investing in collective action and in social control, respectively. Because the target is frequently the state itself, or relies for protection upon the authorities, the resources of the target are usually enormous, compared to those of the challenger. But authorities face legal, political, and constitutional constraints in the exercise of social control.

Social control has three dimensions. *Confrontation* control, social control in the narrow sense, refers to means used by social control agents during confrontations, such as crowd control and riot control. The authorities have considerable flexibility in reallocating agents of social control to trouble spots, mobilizing reserves (calling out the national guard), and using emergency measures (curfews) for reestablishing order. A second dimension of social control consists of measures designed for the *prevention* of nonconventional conflict in the first place: regulations governing meetings and marches, laws dealing with possession and use of weapons, prohibition of certain groups and associations, preventive detention and internment, censorship, and so on. Lastly, social control has a *judicial* dimension consisting of prosecution of law violators and the imposition of penalties. Judicial control comes too late to prevent conflict but has a deterrent effect upon future conflict.

All authorities face constraints in the use of confrontation, prevention, and judicial control. In confrontations, agents of social control will be held accountable for the use of force, and that will discourage the overuse and indiscriminant use of force. Visibility of social control actions, resulting from access by the news media to confrontation sites, and freedom of the press increase accountability and thus also constrain the means of confrontation control. Preventive and judicial control are constrained by constitutional and legal norms for the protection of individual rights, which are backed by domestic public opinion, interest groups, political opposition, and international opinion. Some restraints will be felt even in authoritarian and totalitarian regimes sensitive to international reactions and pressures. Soviet and East European control of dissident intellectuals is constrained by the reaction of Western governments, international public opinion, and Western European communist parties. Thus, the far greater resources of the authorities in a conflict are severely restricted in actual use, especially in a liberal democratic state, and the antagonists are more evenly matched than it might at first appear.

The target will have an incentive to be conciliatory if it is restrained from social control that would make confrontation costly to the challenger, and if repression is counterproductive (that is, if it will create sympathy and support for the challenger). Political opposition that does not condone preventive control and that holds agents of social control accountable, news media that increase visibility of social control, and an independent judiciary that refuses to back up confrontation and preventive control with convictions—all reduce the effectiveness of social control.[7]

CONSTRAINTS ON THE CHALLENGER

As far as the challenger is concerned, his choice of means of conflict will be constrained by his size, by his dependence on outside sources of support, and by the degree to which he is an organized entity. I select these three variables from among dozens of others because they play a key role in mobilization for collective action.

The size of the challenger N will bear centrally on the cost of collective action C_1 and on the probability of success P, as I have already indicated. Thus, size will be positively related to the amount of collective action A. Much collective action increases the visibility of the challenge, which, as we have just noted, increases the likelihood of restraint in the exercise of social control. Much collective action also increases the bargaining power of the challenger, because disruption and embarrassment from even mildly coercive, nonconventional confrontation is then great. The target has an additional incentive to conciliate, because the social control costs are going to be high when there is a great deal of A.

On the other hand, the cost of providing a collective good to a large number is higher than that of providing the good to a small number. Moreover, if the amount of collective action by the challenger is so large as to represent an overwhelming threat to the target, the target may well decide to repress the challenger once and for all, or at least make an intransigent social control response in order to weaken the challenger and force it to abandon its challenge.[8]

The dilemma of a large challenger, then, is that it might appear too threatening. Large challengers able to mount a great deal of collective action have an incentive not to push the target against the wall with costly collective goods demands and destructive collective action, for fear of drawing a repressive response that might make them worse off collectively (G_2 would be much below G_1, and below G_3 as well). Moderation among large challengers could be expected to increase the probability of conciliatory responses and of their obtaining some of their goals.

The dilemma of a small challenger is that its nuisance power is so low that it will not draw a conciliatory response. Consequently, a small challenger may decide to increase the coercive and destructive component of its collective actions, as the Weathermen chose to do after the failure of its call for mass protests in Chicago in 1969 and of other attempts to radicalize youth.

Under ordinary circumstances, a small challenger will be deterred from this escalation by the great personal risk, C_1, of doing so. Outside support, such as safe operating bases from another country or a safe escape route with a skyjacked airliner, will decrease C_1, as has been the case with transnational terrorists. If the outside source of support is only moral, a small challenger, such as the dissidents in the Soviet Union and Eastern Europe, has an incentive to use noncoercive means of challenge, so long as these are highly visible to potential third-party supporters. The leverage of the third party on the target is then expected to increase the probability of a conciliatory response and to moderate social control, despite the small size of the challenger.

To summarize the discussion of the effect of the challenger's size upon nonconventional challenge, I offer some hypotheses. Holding everything else constant:

1. The amount of collective action increases with the size of the challenger.
2. The probability of a conciliatory response by the target to the amount of collective action is curvilinear.

Putting (1) and (2) together:

3. The probability of a conciliatory response to the challenge increases at first with the size of challenger and then decreases.

These relationships are depicted in figure 2.

The second constraint variable, support from without, plays a complex yet important role in conflict. It compensates for resource deficits and the small size of the challenger and is perhaps the principal means by which a weak challenger can overcome the mobilization costs of collective action, C_1. Outside support can, however, be obtained by the target group as well, and its social control costs can thus be shared. The incentive for conciliation on both sides is much diminished when outsiders share in the costs of confrontation. Since World War II, U.S. and Soviet intervention in domestic conflicts in the Third World has

Figure 2 *Challenger Size and Collective Action*

1. Amount of
   challenger
   collective action
   A

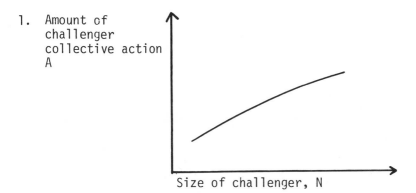

Size of challenger, N

2. Probability of
   conciliatory
   response by
   target P(C)

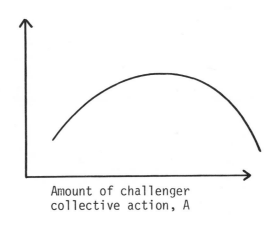

Amount of challenger
collective action, A

3. Probability of
   conciliatory
   response by target
   P(C)

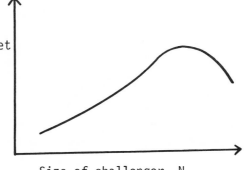

Size of challenger, N

contributed greatly to their destructiveness, their intensification, and their prolongation beyond their "natural" life. Even if third parties decide to withdraw from a conflict that has become destructive, the chances of conciliation are much lower than prior to their intervention, because destructive conflict decreases the likelihood of conciliation, as I have already indicated.

If only the challenger draws outside support, the amount will depend on the means of conflict used by both the challenger and the target. Paradoxically, the target is in a dilemma. To forestall outside support for the challenger, the target may decide to be more conciliatory than would otherwise be the case, given the size and weakness of the challenger. Yet the challenger has little incentive to respond in a conciliatory fashion, because a repressive response by the target will increase outside support, which will further increase the challenger's bargaining power. Maintaining pressure by nonconventional confrontation on even a fairly conciliatory opponent, in order to draw a more repressive response, will be a rational tactic for a weak challenger counting on increased outside support.

To some extent, this was the tactic of the southern civil rights movement. It was too weak to desegregate each city, each separate jurisdiction in the South, in localized confrontations, even with the financial and manpower help of northern liberals. Despite some conciliatory responses in southern towns and cities, the movement's strategy had to be the national one of getting the Congress and the federal government to enact and enforce civil rights legislation that would be applicable across the country. Only confrontations could produce the kinds of beatings and injuries by southern opponents that would outrage public opinion and pressure the federal government to enact such legislation. On their part, many southern politicians advanced their political careers by being nonconciliatory with civil rights groups and by defying the federal government. Thus, both sides in the southern civil rights confrontations had few incentives to conciliate (Oberschall, 1973, chap. 6).

The third constraint on the challenger considered here is the extent to which the challenger is an organized entity. A challenger can be thought of as a social interaction field with zones of varying organizational density (Oberschall, 1977). Organization provides a mechanism for resource mobilization to some central group or agency, which then allocates these resources to the pursuit of collective goals and organization maintenance. There are challengers whose entire social interaction field is encompassed by a social movement organization (SMO). Other challengers are much more loosely structured, with most supporters and many activist part-timers (transitory teams) only weakly linked to a permanent leadership in the SMO. The SMO of a loosely-knit challenger can be thought of as the tip of the iceberg, most of which is under water. The black movement in the middle and late 1960s and the antiwar and student movements were loosely organized movements. A few SMOs (SDS, Mobe, Black Panthers, SNCC) and "media" stars performed leadership roles with but limited organizational resources at their disposal. The blacks who rioted in U.S. cities in the 1960s had no organizational links with civil rights and black power organizations, though black SMOs and leaders had some influence on them. Their situations are in sharp contrast to that of highly organized and disciplined insurgencies, such as the National Liberation Front in South Vietnam, the MPLA in Angola, and the IRA in Northern Ireland.

LOOSELY STRUCTURED MOVEMENTS

Since loosely structured movements have received less attention in the social movement literature than SMOs, I will try to clarify some issues in mobilization for collective action and conflict regulation in the case of loosely structured challengers. Consider first the least organized end of the collective action continuum, food price riots and spontaneous demonstrations and strikes, such as occurred recently in Egyptian cities and in Poland. The situation is that of a large collectivity whose collective welfare has been unilaterally lowered by the authorities. The collectivity is not represented by an existing SMO or political organization with access to the authorities, nor, in the absence of freedom of association and personal liberties, is it possible to create such organization. The first individuals to attempt organization run high personal risks as a result of innovator-loss dynamics; there are free rider tendencies; and the sheer length of time that would pass before SMO efforts might bring relief, even if they could get underway, also make an organized challenge unlikely.

The negatively privileged group does have, however, some important resources at its disposal. It is large in size, and all of its members' welfares have been negatively affected. The potential challengers live in crowded neighborhoods, so that interpersonal communication and interaction among them is routine and relatively cost free. The negatively privileged collectivity possesses solidarity based on a sense of shared fate and opposition to the privileged classes and the authorities and will frequently possess a repertoire of collective action (Tilly, 1975). The collective action repertoire includes knowledge of past collective actions and their degree of success in similar situations, shared norms about the appropriateness of nonconventional protest actions, and a common response to shared symbols.

Participation in collective action will depend on the assessment of personal costs C_1 from overt opposition, the probability of success P, and the opportunity costs C_2. Opportunity costs (lost wages for the most part) can be kept low if the collective action is of short duration, such as a massive demonstration, short-lived riots, and short strikes.[9] Collective action costs C_1 are negatively related, and probability of success P is positively related, to the number of participants N. For pressuring authorities to rescind food price increases, a massive show of collective action and of solidarity is required, and everybody in the challenger groups knows it. Participation of any particular individual is, however, contingent on that individual's assessment of the likelihood of others participating, that is, on strategic interaction.

Roger Brown (1965, pp. 755–76) pointed out the importance of milling prior to rioting and of other forms of spontaneous collective action: "Milling . . . is a process of informal communication, . . . by which members learn that they are of one mind. . . . It is a process of acquainting one another with their preferences. . . ." During milling there occurs a realistic assessment by each participant of how many others will join a collective action.

Aside from the milling of crowds, other processes of strategic interaction, during which preferences, moods, and the likelihood of joining in collective action are communicated, take place in neighborhoods, work places, and casual encounters. These meetings also provide occasions for applying social pressures on those who are timid and fearful. In a relatively short time, then, massive collective action can be mounted without prior organization leadership and SMOs. Because of the collective action repertoire shared by the challengers, they carry in their minds the "battle plans" to be followed.

The target group is not in a position to negotiate with an unorganized entity and can only resort to well-publicized, unilateral concessions if it decides upon conciliation. Its choices are few in any case: usually a rollback of the announced price increases and the dismissal of some particularly disliked officials, who are made into scapegoats. The challenger will in most cases thereupon stick to its side of this tacit bargain and stop coercive collective action. In most such confrontations, destructive escalation of conflict is avoided by both sides.

AN ILLUSTRATION: THE 1960s' BLACK RIOTS

An explanation of black rioting in the 1960s in the United States can also be made along these lines, though what marks them off from the food price riots just discussed is their spread over a number of years, from 1963 to 1968; the increase in the frequency and severity of riots during these years; their outbreak in the late spring and summer months; and their higher incidence on weekends than on weekdays. One consistent finding from riot analyses (Spilerman, 1970, 1976) is that the two structural variables that explain frequency and severity of rioting in United States cities are the absolute size of the black population and location in the non-South, with other variables measuring absolute deprivation, relative deprivation, social disorganization, and political access explaining little or no variance.

During the mid-1960s, lower-class blacks were exposed to frequent and intense stimuli about their negatively privileged condition and the injustice of that state of affairs, communicated through the mass media and proclaimed by civil rights and black power leaders, by white liberal activists, and by elected national political leaders. Thus, black political consciousness grew, especially among youth. Yet none of the existing political parties, black organizations, and New Left groups succeeded in penetrating the black ghettos with an effective organizational network.

The situation was more critical outside the South because the two most visible and important reform measures, the Civil Rights Acts of 1964 and 1965, benefited southern blacks collectively but made little difference for the status of blacks elsewhere. Rioting as a means of applying and maintaining pressure on the white political leadership, both national and municipal, became the collective action response (some refer to it as the growth of a riot ideology) for exercising this pressure, in the absence of effective institutional and organized channels of political demand making.

Rioting occurred precisely where and when the conditions for strategic interaction were present and would lead to massive participation and low collective action costs: large size of black population ($\partial p/N>0$; $\partial A/\partial N>0$; $\partial C_1/\partial N<0$); ease of informal communication in black neighborhoods in the warm months, when people hang out in the streets; and weekends, when opportunity costs are low. The growth of a riot ideology, that is, of a collective action repertoire of rioting, helps explain the increase in frequency and severity over the years. The probability of others' joining in a riot would increase as this ideology became the norm; strategic interaction would thus set off positive bandwagons in riot participation. The nationwide riots following the assassination of civil rights leader Martin Luther King, Jr., point also to the explicitly political dimension of the black collective action repertoire that had developed during the 1960s. These riots meant that blacks expressed support for Dr. King's civil rights goals and were determined to press ahead to greater equality, even without their most prominent national spokesman.

One may well ask how and why such a riot wave came to a rather abrupt end in 1969, as neither the conditions for strategic interaction, nor the size of the black population, nor the riot ideology, nor indeed

Protracted Conflict   **65**

the socioeconomic condition of blacks could possibly change so abruptly from one year to another, and indeed did not. If rioting was a calculated means of gaining unilateral concessions from political leaders to whom lower-class blacks had no effective means of access and nothing positive to offer by way of exchange, then one has to take seriously the notion that the costs of rioting (fairly substantial when measured in terms of property damage, injuries, deaths, and arrests, borne principally by blacks and some white merchants) might outweigh the expected benefits once the political leadership was no longer responsive to this form of tacit bargaining. Nineteen sixty-eight was an important turning point in the sixties, for in that presidential election year the Wallace candidacy and backlash, the law and order theme stressed by all three candidates, the priority that the Vietnam issue had come to occupy over the black issue for the New Left, and the final Nixon victory were visible signals to blacks that the coercive pressures that appeared to be effective against liberal democratic administrations in Washington would no longer work and might even be counterproductive.

Thus, it was not more severe and more efficient social control that would account for the cessation of riots (I know of no information that would lead one to believe that such changes in social control occurred in the first place), nor the achievement of important collective goods breakthroughs by blacks between 1968 and 1969 (though evidence of gradual socioeconomic and political gains for blacks throughout the 1960s does exist). It was rather a realistic assessment that the probability P of a favorable response to rioting had considerably decreased between 1968 and 1969, and thus also the net benefits from rioting.[10]

Nonconventional conflict with a loosely organized challenger cannot be resolved by negotiated agreements, for there is no agent or group that can speak for the challenger and enforce compliance with the agreement. Authorities will therefore make unilateral concessions exacted under pressure and rely on social control. The individual incentives from participation in a loosely structured movement made up largely of part-timers with weak affiliation to SMOs and movement leaders are going to be quite modest, compared to the expected benefits from obtaining the collective good itself. Participants cannot be provided with selective incentives by an SMO if they are not formal members (it often happens that the SMOs cannot even identify their supporters individually), and part-time participation provides less "solidarity" benefits than in the case of permanent membership in a group dedicated to a common cause. Nor do participants in a loosely structured movement ever burn their bridges for a safe exit from the movement. They can withdraw from the movement into anonymity without fear of penalty, whereas members of SMOs may not be able to do so, because the social control agencies are more likely to have identified them, to keep track of them, and to harass or prosecute them. Finally, the opportunity costs of part-time participation are going to be quite low compared to those of full-time, dedicated SMO members, who may give up their jobs and professions altogether.

For the case of loosely organized challengers, the differences between G_1^*, G_2^*, and G_3^* are going to be much smaller than for highly organized movements, and C_2 less negative. Consequently, the decision to participate and to continue with a loosely organized challenger will depend heavily on G_1, G_2, G_3, P, and C_1. The three G_1 are subject to manipulation by the authorities by means of unilateral concessions. P and C are sensitive to the number of challengers N and to strategic interaction. Thus, the decline of a loosely organized challenge will be very rapid, as a result of the reverse bandwagon set in motion by a decreasing number of challengers if unilateral concessions satisfy and demobilize some of them. The remaining challengers, consisting of more radical and full-time activists who wish to pursue the struggle, may then turn to more violent and anonymous means of conflict. For them G_1 and G_1^* are still very much higher than G_3 and G_3^*, compensating for the lower probability of success P; and G_2^* still remains high, counteracting the more negative C_1 from loss of membership (only partly compensated by going underground and engaging in unpredictable hit-and-run actions against selected targets).

Unlike the short-lived food riot that ends in tacit bargaining between challenger and authority, the sustained, loosely organized challenge will end with the demobilization of the majority of participants as a result of substantial collective goods gains, even as a small group escalates the conflict by means of violent actions. Eventually, this small group will abandon the challenge unilaterally or will be tracked down by authorities, or, more likely, both.[11]

CONCLUSION

Though I hope that this application of the rational choice approach and of mobilization theory provides useful insights into conflict dynamics and conflict resolution, much more theoretical work remains, aside from empirical tests of deductions and generalizations. A fully articulated, dynamic analysis of social movements and of social conflict will have to specify the most important resources—material, psychological, and structural—that are assembled for, and used up in, organizational and collective action. It will have to specify how resource stocks constrain the protagonists' choices in conflict. It will have to incorporate analyses of strategies, bargaining, alliances, and coalition formation to explain the changing structure of social movements and of their targets. The goals of participants, their assessment of gains and losses, their perceptions of chances of success, their responses to incentives, both selective and collective, will have to be systematically grounded in social psychological theory. Lastly, a complete theory will have to specify the sources of conflict in the larger social and cultural environment, and spell out the impact of social movements upon the larger societal environment.

ENDNOTES

1. For simplicity's sake, I assume that both challenger and target are a single entity. In the theory of mobilization and collective action, it has been found useful to think of the challengers as consisting of activists or political entrepreneurs (Frohlich, Oppenheimer, and Young, 1971), or transitory teams, a conscience constituency, and other sympathizers (McCarthy and Zald, 1973b).
2. Collective goods and bads enter into G_1, G_2, and G_3. Selective incentives enter into G_1^*, G_2^*, and G_3^*. The point of reference for measuring gain (or loss) is the state of the chooser at the time of choice. If net benefits were to be expressed in utilities, the last terms, C_1 and C_2, would have to be expressed differently. The analysis that follows would remain the same regardless of the notation used.
3. I have assumed for the sake of simplicity that the probability of obtaining the collective good and the probability of individual success are the same. Though not likely, it is nevertheless possible that a challenging group might be successful in obtaining the collective good, and yet an individual participant in the challenge might not obtain the individual benefits associated with a successful group challenge with the same probability. To allow for this contingency, the expression for net benefit could be rewritten as

$$NB = PG_1 = (1 - P)G_2 + QG_1^* + (1 - Q)G_2^* - C_1 - C_2 - G_3 - G_3^*,$$

where P is the probability of obtaining the collective good, and Q is the probability of obtaining personal benefits from a successful challenge.
4. I have assumed only two outcomes, success and lack of success, associated with gains G_1 and G_2. The approach can be extended to a number of outcomes, each associated with a probability and a gain (or loss), without changing the conclusions. A second assumption is that net benefits depend on the expected value of the gains and losses. If one were to describe the choices of risk averters or risk takers, a more complicated probability expression would be appropriate.
5. In these benefit and cost calculations, I have not included the cost of providing the collective good, because it is not borne by the challenger, should he be successful. The type of group conflict analyzed here involves situations in which the challenger undertakes collective action of some kind,

which is a cost for him, in order to have the target group supply the collective good, which will be a cost to the target. A movement that is successful in legalizing abortion does not supply the abortion service itself, nor contribute to the costs of these services. It is health insurance, the users of the service, or a national health service that pays for the collective good, the abortion.

This formulation of the benefits and costs differs from Olson's (1968) and Frohlich, Oppenheimer, and Young's (1971) analysis of collective goods provisions, because the group conflict situation differs from those they dealt with. But insofar as the challenger supplies collective action to obtain the collective good, the collective action *is* a collective good for the beneficiary group. Thus, the Olson and Frohlich, Oppenheimer, and Young analyses apply to the question of contributions to collective action by those who would benefit from the collective good.

6. To continue with the IRA example, the best benefit to the British government of a conciliatory policy would depend on the governments assessment of the probability P of success of that policy; G_1, gain or loss to the government from a peaceful Britain; G_2, gain or loss from the state of Britain should conciliation fail; G_3, gain or loss from the state of Britain should the government continue a policy of repression; G_1^*, the political advantage of successful conciliation; G_2^*, the political costs of unsuccessful conciliation; G_3^*, the political gains or losses from taking a hard line; C_1, the political cost of social control in lives lost and resources expended; and C_2, the political advantage given up had these resources been invested in economic and social programs rather than in conflict.

7. In the late 1960s and the early 1970s in the United States, as I have elsewhere shown (Oberschall, 1977), judges, juries, and courts repeatedly refused to convict or else set mild penalties in cases involving antiwar, New Left, and black activists; and university administrators and faculty disciplinary boards did the same for students in campus confrontations. Despite their vast scale, the FBI, military intelligence, and police efforts proved singularly ineffective in curbing dissident groups. Moreover, the legal and illegal social control activities of the authorities did not succeed in intimidating civil liberties groups, such as the ACLU, the news media, and the political opposition to the Johnson and Nixon administrations. Unable to repress the antiwar movement, the Johnson and Nixon administrations were constrained to make conciliatory responses to the antiwar and other protest movements (bombing halts, Paris peace negotiations, Johnson's decision not to run for president, U.S. troop withdrawals, termination of the draft).

8. A more complete treatment of the size variable would have to take into account not only absolute size but the relative size of the challenger and of the target and the size of the active, mobilized portion of the challenger.

9. The longer the duration of collective action, the greater the opportunity costs.

10. There exists some evidence of the growth of a similar collective action repertoire in the student and antiwar movements in these years, touched off not by greater organizational mobilization of challengers and the

emergence of a central leadership and disciplined cadres, but by conditions favoring strategic interaction and bandwagon effects made possible by costless communication among challengers through the mass media, especially television (Oberschall, 1977).

11. This conclusion does not apply to the more complicated case of a highly organized movement emerging out of an initially loosely structured challenge.

Media and Movements

Harvey Molotch

A social movement must create a societal context in which it can survive, prosper, and ultimately, triumph. One important resource in providing for this fertile context is the mass media and, in particular, the print and broadcast news. Social movements represent those portions of society that lie outside the ordinary routines of exercising power and influence. For them, the mass media represent a potential mechanism for utilizing an establishment institution to fulfill nonestablishment goals: communicating with movement followers, reaching out to potential recruits, neutralizing would-be opponents, and confusing or otherwise immobilizing committed opponents.

For the mass media, the movements have their uses as well. Journalists working "on the line" find that, at least at certain times and places, reports on activists' doings are received as competent copy by their editors. Editors, at least under certain conditions, find movement activities "interesting" and matters that ought to be known about by mass audiences as a matter of civic benefit. News of movements can help fill the daily news hole and aid the medium in its key business of selling attentive audiences to advertisers. The media and the movements hence often need one another, but in a context with high potential for tension. The remainder of this essay attempts to elaborate the ways in which these needs intersect and the consequences that follow from the contingencies framing these intersections. Although a more complete treatment would include within this analysis a wide range of mass media (including TV talk shows, comic books, phonograph records, drama, etc.), this discussion focuses almost exclusively on "straight" news.

I am especially indebted to Richard Peterson for his detailed critique.

THE SALIENCE OF MEDIA TO ACTIVISTS

Within the rather diverse group of movements I have either studied or participated in, activists have seemed generally aware of the significance of media in their work, although this awareness was different in content from what is now my own. By briefly describing these groups I can use them to provide a few illustrations of the salience of media in the lives of movement activists.

1. *South Shore* was a gray area of Chicago led by upper-middle-class professionals committed to stemming black immigration into their community. Although only marginally constituting a social movement, because of their close ties with local establishments, they considered themselves embattled and courageous, and hence much of their behavior had characteristics ordinarily associated with social movements. In my study of their attempt to "preserve racial integration," I was struck by a paradox: regardless of the clarity of the evidence made available to them that they were failing, the activists were high in morale and hopeful of success. I concluded that although the organization was indeed failing in its formal goals, it was succeeding in its mobilization of resources—for example, increasing operating budgets and gaining access to politicians and, particularly, to media. Articles in local and national papers chronicling alleged success (even when based on fabrications developed by the activists) brought bolts of euphoria to the leadership and seemed to cause a redoubling of commitment (see Molotch, 1967).

2. *Students for a Democratic Society* (SDS) displayed the same sort of interest in media coverage. This impression, gained from my years as an SDS participant, seems confirmed by the subsequent descriptive analyses and histories of the student movement (see particularly Gitlin, 1977; Mairowitz, 1974). The effect of coverage was to enliven the movement and increase morale. Even when coverage was unsympathetic (as it usually was), the result was animation and increased energy. Coverage per se tended to be an organizationally constructive force, and the denunciation of the media that often followed coverage of a specific event was another way of discussing and getting motivated for "what must be done." Generally speaking, no news was bad news.

3. *Get Oil Out* activists in Santa Barbara came into being after the 1969 oil spill. They consistently saw their clear function as the manipulation of the national media in order to mold national energy and environmental policies to the advantage of their local community. Unlike student movement participants, these were adults established in business and professional careers; unlike middle-class South Shore leaders, the antioil activists were attempting to influence national decision making

and were, at least in relation to national energy and environmental policy, quite definitely antiestablishment (Molotch, 1970).

Again, I stress that these movements were rather diverse, and, with some help from supporting literature (including others' contributions to this volume), I make a good deal of their common reliance upon, sensitivity to, and celebration of, media coverage.

Perhaps, as I have previously implied, this abiding interest in media derives from activists' own knowledge that media are a means for organizational goal attainment. But there is also the activists' sense that media coverage means that what they do *matters in the world*. Especially for people who are more used to making life than to making history (see Flacks, 1976), there is a special euphoria that comes from seeing in mass media the results of their own actions. It provides for a sense of dignity and effectiveness—regardless of the type of coverage received. For those observers unsympathetic to the movement, or at least to a particular movement strategy, this energizing force of coverage is seen to display "merely" the "politics of kicks," or the "politics of masturbation," or the politics of people who "just want to see their names in the newspaper."

I do not see psychic gratification as an extraneous quality of political activity; it is a necessary concomitant, just as psychic motivation is a requisite for any human behavior. Nor do I see any analytic conflict between viewing social movements as actors whose motivations are taken as problematic and seeing social movements as structurally determined phenomena in which actors struggle for resources in critical contexts molded by many forces outside their own control. In their use of media, activists seek to achieve concrete goals and they are aware —to some degree—of the significance of media in achieving those goals. At the same time, the ability to use media, to see their names in print, further vitalizes the range of activity—some of it, like licking envelopes or making bombs, quite arduous and unpleasant—that leads to the events gaining the coverage, which further provides for activists' morale.

The movements with which I am most familiar, and which hence form the context of this discussion, are recent and are American; it is quite possible that at other times and places the role of mass media is less pervasive. But among the modern American movements, the news media do seem to play a critical role in linking psychic motivation with resource context, biographies with history, the have-nots with one establishment institution. In order to continue developing these linkages, my plan for the remainder of this essay is to (1) define what news is; (2) further elaborate what movements are in terms of their uses of news media; (3) describe the counterstrategies of media in opposition to movement goals; and (4) provide for more complex models of changing media-movement relationships.

NEWS AS SPECIFICALLY ANYTHING

News is often defined as a coverage of objectively important things in the world (see Tuchman, 1972), in its temporal relation to those events—that is, news is "fresh," compared to, say, history. In contrast, I wish to define news interactionally, rather than as a *thing* in the world.

I view news as a peculiar form of information, peculiar in that it is, at least in formal terms, *specifically about nothing in particular*. Unlike washing machine instructions, a genetics textbook, or a history of England, the content of a newspaper or newscast is unspecifiable in substance. What it will consist of is unknown, and in this sense there is a critical element of surprise; both the news consumer and the news producer have *no specific expectation of content*. This is the attitude at the outset; it is this open-ended quality of news that I take to be its defining characteristic and that makes it so rich a basis for interaction study.

From this definition, it follows that news can happen anywhere—in the mass media, of course, but also in a two-party conversation. The question "What's new?" can, *in formal terms*, elicit anything. But as Lester and I have tried to point out elsewhere (Molotch and Lester, 1974, 1975), the "anything" is contextually structured in complex and interesting ways. As a formal matter, news is about anything; as a practical matter, it is not. It is artfully constructed as an interaction between two or more human beings, and it is the nature of the participants, their power relative to one another, the historic moment they share, and all other particulars of their situation that will determine what is or is not news. Therefore, it is the social context, energized by actors' purposes-at-hand, rather than the substantive content of a given event, that is the practical source of news.

Hence, if a faculty colleague asks me "What's new?" I will make use of a sense of relevancies derived from our common life—my colleague's biography, my biography as it is known to her, the particulars of the context we share. So I may answer with talk about a paper I am writing, a student who passed an exam, a piece of dirt about an administrator we both dislike. Although I am called upon to talk about "anything," I *know* that not anything will do. I do not, for example, tell my colleague about my love life, my most recent meal, my sister's operation, or my growing dislike of my colleague's best friend. Yet all these details might, in a different context, be the appropriate and called-for reply to the question "What's new?"

I am not trying to say that in not bringing up certain matters in a given context, one is telling half-truths, withholding information, or distorting the facts. One is instead merely being responsive to the goal of being *interesting*. And what strikes one as interesting emerges from the context surrounding both the speaker and the listener. Ordinarily, a piece of information that does not facilitate my own goals is less interesting to me than one that does. The fact that a highway I use on my way to work is closed to traffic is more interesting than the fact that another, "irrelevant" highway is closed. My listener has an analogous set of *news needs*, and my ability to provide for those needs is the degree to which I am interesting to him. The skilled conversationalist apprehends things as "interesting" based on these two criteria.

Two things are hence at work when I do news: I must provide replies that suit the relevancies and news needs of the other; and I must strive to provide self-serving particulars that will enhance my own goals or at least be neutral to them. News is, accordingly, purposive behavior, and doing news is important survival work. Certain people are more skilled than others because they have more talent, are structurally located in an advantageous power status, have greater access to knowledge of particulars and alternative schemes of relevance, and—most important in the present discussion—have easier access to media, which provide an opportunity to serve the news needs of others while simultaneously enhancing goals of one's own. They can be interesting on a massive scale.

THE CLASS BIAS OF "INTERESTING"

Mass media provide those with access to them a means of multiplying the doing of news in a significantly more effective way. The process is the same as in a two-party conversation, but the scale of the operation and therefore the significance of the consequence are very different. Hence the struggle for access.

Mass media in the United States are under the control of a certain class—let us call it the ruling class. I say the ruling class controls because the owners of newspapers and of TV and radio stations either are themselves members of this class or aspire to such membership. The class controls because the revenues of the media are heavily dependent upon advertisements and grants from members of this class. The members of this class control because they are the single most important social influence on the national government, which "controls," through its regulatory agencies, the electronic media, and through the courts, the rights of the print media as well. Finally, they control because they are the single most important social force in structuring the national ideology through mechanisms such as education, voluntary associations, religious organizations, theater, films, and so on—the other media that socialize news producers and news consumers.

It is a part of the genius of the American system that its ruling class does not control through day-to-day edicts or bureaucracies that formally mobilize resources on its behalf. Our system is relatively open, loose, sloppy. Visible legitimacy, the consent of the governed, is taken as critically important by many members of the ruling class, and society's institutions reflect this commitment. The doctrine of editorial freedom means that certain noxious publications must be allowed to exist (up to a point) alongside the major dailies and networks. It is at least tasteless to fire a reporter or to censor a story by making explicit reference to the ideological needs of a ruling class.

But I take it that the news-generating process in the mass media is essentially the same as in a two-party conversation. Those who control the media (whether the medium is NBC or an individual's mouth) will, over the long haul, attempt to generate news that serves the two critical functions of meeting the news needs of the listener-hearer while sustaining the power and efficacy of those who control the medium. So what I am saying is that, of a wide range of "things" to publish and broadcast, the thrust of publication and broadcasting will serve the ruling class and the status quo.

The reporter's "nose for news," I am saying, includes as a critical component the sustenance of the ruling class. This nose has been subtly shaped through a complex array of mechanisms and institutions: political science, which teaches future news reporters that the power and influence structure of the United States is reflected in the organizational chart of governmental institutions; economics, which teaches the same people that the assumptions of a free market economy are sacred and that prosperity is best measured by such indexes as GNP; sociology, which teaches them to make a fetish of fact, to ritualize objectivity, and to see the poor as a source of human interest stories but not as a class with potentially insurgent behavior and goals. The nose is also shaped, when need be, by editors who find reporters' stories unworthy of publication by seeing them as uninteresting, unconstructive, or speculative. The most proximate force shaping the nose for news is the unrelenting demand that reporters provide large quantities of copy each day, a requirement that causes them to rely upon official press conferences, public relations men, and politicians' news representatives. They have little time for anything else. Reporters become locked in establishment bureaucracies because only these institutions both have prima facie legitimacy and are dependable sources of column inches of copy. As Mark Fishman argues in a forthcoming study, news is therefore bureaucratized. Collecting the routine droppings of these legitimated bureaucracies somehow comes to be the safest and most reliable means available to the newsworker of displaying objective professionalism.

This is part of what social movements are up against. Because a social movement is, to one degree or another, antiestablishment, it must find a way to enter media that are, as a matter of routine operation, not suited to provide it with coverage. What is "interesting" to the movement is not necessarily "interesting" to the media. Unlike news from the established institutions, movement news is not prima facie interesting, important, and defensible to work supervisors as worthy of publication. Unlike news from the established institutions, news from the movements is not made available to the media in a dependably usable format, or produced at a dependable time and length with follow-up information securely available at phones answered by secretaries who leave messages for media-skilled bosses. Only news of movements made available by the bureaucracies (e.g., police or politicians) has these qualities, but then it also partakes of news needs opposite to those of the activists.

Movement activists must somehow overcome these difficulties to achieve useful coverage. They must do this by somehow, in some striking way, fulfilling the news needs of those in control of media—that is, they must become interesting. Obviously, calling a press conference will not do. The movement must shape its behavior in such a way that the media find it useful to report that behavior; and at the same time, to serve its own interests, the movement must succeed in portraying itself in a somewhat effective way. The movement must achieve visibility and end up stronger as a result of coverage than it would have been without the coverage. Coverage brings strength in the form of morale boost; it also brings strength—at least potentially—in its ability to affect others. The media cover the activists, but when they are in tension with the movement (as is usually the case), they do so with opposite goals in view. From their vantage point in the game, the media "win" if the status quo is enhanced as a result of the media coverage. Hence, a typical movement story results from differing estimates of the consequences of coverage; the activists stage rallies, sit-ins, pickets, marches, or whatever, because they think a net gain in social change will result; the media make the opposite estimate of the situation and therefore provide the coverage. Somebody is wrong in this situation, but it is often very difficult for the participants to know which side is in error.

MOVEMENTS AS ANTIROUTINES

From my definitional standpoint, a social movement takes its form, is indeed defined in terms of, its juxtaposition to the normal functioning and structural characteristics of the society at large. A social movement is "abnormal" rather than normal, episodic rather than continuous, extraordinary rather than routine, illegitimate rather than legitimate, and powerless rather than powerful. This is the position from which a social movement ordinarily begins its struggle for access.

Members of the ruling class are not typically participants in social movements. They have no need to be. The mass media, just as with societal institutions generally, are organized to serve their needs. What Lester and I have elsewhere (Molotch and Lester, 1974) called "routine news" is a system that provides for their news needs, just as their country clubs provide for their recreation. They also buy coverage they need through product, corporate institutional, and voluntary association advertising.[1] When they have grievances against the status quo, those grievances are immediately translatable into institutional formations that bear little resemblance to social movements. High-status people can act individually and quite directly: they can purchase what they want, they can phone in a complaint, they can buy a politician. They can mobilize the existing institutional structure by having appropriate legislation introduced or by mounting a lawsuit. Where public support is necessary, they can create propaganda arms that feed into a news media always responsive to their institutions; they can form commissions to investigate, blue-ribbon committees to recommend, fact-finding task forces to mobilize opinions. As Lester and I have tried to demonstrate empirically in previous work (Molotch and Lester, 1975), when they speak, their words are widely disseminated by mass media.

When their interests are directly confronted—as with cases of theft, murder, industrial sabotage, political insurrection—they find themselves supported by a criminal justice system existing for their benefit. "Crime" can be defined in just such terms; it consists of those acts as a result of which societal resources are mobilized to bring moral support to a "victim" and to eliminate such support from an "offender." Crime victims, by this definition, are able to make legitimate claims for retribution, sympathy, revenge.

As opposed to crime victims, there are those who, although aggrieved by human acts in the society, by something being done to them, have no warrant to claim prima facie legitimacy for their complaints. These are *crimeless victims*, and their situation is very different from that of victims of crime. Unlike the latter, they have an unrecognized grief. Members of social movements are made up of such crimeless victims or of those who act on behalf of crimeless victims. The claim to victimization often raised by members of social movements hence has a status very different from that of the claims of crime victims. To the extent that the society is generally presumed to be legitimate, such claims will be seen as self-evidently irrational. Rather than generating sympathy, retribution, and revenge, such victims bear the burden of showing that they themselves are not incompetent, irrational, or otherwise dangerous. Ideally, their access to media should permit them the ability to portray their situation substantively to overcome this initial disadvantage.

This is not, however, what typically occurs. Hence it was that the women's liberation movement was first met with a variety of media responses tending toward a view of women activists as deviant or incompetent. It was asked why women should complain when, after all, their lives were so good: lived on a pedestal, free from the rigors of the work world, with a longer life expectancy than men. The spokespeople of the movement were seen as peculiar variants of women—malcontents (perhaps in need of some good sex), lesbians, or women who were in some other way clinically suspect. The one action of the women's movement that received the most extensive, dramatic coverage, bra-burning, was an act that never occurred at all (see Martin, 1971, as cited in Freeman, 1975, p. 112). But bra-burning, mythical or not, was too good not to be fit to print: it involved no analysis of the actual social, economic, or sexual subjugation of women; it provided a way to portray "libbers" as deviant women; it catered to men's locker-room eroticism, which finds interest in anything having to do with female breasts or underwear. In other words, it was interesting to men; it fed their news needs; it was good copy.

The civil rights activists, similarly, were met with initial claims that "progress was being made," that blacks had it better here than in Africa, that this was the greatest country on earth. Accordingly, blacks' claims of victimization in this context of generalized legitimacy were blamed on some form of pathological deviance (the activities of "outside agitators," violent personality structure, or cultural deprivation). The student movement received parallel treatment from those who asked how children raised in affluence and provided with the finest educations could nevertheless rebel. Their answer was to see the students as spoiled or—in the case of movement leaders—actually crazy.

These views of dissidents shape the nose for news. That is, the kinds of things that can get covered and the kinds of questions that are asked of the dissidents emerge from this world view of the victims. The "angle" and the "theme" of coverage are determined from these perspectives (see Altheide, 1976). The media become preoccupied with the personal biographies of the dissidents—how they went wrong; their sexual mores, personal cleanliness, and physical attributes; and their potential threat to the system. We need to know whether women's libbers are lesbians—that is, does the "threat" of liberation for women mean that men's heterosexual erotic lives are going to suffer? Or that the sexual and interactional subjugation of women will end? We need to know whether blacks who clench fists are violent and the degree to which they are intent upon destroying the system. We need to know whether student activists are similarly possessed of violent intentions and the extent to which they will in other ways betray the system, if in no other way than in withholding their allegedly special talents from the functioning of that system.

On the other hand, media are not preoccupied with the issues important to the movement activists themselves. They do not find interesting the actual, thought-out reasons motivating feminist politics; students are not asked in substantive terms why they rebel—why, for example, they opposed the war in Vietnam. Black leaders are not asked to explain the meaning of institutional racism or the thesis of internal colonialism. Nor are the journalists' skills of popularization applied to make such ideas comprehensible to mass publics.

Movement activists are presented with a difficult challenge in attempting to deal with media. They are confronted with an intellectual agenda completely foreign to their own way of thinking. That agenda derives from a world view that sees them, in some sense at least, as insane and/or dangerous. I have seen activists become very frustrated under such conditions—finally to explode in a rage that the issue is *not* whether or not they intend violence, whether or not they burn their bras, whether or not they are homosexual, whether or not they were neat in the dean's office, whether or not they grew up in permissive households. But this explosion comes in response to what is generally seen as a "perfectly reasonable" question that can be answered simply as a matter of fact. And because we all have, as a matter of practical, interactional ethics, the responsibility of answering perfectly reasonable questions with the simple facts of the matter, the explosion is seen as further evidence of pathology. This evidence of emotional instability or irrationality adds to the case, sustaining the original conception of insanity/incompetence/danger.

Confronted with this situation, the activists can move in one of two directions. The most common is that of feeding the agenda of the establishment by providing acts and utterances that generate its curiosity —activities that are ordinarily not ignored, because of the news needs of the higher circles. Accordingly, they create nonroutine events that break or threaten to break the routines of the status quo system. Activists do the inexplicable: lie on the ground, clog the streets with marchers, run around naked. Media are brought in and the inane questions are asked, the inane issues are raised. Confrontation politics, in particular, sustain the drama over a rather long period of time. The activists' hope is that they will be able to "work in" substantive points of use to them. They hope that, as they receive coverage, the very fact of their existence will cause the movement to spread, will embolden others, will sustain their own ranks. But it is not the kind of coverage they would ideally like to have.

In a second type of movement strategy, activists dispense completely with any attempts to render the appearance of rationality or to inject "serious" discussion into the coverage. Here the assault on the status quo is most direct. The presumed insanity of the movement is capitalized upon rather than dealt with as a liability. In order to display the status quo as absurd, the activists display themselves as completely unresponsive to normative ordering of behavior. Their strategy is to render the world meaningless by displaying a deliberately cavalier attitude to the sacred symbols and procedures of the legitimated order. This sort of behavior, rooted of course in anarchistic thinking, finds its American manifestation in the Yippies. The strategy is to behave absurdly in order to pose the possibility that the established world is an absurd one. The American variant, especially, seeks to build converts by a display of political action that is downright fun. Again the risk is that the media, through ridicule, will be successful in denigrating the dissidents—through pronouncements of pathological insanity or destructiveness (e.g., by linking Yippies with dangerous drugs and random destruction). Once again the bets are placed, and, other than observing that this technique will have the least success in a context of high generalized legitimacy, there is no general rule on its intrinsic effectiveness or lack of effectiveness.

This difficulty in assessing whether a certain form of coverage will provide net benefit constitutes much of the internal politics of the movement organization. Debated options include the possibility of dealing with only certain "trusted" media (e.g., the underground press or certain left-liberal establishment organs) or certain favored media individuals. Similarly, it can be decided to trade off widespread coverage of "outrageous" actions for more limited coverage of activities that would generate a more positive understanding of movement goals. Finally, it can be decided to forgo coverage completely in favor of a strategy that emphasizes direct face-to-face organizing. The debates can often be extremely bitter, causing deep schisms and resulting in organizational dissolution.

The outcome of these decisions not only affects the success of the movement but also shapes its leadership and its meaning to the general public and to its own adherents—in short, what the movement actually is. Strategies involving media-oriented outrage will provide leadership potential for a Jerry Rubin or a Bobby Seale, but less for a Dave Dellinger or an Andrew Young. Strategies feeding the interest agendas of the establishment media will fashion the organization into one that is engaged more and more in developing such strategies, celebrating the success of such strategies, and honoring those who made them happen. In a sense, the medium becomes the movement.[2]

A concrete illustration can be taken from Huey Newton's 1973 account of the development of the Black Panthers—a group that apparently felt these dilemmas quite keenly. Because of the dangerous conditions they considered themselves to be in, the Panthers began carrying weapons for self-defense—certainly not as a means for random terrorizing of white people. But the fact that blacks had armed themselves was the major basis of Panther news coverage in white media; indeed, the Panthers came to national attention more or less as a new kind of black militant—a group rejecting the nonviolence that was the hallmark of previous civil rights organizations. Although carrying arms was not a critical point in Panther ideology and certainly was not a strategy for generating media attention, the Panthers came more or less to accept the media's portrayal of their own organization. The Panthers could have tried to correct the story by providing assurance that no violence was intended against whites or authorities, and so forth. These denials would likely have provided much publicity—especially because they would have had to be repeated many times before the white media would have believed them. But once they were accepted as true, there would have been no more publicity for the Panthers. Instead, the Panthers took the risk: they accepted the media's definition of them and continued to "enjoy" publicity. In so doing, the organization's internal organization was shaped, and its leaders became subject to brutal repression from the authorities.[3]

MEDIA STRATEGIES

Why would the establishment media provide any coverage at all to dissident groups? What do they have to gain?

1. They must alert the public, other members of the ruling class, and those bureaucrats and professionals particularly responsive to ruling-class needs of impending danger to the status quo. It *is* interesting when blacks rebel in the slum streets—especially when they have been "given" welfare, urban renewal, and job training; it *is* interesting when students lie down in the administration building, especially when they have been "given" access to a good education, a pleasant student union, and a fine library. It is important to know about such things so that corrective action can be taken: increased jail sentences (conservative) or school integration (liberal) for blacks; mandatory expulsion (conservative) or more favorable student-faculty ratios (liberal) for students. As is often pointed out in the journalism texts, the media operate as an early warning system of troubles arising. I only add the comment that what is trouble to some is solution to others. And control of the media determines what is a trouble to be "warned about" and what is a solution to be celebrated.

2. A much less subtle case involves establishment attempts to destroy social movements that either operate without media coverage as a strategy or attempt to retreat from the media because coverage is seen as resulting in a net loss to the movement. During the McCarthy period, the Communist party was in such a predicament—hounded by establishment repression, including uncritical media coverage of staged inquisitions. Routine news procedures were turned against the movement and used aggressively to destroy it.

3. Media are diverse in a number of ways, including the nature of audience and the source of advertising revenues. Hence, a magazine for surfers may well be more sensitive to certain conservationist movements than, say, a national business magazine. When such a fusion of interests occurs between advertisers and readers, a publication can be expected to display this fusion—within the confines of general loyalty to existing institutional arrangements—and to provide favorable coverage to relevant movements. Similarly, advertiser considerations may cause one segment of a movement to receive attention at the expense of other segments. It would be expected, for example, that the traditional women's magazine (like *Vogue* and *Mademoiselle*) would provide positive coverage only for those aspects of the women's movements that foster support for advertisers (i.e., the cosmetics and fashion industries): such magazines view feminism as a woman's right to equal pay—money that can then be used to buy still more cosmetics and fashion (see Coleman, 1977; Benet, Daniels, and Tuchman, forthcoming). Those portions of the women's movement that stress feminism as antifashion would, it is hypothesized, receive little coverage, and certainly very little positive coverage.

Related to these considerations is the fact that media differ in the general resource bases within which they operate. Besides differences in advertiser and audience constituencies, media are usually locally grounded, and the nature of these local groundings—as economic resource bases—can differ. As I have argued elsewhere (Molotch, 1976), local media are enthusiastic supporters of the urban growth machines that act to sustain and enhance local economic development. In the case of local media, such growth carries the crucial consequence of larger audiences (often captively held through monopoly or near-monopoly conditions) and thus higher advertising revenues. Media can therefore be expected to respond negatively to any movements that threaten their surrounding economic base and to be sympathetic to those movements, on the relatively rare occasions when they exist, that are seen as enhancing the future of that economic base.[4]

Two contrasting cases in point can be offered. Following the accidental escape of nerve gas at Dugway Proving Grounds in Utah, Lester (1971) found that the Salt Lake City newspaper gave the incident relatively little coverage and devoted little space or sympathy to the incipient local movement opposing further nerve gas experimentation. Indeed, certain nonlocal media (e.g., the *New York Times*) gave the incident more coverage and, just as significantly, coverage that was of substantive use to nerve gas opponents. The contrasting case is the Santa Barbara oil spill, which resulted in an enormous amount of local coverage (far more extensive than in any nonlocal medium) and coverage extremely sympathetic to antioil conservationist movements (Molotch, 1970). The difference between Utah and Santa Barbara is that the former region is heavily dependent upon federal defense experimentation as part of its economic base, whereas the latter has its economic future and the prosperity of its media tied to tourism, trendy higher education, and amenities for the well-to-do retired. In Santa Barbara the movement and the media were virtually indistinguishable in their message content (a source of bitter oil company complaint); in Utah, the media hardly recognized the movement as existing, and hence it hardly came to exist at all. The point here is that a particular medium can find a particular movement particularly useful, and coverage will display this utility.

4. Still a fourth function of coverage, from the establishment's point of view, has to do with the perceived legitimacy of the medium itself. Events are often seen by some eye witnesses, and those eye witnesses, however small in number, will think something is amiss if there is no coverage of events that seem to fit their own news needs or that seem to be customarily covered by media. Similarly, the workers on the line in the news business are—to a degree—deferred to in their news judgment. Not being as sensitive to the news needs of the ruling class as are members of that class themselves, they may at times make coverage decisions at variance with those that would be made by higher-ups.[5]

Reporters also sometimes develop affection for activists through shared contacts and stresses (perhaps like the affection between hostages and terrorists under common siege), resulting in rapport that can also be of potential use toward developing a professionally rewarding "big story." The sort of staff-line differences that can result in varied attitudes toward movement coverage can result in occasional firings or principled resignations by reporters. Instances of this sort of internal media dispute were reported on occasion in the journal *More*. Especially when there is a decision from the top to *change* the degree to which a movement is to receive coverage, a journalist is in a position to see resulting editorial policy as "arbitrary" or "political" or otherwise unobjective, that is, unprofessional. This is a cost to be avoided by editor and publisher, but also one evidently to be paid when circumstances demand.[6]

SELECTIVE INSIGHT: PULLING OUT OF THE GAME

It is by no means clear how a given story will suit the news needs of a given party. Liberal members of the ruling class typically allow their media to risk more than conservative members. This is because generalized legitimacy of institutions is more critical to liberals, and they are willing to sacrifice short-term goals such as smooth-running, efficient institutions for the sake of the long-term goal of preserving, in its rough outline, the structure of American capitalism.

But it seems that when coverage of movements is seen as generating net loss of the status quo, the media—as a conscious, deliberate policy—pull out. This is what appears to have happened in response to coverage of the black ghetto insurrections: when coverage of such incidents was seen as perpetuating them, the coverage was curtailed as a matter of *journalistic responsibility* (see Tuchman, forthcoming, chap. 5).

One illustration of noncoverage is available to me through my direct experience with a political firing at the institution where I have taught for the last ten years. During the late sixties, UC Santa Barbara was the scene of large-scale student disturbances—second in California only to Berkeley in numbers involved, arrests, and injuries over the course of the period. The events received widespread national coverage —again, coverage that was a source of elation and organizational sustenance to participants. In the fall of 1970, the sociology department hired Maurice Zeitlin to teach as a visiting professor. Before Zeitlin arrived, but after contracts and loyalty oath had been signed, the campus administration fired Zeitlin—or in its words "withdrew the invitation to the courtesy use of University facilities." Court action followed. It was obvious that this unprecedented action was caused by Zeitlin's reputation as an antiwar activist at Wisconsin, and hence the details of the case were appropriate for an academic freedom *cause célèbre*—more significant, in many ways, than the previous extraordinarily well-covered firing of Angela Davis from UCLA or the hiring/unhiring of Herbert Marcuse at UC San Diego. Yet there was virtually no coverage of the Zeitlin case in either the local or the state newspapers. The student paper (the *Nexus*) provided extensive, detailed, and at times angry coverage. An education editor of the *Los Angeles Times* (California's prestigious and generally liberal paper) visited the campus for several days and carried out extensive interviews, yet no story was printed.

I wrote to the *Times* managing editor and asked why no story appeared, insinuating that the reporter was hiding from those who called him from the campus and charging the *Times* with blocking the news. This is the body of the reply I received, in its entirety (the last two paragraphs are the critical ones):

Dear Prof. Molotch:

Frank Haven, our managing editor, has shown me a copy of your Dec. 28 letter to him. He may be planning to write a separate reply to you, but there are a couple of points I want to make.

First, it is untrue that I have failed to return phone calls regarding the Zeitlin case. Among others, I have discussed with Zeitlin's attorney and Larry Boggs, editor of the *Nexus*, the reasons why no extensive story on Zeitlin appeared. I don't know who told you I'm not returning phone calls, but that is sheer poppycock.

It is untrue that no Zeitlin stories have appeared since I visited the campus. In fact, most of the brief pieces that we have run on the case were published after my visit, not before.

We have not run an extensive story on Zeitlin because of the judgment of my editors that because the Zeitlin case has not become an issue of major proportions enveloping the campus community, we might be accused of creating an issue if we give it full-blown treatment at this point in time.

It is not a case of holding back information, but the concern that my editors have for trying to avoid the situation where something becomes a major issue *because* a large daily newspaper has written about it at length. [Emphasis in original.]

This response is worth some detailed analysis. The ideological underpinning of newswork—from publisher to cub reporter—is objectivity, and this reply makes indirect use of that principle. The objectivity principle is the notion that there is a world "out there" of concrete things. News is a reportage of those things. Although everyone recognizes that there are too many things to report, the argument goes, there are some things that are *objectively* more important than others. Reportage consists of these important things. These things can be known and known to be important quite irrespective of the social, cultural, and political contexts in which they exist and the social, cultural, and political identities of the reporter. Of course, there is "bias," and no reporter can ever completely keep his "values" out of his judgments, but he can come near the mark; he can approximate the goal. Perfection is not possible, but the goal is valid, the goal is not an intellectual absurdity, the goal is a thing in the world to be approached. News media are hence a *mirror* of *the* important world. Exceptions are departures from a sought-after, practically unachievable, but theoretically conceivable state of affairs.

Especially when trained for this purpose, either in a journalism school or on the job, the conscientious *professional* can know the important from the trivial, can separate out her values from her reporting job. The whole argument parallels the value-free controversy in sociology and has, I would argue, the same professional and social structural consequences.

This objectivity assumption is also basic to everyday life and is thereby strengthened in its incontrovertibility. It is one of those tacit procedures of doing the world that is indispensable, and the tacitness is likewise indispensable.

Yet, at times in the functioning of practical affairs, there is a sense that the objectivity principle will not do. We sometimes admit, "It all depends on how you look at it," or "You had to be there," or "Men eat before they reason." In everyday life, as it is practiced, these are exceptional insights reserved either for extraordinary moments of "ivory-tower" philosophizing or for very special situations. I want to emphasize that it is critical that these insights be reserved for special occasions; to see contingency rather than objectivity as the general state of things is to eliminate the prerequisite for carrying on as a sane, competent member of society. Objectivity is hence coerced as a general rule of thumb.

Quite on its own, and quite voluntarily, the *Los Angeles Times* saw, *in this instance*, the possibility that "something [could become] a major issue *because* a large daily newspaper has written about it." This comment raises the possibility that news media do not mirror a world but constitute it. And, indeed, from my perspective, news media always and inevitably constitute the public world. The question is why this medium gathered this insight at the moment it did.

The perception of an exception to the general rule of objectivity is not coerced. In the example at hand, the *Los Angeles Times* found a propitious moment and a propitious case for such creative manipulation of the world, for a quasi-bracketing of an everyday assumption. But just as in other realms of voluntary, discretionary, playful activity in a society of class and caste, the voluntarism of some counts for much more than the voluntarism of others. The editors of the *Times* are in a powerful position to do this sort of work. In the case at hand, they "see" the reflexive nature of news, just as they could see the same phenomenon at work in any potential news story. The "bias" of the medium can thus lie in its selective perception of the phenomenological bases of communication, rather than in its direct selective perception of news content itself. It is because of this very indirectness of the bias process that the publisher is insulated from a charge of bias. That is, because the groundings of communication are themselves not a part of public discourse, they cannot readily be used to charge bias. Such charges must derive from folk knowledge, must take place within the context of the objectivity assumption, and must, therefore, often miss their mark. The tacit nature of the groundings of communication, in the context of formal freedom, is thus a tool used by the powerful to repress unaccountably. And because tacitness is a requirement of normal procedure, there is a great problem for those wishing to neutralize such power. How can one argue against the *Los Angeles Times* when it takes the position that it does not want to make news, only to report it? The *generally* reflexive nature of news would have to be the accepted view before an effective answer could be framed. And the *Los Angeles Times* and the sociologists (among others) are loathe to encourage such world views among the folk.

Once there is a blackout of coverage of a certain type of movement activity, the movement must develop new strategies—perhaps involving an escalation of its threats to normalcy or some other creative means of fitting the news needs of an establishment that is becoming increasingly skeptical of its potential to gain by providing such coverage.

THE BEDFELLOW DIALECTIC

The establishment does not always win, or at least it does not always win neatly. The establishment has incompetents within its ranks, including those whom it selects to represent its interests (like Nixon) but who fail to do so adequately. The establishment similarly makes planning errors, as in the case of Vietnam, where it grossly miscalculated the resources of the Viet Cong. Further, the establishment has cleavages within its ranks, such as conservatives and liberals, who debate (sometimes publicly) the best means of achieving a stable, capitalist system. And there are other bases of cleavage as well, including region, social networks, and ethnicity (rich Jews are still excluded from the "best" clubs).

Such resulting vulnerabilities can provide movements with the openings they need. The antiwar activists were able, I think, to exploit media creatively to a point where the war was rendered generally unpopular. Of course, the staying power of the Viet Cong was the more critical force, but I think a relatively inexpensive war, such as that waged in Vietnam, could have been tolerated by the American public for an almost infinite period of time. I see the change of American popular opinion as initiated by the Left, which had an effective strategy (confrontation politics) for dealing with this limited issue. Increasingly, so many thousands became involved at the grassroots level that overall legitimacy was threatened and repression of a "small minority" ceased to be a viable alternative. As is common to the pattern, the liberals were first to make the decision to end "the mistake" in Vietnam, and it was they who supported the antiwar movement through finance and through increasingly favorable treatment by media under their control. The conservatives, on the other hand, determined to stick it out and urged increasingly punitive measures against dissidents. Dominant U.S. media talked less of preserving freedom in Southeast Asia and more about corruption of the Thieu regime. Body counts gave way to dollar counts of the war's costs. And the Right developed increasingly bitter criticisms of the media.

This liberal-conservative cleavage was, in the context of the Nixon administration, a media-administration cleavage. The leftist activists caused legitimacy to deteriorate, perhaps more through the cavalier bad taste of the administration's reactions than through the wisdom of the activists. Agnew was right; the press *was* out to get Nixon. Nixon's main failing was not that he broke into buildings or cheated on his income tax. His failing was that he did not know how, or care to know how, to preserve legitimacy. He tried, with no apologies, to appoint racists and mediocrities to the august Supreme Court; his attorney general, when told that mass arrests of demonstrators was unconstitutional, told reporters he would worry about the Constitution in the morning. The media had to cover the presidency; such coverage is built into its news routines and is central to its larger ideological purpose. But what the president said was having effects contrary to that purpose. Nixon's failure was an inability to exploit his office properly to serve larger class interests. The existence of the movements, in part, made this failure possible. The liberal media used the movements, just as the movements used the media. In their limited goal of ending the war and in their civil libertarian disputes with the Nixon administration, the movements increasingly had the same news needs as the media. Near the end, the media released staff from the debilitating rigors of bureaucratized journalism and set them loose on the biggest enchilada of them all. The media became the movement, and the Left was at least temporarily finished, as its role was increasingly taken over by the establishment during the Watergate prosecutions.

In the case of the civil rights movement, an analogous movement-media dialectic played itself out, but with some interesting differences stemming, in this case, from *regional* variation in elite interests within the United States. Until the end of World War II, there was general elite acquiescence (if not enthusiasm) for regional variation in race relations, that is, de facto segregation in the North, de jure segregation in the South. Misgivings on the Democratic Left (personified perhaps in Eleanor Roosevelt) was sometimes enthusiastically expressed, but the ruling Democrat coalition rested on the sanctity of the arrangement.

The civil rights movement, initially oriented to the South, exposed "the American dilemma," and under the battle cry of "bringing the South into the United States," northern liberal opinions (including some significant money and significant media) rallied to the cause. Again, I see the key issue as legitimacy: important segments of northern opinion saw the continued exposure of blatant inequities as damaging to the larger legitimacy of U.S. institutions, and hence their interest matrix included media coverage of such inequities and the methods used to redress them. Such coverage was both interesting and, despite the potential for violence, journalistically responsible.

Southern elites were, quite reasonably, more slow to join the cause, and when they did so they were motivated not so much by the need to maintain legitimacy (such matters had always been of more concern to the sophisticated liberals of the North) as by the need to provide for the kind of social and economic climate that would facilitate a profit renaissance on southern turf. That is, the northern-originated ("outside agitators") movements for an end to de jure segregation were tolerated and supported by a portion of the nation's elite, which saw cracker bourgeois interests as expendable, compared to the growing crisis in national legitimacy. Southern elites modified their positions accordingly and increasingly saw the racial social code as itself expendable, compared to their regional economic interests, which were, to some degree, shaped by northern liberal opinion. Therefore, although the southern elites never joined the North in enthusiasm for Martin Luther King, Jr., he became legitimized as a figure with whom reconciliation should occur.

Northern liberal elite acceptance of King was initially limited to the single issue of race relations in the South. As King expanded his issue base, his northern support fell away. When King first spoke out against the Vietnam war he was denounced by the *New York Times* (among other liberal northern voices) for, in effect, putting his nose where it did not belong. I read this denunciation as caused by the fact that *at that historical stage*, King—erected in large part as a public celebrity by northern media—was using that celebrity in a counterproductive manner. That is, he was not being useful in feeding the news needs of those guarding the *national* status quo.[7] Similarly, King lost media support when he expanded his civil rights campaign to ending de facto segregation in the North. The key point is that as he expanded his public concerns into new areas, the effect was to undermine, rather than enhance, national legitimacy.

After King's death, as his movement withered away, his charisma was harnessed—through the media's romantic Americanization of his life—to the continuing effort of "binding wounds," an effort very much aided by the demise of King. The eulogies to King—continuing in one form or another to the present day—were part of the growing effort to secure legitimacy (and thereby undermine the radical elements of the sixties' movements) by ending the war, purging Nixon (after the greater danger of McGovern was dispensed with), and casting a new ideological net over the deprived minorities (in both regions), along with the suspicious middle classes. Jimmy Carter, as though sent from central casting (which he was), is the personification of this new arrangement, and the movements are today at bay in the context of this dramatic ruling-class public relations success.

SUMMARY

These somewhat disjointed comments can perhaps be connected through a series of assertions that put forth the argument in more succinct terms:

1. News coverage is critical to sustaining social movements.
2. The open-ended quality of what is news allows socially contextual factors to structure its content.
3. The objectivity assumption shields these social determinants from view.
4. These social determinants are rooted in class interests.
5. Because they are, by definition, alien from the routines of power and news, social movements must take recourse to extraordinary techniques to gain coverage.
6. The use of such techniques runs a high risk that illegitimacy and/or incompetence among the activists will be documented.
7. When the media perceive the movements as nevertheless gaining strength through coverage, this coverage can be curtailed through a variety of public and self-justifications, including those based on the capacity for selective phenomenological insight.
8. Cleavages within the ruling class are reflected as *issues* in the media; in the case of the war, movement activists helped promote such cleavage and, by displaying the president's incompetence as a class functionary, encouraged and facilitated his destruction. Regional elite cleavages were critical in shaping coverage of civil rights activists and in the temporary resolution of that issue.
9. Media and movements, particularly in the modern American context, are part of a single process through which one social class acts to guarantee stability in the face of continuous challenges to that stability. The media would be a different "thing" in the world without the existence of movements, and the movements, as we know them, would not be the "thing" they appear to be without the media. Media and movements are not discrete phenomena but part of a single unfolding process in which energy and constraints emanate from a single source: the endemic conflict between the haves and the have-nots.

This analysis has pushed a certain perspective quite hard and has been, at times, quite speculative. My goal has been to encourage a way of thinking about media and movements. My main attempt has been not to offer research findings, but to offer antifindings. I do not think it can be said as a generality that media help movements or that media destroy them. Nor can the content of coverage or the class usefulness of a given type of content be specified in a *general*, that is, ahistorical, acontextual way. My way of thinking has no predictive value. All that I can offer as general are the contingencies enforced by class, power, and struggle within which actors develop their diverse strategies and justifications. Alert and graceful, they move in response and in anticipation of one another's actions. Media and movements are dialectically bound, always in motion and alert to one another's motion—be it embrace, flight, or thundering blow. The most appropriate metaphor to describe their relationship is dance—sometimes a dance of death.

ENDNOTES

1. Movements often have trouble *buying* media advertising even when they have the money. The print media, in particular, can quite legally (drawing upon constitutional protections) refuse advertising or can force advertisers to modify ad copy, generally on the grounds that wording is "irresponsible," "inflammatory," and so forth. For an acount of how the Miami newspapers frustrated efforts of the Dade County Coalition for Human Rights (in its counter-campaign to the "Anita Bryant referendum"), see Solomon (1977).
2. For an important discussion of these issues, see Gitlin (forthcoming).
3. I am indebted to David Bouchier of University of Essex for this analysis of the Panther case.
4. Such a movement can theoretically exist because it is possible for a group to have goals consistent with those of a local elite, but inconsistent with those of the national elite. The Santa Barbara antioil activists were a case in point. A contrasting instance of the same basic phenomenon was the moderate civil rights movement in the South, which was often in opposition to local elites but supported by national elites.
5. Among the typical media, there is a tendency for staff reporters to be to the political left of the media executives for whom they work—a pattern not found, however, within the more prestigious media organs (see Johnstone, Slawski, and Bowman, 1976, p. 93; cf. Breed, 1955).
6. Perhaps the most famous recent instance of this phenomenon involved neither reporters nor news media but the political content of an entertainment show—the Smothers Brothers CBS series. The resulting bad publicity cost CBS and the big media generally in legitimacy, but it also provided clear warning to other entertainers (and newscasters as well, I would argue) of the limits to the permissible range of political viewpoints that would be tolerated by the liberal media.
7. As a result of his assasination, and also as elite opinion began changing toward the war, King was to be celebrated for his antiwar stance as well. In its 7 April 1967 editorial, the *New York Times* condemned "Dr. King's error" in linking "his personal opposition to the war . . . with the cause of Negro equality in the United States. . . . This is a fusing of two public problems that are distinct and separate. . . ." One year later (to the day—

7 April 1968), the *Times* editorially eulogized King because he had "felt obliged to extend his personal philosophy of nonviolence from the streets of Selma and Memphis to the rice paddies of the Mekong Delta. . . . He saw the impediments to race and economic progress at home while a war was raging abroad."

External Efforts to Damage or Facilitate Social Movements: Some Patterns, Explanations, Outcomes, and Complications

Gary T. Marx

In spite of the impression left by much of the literature through the 1960s, social movements are not autonomous forces hurling toward their destiny only in response to the oppression, intensity of commitment, and skill of activists. Nor are they epiphenomena at the mercy of groups in their external environment that seek to block or facilitate them. Instead movements represent a complex interplay of external and internal factors. Until recently researchers have tended to focus much more on the latter than the former, but both must be considered.

McCarthy and Zald (1973b), in focusing on external factors, have helped to redress the balance. They note how broad social trends in the United States are conducive to the emergence and growth of social movements, regardless of the nature and type of deprivation felt by the beneficiaries of the movement. However, we can also note that many of the same factors are equally conducive to the emergence of counter-movements and to efforts on the part of the government or private groups to block, damage, inhibit, or destroy social movements. The resources are clearly there in greater abundance than ever before; how they will be used is another question. Our perspective on the external environment must be broad enough to include repressive as well as facilitative actions.

I will consider how selected elements of the external environment may seek to affect social movements by examining some strategies and

I am grateful to Jo Freeman, John Howard, Bob Ross, and Dick Wilsnack for their suggestions. A longer version is available from the author.

tactics intended to facilitate or damage social movements, looking at some questions raised by these activities and some efforts at explanation, and showing some of their intended and unintended outcomes. My attention will focus on the actions of government because more is known about this area and a consideration of it can suggest concepts more generally applicable to the actions taken by nongovernmental groups. Beyond this, one of the insights to emerge from recent hearings and court cases is that some elements of the media, some interest groups, and some social movements can be extensions of government.

My concern is primarily with social control or facilitation efforts that have appeared with respect to specific movements in the United States. Of less concern are aspects of culture and social structure or general actions taken prior to the appearance of a movement that affects grievances and possibilities for collective action.[1] For example, our legal system, with the protected freedoms of the Bill of Rights and local ordinances regarding parade permits, is a more distant form of facilitation and control. It is part of the societal framework within which a movement operates. In principle such forms of control and facilitation apply universally. They can be separated from the specific actions at the micro-level taken by government in response to a given movement.

STRATEGIES AND TACTICS INTENDED TO FACILITATE OR DAMAGE SOCIAL MOVEMENTS

To highlight the issues involved, let us take the least ambiguous, extreme case where an outside group such as the government either wants to damage or facilitate a movement. A review of the last two decades suggests a number of broad strategies and specific tactics that have been undertaken to achieve the desired goal. Many of the actions taken with the aim of damaging a movement are the reverse of those taken to enhance a movement. These can be characterized in terms of opposing organizational, tactical, and resource mobilization tasks. The actions of those seeking to further the cause of the social movement lie on the left side of table 1, and those seeking to damage the movement lie on the right side.

Although analytically distinct, these factors are obviously related. Some—such as inhibiting the capacity for corporate action, directing energies to maintenance needs, and damaging morale—are general and include most of the others. Obtaining one end, such as the application of legal sanctions, can be a means to other ends, such as creating an unfavorable public image or destroying leadership. One end can be pursued by multiple means, and the same means, such as the use of agents provocateurs, can serve a number of ends. These represent the point of

Table 1 *Some General Strategies for Facilitating or Inhibiting a Social Movement*

To Facilitate the Movement	To Inhibit the Movement
Facilitate capacity for corporate action	Inhibit capacity for corporate action
Make it possible for energies of movement to go toward pursuit of broader social change goals, as well as maintenance needs	Direct energies of movement to defensive maintenance needs and away from pursuit of broader social goals
Create favorable public image; develop and support ideology	Create unfavorable public image and counterideology
Give information to movement	Gather information on movement
Facilitate supply of money and facilities	Inhibit supply of money and facilities
Facilitate freedom of movement, expression, and action; offer legal immunity	Inhibit freedom of movement, expression, and action; create myth and fact of surveillance and repression; apply legal sanctions
Build and sustain morale	Damage morale
Recruit supporters	Derecruitment
Build leaders	Destroy or displace leaders
Encourage internal solidarity	Encourage internal conflict
Encourage external coalitions with potential allies and neutral relations (or conflict only insofar as it is functional) with potential opponents	Encourage external conflict with potential allies and opponents
Facilitate particular actions	Inhibit or sabotage particular actions

view of the outside analyst, although they are likely to overlap considerably with the point of view of the actor.[2] Let us first consider the far more prevalent efforts to damage movements.

Creation of an Unfavorable Public Image

Public labeling of a social movement, its leaders, and its activities is affected by what leaders say about it (Nixon's references to antiwar protesters as bums and Johnson's "we shall overcome" speech are examples), as well as by more covert actions designed to affect how its image is projected by the media. What and how the media report are crucial topics for understanding social movements, independent of government pressures. For example, advertisers and the beliefs of those working in the media can be crucial to what is said—and not said— about a social movement.[3] Our concern here, however, is government actions.

We do not know with certainty what effect recent Federal Communication Commission pressure or Vice-President Agnew's attack on the "liberal media" had. Yet real or anticipated pressures from government on the media may make it more difficult for a movement to communicate accurately with the public. Easier to identify than self-censorship in the presentation of news are more direct tactics that may be undertaken by social control agents in efforts to affect actual media content.

Image-damaging information may be given to friendly journalists or supplied anonymously. This may involve passing on information about arrest records, associations, life-styles, and statements of the targeted person or group that are thought likely to hurt the movement. For example, information obtained from electronic surveillance supposedly dealing with Martin Luther King's sexual behavior was offered by the FBI to various journalists. Or control agents may write their own stories and editorials, which they pass on to the media. For example, the FBI planted a series of derogatory articles about the Poor People's Campaign (Select Committee, book II, 1976, p. 16). The media are not necessarily aware of the source of such material.

The information given to the media may be fabricated, it may be accurate yet privileged information known to authorities only as a result of wiretaps, informers, and other forms of surveillance; or it may be accurate but only in a contrived sense (as when authorities have taken covert action to create events whose reporting will reflect negatively upon the movement). Examples of this would be provoking the movement to illegal actions, carrying out illegal actions themselves that will then be attributed to the movement, or tempting leaders with vice opportunities.

Efforts may be undertaken to block or counter the publication of materials favorable to the movement. "Disinformation" and counter-propaganda arguing that the movement's ideology and claims are empirically wrong, illogical, in conflict with basic American values, or linked to foreign or disreputable sources may be published.

For the FBI, such activities go back at least thirty years. In 1946 the head of the FBI Intelligence Division suggested that "educational material" be released through "available channels [to] influence public opinion" about American communists. Propaganda efforts were carried out that aimed to bring the U.S. Communist party and its leaders "into disrepute before the American public" (ibid., p. 66).[4] In the case of the New Left, FBI agents were told that "every avenue of possible embarrassment must be vigorously and enthusiastically explored." In efforts "to discredit the New Left and its adherents," agents were requested to send information for "prompt dissemination to the news media" (ibid., p. 16). Among specific instructions given agents were:

> a. Prepare leaflets designed to discredit student demonstrators, using photographs of New Left leadership. . . . Naturally, the most obnoxious picture should be used.
> b. Send . . . articles from student newspapers or the "underground press" which show the depravity of the New Left to university officials, donors, legislators, and parents. Articles showing advocation of the use of narcotics and free sex are ideal.

Many examples indicate that this advice was followed for the New Left, as well as for other groups. For example, the FBI circulated a flyer headlined "Pick the Fag Contest," which contained a list of mock prizes and pictures of four New Left leaders (Wise, 1976, p. 317). It also sent an anonymous letter to a Hollywood gossip columnist claiming that activist Jane Fonda led a Black Panther rally in obscene and violent chants involving Richard Nixon. Fonda has denied this charge and filed a $2.8 million lawsuit. The agent in charge of the Los Angeles FBI office wrote to J. Edgar Hoover, "It is felt that knowledge of Fonda's involvement would cause her embarrassment and detract from her status with the general public" (ibid., p. 316).

The CIA in its foreign activities appears to have gone even farther in media manipulation by becoming, rather than merely trying to influence, the media. The CIA supported two European news services used by U.S. newspapers, and as of February 1976, about fifty U.S. journalists and other news organization workers were employed by or had a covert relationship with the CIA. In a few cases regular CIA agents also posed as journalists (Select Committee, book I, 1976). When asked whether the CIA ever planted stories with foreign news organizations, former director William Colby replied, "Oh, sure all the time" (*New York Times*, February 4, 1976). When foreign sources such as Reuters are used, this material can help shape American public opinion, as can books paid for or affected by the CIA.[5]

Information Gathering

The largest single activity of control agents with respect to social movements has probably been in information gathering. Indeed it is a prerequisite for most other activities. Information-gathering techniques developed for criminal investigations have been applied to social movements. In roughly decreasing frequency, they include:

Collection of news items, movement documents, and membership lists.
Informers developed through infiltration, *"turning around"* those already in the movement, or drawing upon individuals in the movement's milieu.
Attendance at public meetings and demonstrations.
Still photography and videotape.
Background investigations using public and private records and interviews.
Wiretaps and other forms of auditory electronic surveillance, often requiring breaking and entering and monitoring international telephone calls.
Physical surveillance of persons or places.
Police posing as journalists and photographers or the latter giving information to police.
Grand jury investigations.
Mail openings.

The reasons for which such information is collected vary: search for subversion, conspiracy, and espionage; information needed in a criminal investigation; harassment; names to put on a dangerous persons' or organization's list and in computer banks; information to aid in the preparation of counterintelligence actions; or ritualized bureaucratic work to meet information quotas, which are taken as evidence that agents are working. The vast majority of the information gathered is not used, is often of questionable validity, and is rapidly dated. To be useful beyond its harrassment function, it must be organized, evaluated, and interpreted. Knowing that agents are gathering information on it may make the social movement less open and democratic, require that limited resources be devoted to security, and may deter participation.

Inhibiting the Supply of Resources and Facilities

Social movement organizations need money, means of communication services and supplies, and physical space. Government actions may be taken to deny or restrict a movement's access to these, particularly insofar as they come from sources external to the movement. Where the government was the sponsor and an organization comes to be seen as too threatening, funds may simply be withdrawn, as was the case with Office of Economic Opportunity programs (Donovan, 1970). The social movement organization may experience direct pressure and threats from private funding agencies, which themselves may anticipate government sanctioning. As Goulden (1971) has noted for the Ford Foundation, even the accusation that a foundation is funding a radical group can lead to pressure on the group to become more moderate.

The government may seek to discover the source of an organization's funding. Efforts of varying degrees of legality may then be carried out to dry up larger sources of contribution. For example, the FBI considered its attempts to put a stop to a Southern Christian Leadership Conference funding source as "quite successful" (Select Committee, book II, 1976, p. 15).

The tax-exempt status of social movement organizations or those contributing to them may be chosen for auditing on strictly political grounds and then revoked. Contributors and activists may be subjected to special audits (ibid.). Recent general congressional inquiries into laws regarding the tax-exempt status of foundations appear to have resulted in greater caution in their funding activities.

Those renting offices or providing office or meeting space to a movement may be encouraged by the government not to do so. For example, the FBI tried to prevent the holding of a forum by an alleged Communist front on a Midwest campus. It then investigated the judge who ordered that the meeting be permitted (ibid., p. 17). The FBI claimed in a 1965 report that "as a result of counterintelligence action, many meeting places formerly used on a regular basis by the communists have been barred from their use" (Berman and Halperin, 1975, p. 28).

As McCarthy and Zald (1973b) note, the more than subsistence income, fringe resources, leisure, and flexibility offered by many jobs can indirectly be important in facilitating social movement participation. Conversely the denial of such employment to activists can be a means of indirectly damaging a movement. Authorities have attempted to get activists fired from their jobs and to affect their credit standing negatively. Those whose names are in security files may have difficulty finding new employment.

During the McCarthy era, more than 490 persons lost government jobs on loyalty grounds though no cases of espionage were found. More recently, the Select Committee to Study Governmental Operations with Respect to Intelligence report cites examples such as FBI records being given to employers and their receiving anonymous letters about activist employees.

Such activities can damage morale, shrink resources, and make sustained actions difficult or impossible. For some activists, the cost of continued participation may become too great, and they may quit. But more direct efforts toward this end may also be undertaken in the form of explicit derecruitment activities.

Derecruitment

One way to create an unfavorable public image is to keep potential recruits away. The public sanctioning of activists may also be a means of deterring new recruits. But beyond trying to stop a movement from expanding, the government may try to reduce the movement's size and weaken the morale and degree of commitment among those currently active. Obtaining membership and mailing lists have been given high priority by authorities, even where this practice necessitated breaking and entering.

Once the identity of activists is known, employers, parents, neighbors, friends, or spouses may be contacted, sometimes anonymously, in hopes of encouraging them to dissuade or threaten activists. A policy directive advising FBI agents to make such contacts expressed the hope that "this could have the effect of forcing the parents to take action" (Select Committee, book III, 1976, p. 26). For example, in 1968, the FBI sent anonymous letters to the parents of two Oberlin College students involved in a campus hunger strike against the Vietnam war urging them to intervene to prevent their children from becoming dupes of the Young Socialist Alliance (Berman and Halperin, 1975, p. 30). It has also sent anonymous letters to the spouses of activists in the Ku Klux Klan, the Black Panthers and other groups accusing their marital partners of infidelity (ibid., p. 51). A Klan informant testified that he was instructed "to sleep with as many wives as I could" in attempts to break up marriages and gain information (Select Committee, Hearings, 1976, 6:118).

Activists may encounter direct appeals from government agents who point out the risks they face, argue matters of ideology, give them damaging information about others in the movement, and threaten them. There may be efforts to maneuver activists into situations (such as of a sexual nature) from which they can then be controlled under threat of exposure or arrest. They may seek to persuade them to become informants. An FBI directive tells agents, "There is a pretty general consensus that more interviews with these [New Left] subjects and hangers-on are in order for plenty of reasons, chief of which are it will enhance the paranoia endemic in these circles and will further serve to get the point across that there is an FBI agent behind every mailbox" (Wise, 1972).

In at least one case, FBI agents appear to have kidnapped an antiwar activist in hopes of scaring him into ceasing his protest actions (*New York Times*, July 11, 1976). During preparation for a large Washington, D.C., antiwar demonstration, another activist recalls: "We were followed more and more. The Feds came to a lot of different people's apartments in the middle of the night with keys. They grabbed people as they were getting into their cars in parking lots and threw them into the car and drove around for a few hours, bribing them, telling them they'd give them thousands of dollars and a new passport if they'd only sing a song. And it didn't make any difference whether they did or not, cause their goose was cooked, they had information on us—it just went on and on" (Wise, 1976, p. 377).

An example of derecruitment efforts in a private context is provided by attempts to deprogram youthful converts to religious movements, such as Reverend Sun Myung Moon's Unification church. A new class of countersocial movement specialist has emerged here, the functional equivalent of those playing recruitment roles from within the movement. In the rural South there were many privately initiated efforts to apply, and threats of applying, economic sanctions against civil rights activists. Private police in their campaign against labor radicals and union organizing had a marked degree of success here, at least until the reforms of the New Deal. For example, according to one estimate, labor spying was a major factor in a one-third decline in labor union membership between 1920 and 1929 (Bernstein, 1960).

Destroying Leaders

Because social movement leaders are symbolically and instrumentally important, movement-damaging activities often focus on weakening them as the most visible and presumed central part of a movement.[6] Visibility as a social movement leader may offer the person some protection from some of the more nefarious and illegal tactics, yet leaders have been targets for most of the movement-damaging strategies we are considering. They may be subject to image-damaging efforts, surveillance, harassment, assaults, and threats. They may face a variety of legal sanctions, such as injunctions against demonstrating, grand jury inquiries of a fishing expedition nature, arrest on false or vague conspiracy charges, and excessive bail and sentences. Tax difficulties may be created for them. They may be the principal figures in efforts to create internal and external conflict. There may be efforts to maneuver them into compromising positions where they can be made informers or at least be forced into cooperation with the government. Co-optive efforts may be undertaken. There may be efforts to displace them, as the government infiltrates its own people into the movement who become leaders or builds up a rival group. The campaign against Martin Luther King included most of these tactics—plus some others—and Communist, Klan, black militant, and New Left leaders have faced similar efforts.

Internal Conflict

A major aim of domestic counterintelligence activities has been to create internal conflict by encouraging factionalism, jealousy, and suspicion among activists. Schisms based on disagreements over tactics, goals, or personalities may be created and encouraged. Agents were encouraged to create "personal conflicts or animosities" between leaders (Select Committee, book III, 1976, p. 26). In some cases government agents within opposing factions exacerbated tensions between them. This was apparently the case with the major split in the Black Panthers between the Newton and Cleaver factions and splits within the New Left between Students for a Democratic Society and groups such as the Progressive Labor party.

Key activists or those known to be violent may be anonymously and falsely accused of being informants or set up to make it appear that they are, in the hope that they will be attacked, isolated, or expelled. Beyond generating internal conflict, this tactic can be a means of derecruitment and efforts to destroy leadership.

William Albertson, a Communist party leader and member for almost thirty years, was drummed out of the party as a "stool pigeon" and one who had led a life of "duplicity and treachery." The FBI had planted "snitch jackets" (forged documents) on him to make it appear that he was an informer. One letter offered an FBI agent information in exchange for a "raise in expenses." After this episode, Albertson was unable to find work or to remain active in the movement he had given his life to, he was ostracized by his friends, and his home was burned after arson threats. He was ironically later approached by the FBI about becoming an informer and refused. Its assumption perhaps was that he would cooperate out of anger in response to the group's falsely accusing him (Donner, 1976). In describing this action and assessing its consequences, an FBI memo noted:

> The most active and efficient functionary of the New York District of the Communist Party USA and leading national officer of the party, through our counterintelligence efforts has been expelled from the party. Factors relating to this expulsion crippled the activities of the New York State communist organization and the turmoil within the party continues to this date. Albertson's exposure as an FBI informant has discouraged many dedicated communists from activities and has discredited the party in the eyes of the Soviets (p. 12).[7]

Encouraging External Conflict

Conflict between the movement and groups in its environment may be encouraged in the hope of damaging it and diverting it from the direct pursuit of broader social change goals. In extreme cases, this strategy involved the encouragement of armed conflict. In San Diego, four people were wounded and two killed during a summer of clandestinely encouraged FBI fighting between rival black groups (U.S. and the Black Panthers). A 1969 memo to J. Edgar Hoover on this episode stated, "Shootings, beatings, and a high degree of unrest continues to prevail in the ghetto area of southeast San Diego. Although no specific counterintelligence action can be credited with contributing to this overall situation, it is felt that a substantial amount of unrest is directly attributable to this program" (Wise, 1976, p. 319).

Actions aimed at preventing coalitions and cooperative actions may be undertaken. For example, after Malcolm X's assassination, the Socialist Workers party attempted to gain new recruits from the Black Muslims. FBI informers within the New York Black Muslims were encouraged to speak out against the "anti-religious" Socialist Workers party and to thwart their recruitment efforts (Berman and Halperin, 1975, p. 26).

Rather than encouraging conflict between organizations under the umbrella of the same social movement, conflict may also be encouraged among social movements with very different ideologies. Thus an FBI informant organized the right-wing Secret Army Organization in San Diego, a group that attacked leftists (Viorst, 1976). In Operation Hoodwink, the FBI sought to encourage conflict between the Communist party and elements of organized crime. According to an FBI memo, it was hoped that this action "would cause disruption of both groups by having each expend their energies, time, and money attacking each other" (Donner, 1976, p. 19).

A related tactic involves creating alternative social movement organizations. For example, during the 1960s and early 1970s, U.S. authorities created Communist, student, Klan, and anti-Communist type groups. These may compete with the target group for a limited resource base, fight with it over matters of doctrine and policy, and offer authorities unprecedented control over the movement since it is a government front. There are some parallels to the trade unions sponsored by the Russian police.

Sabotaging Particular Actions

When social movements take public action, they often seek to expand their base to include sympathetic but nonactivist members of their presumed mass constituency, as well as enter into coalitions with other social movement organizations whose members are not well known to them. Movements often have a loose and shifting nature, are geographically dispersed, and frequently lack specialized internal resources.

When national or regional meetings or demonstrations are held, out-of-town members must be housed and fed. Goods and services must be obtained from secondary sources. Strangers are brought together ostensibly in cooperative action but without the usual means of verifying identity. These factors make public social movement events vulnerable to disruption. Those seeking to disrupt a movement are offered a rich field for intervention.

Tactics of misinformation have been used to notify members falsely that events were cancelled, that they were being held elsewhere, or that times had been changed (Select Committee, book II, 1976, p. 10). Fake orders have been broadcast over the same citizen's band frequency used by marshals trying to control demonstrations, and CB communications have been jammed.

For large demonstrations planned in Chicago and Washington, FBI agents obtained and duplicated housing supply forms, which they filled in with fictitious names and addresses of people supposedly willing to offer housing to demonstrators. After "long and useless journeys to locate these addresses," demonstrators found themselves with no housing (ibid., p. 10).

Particular protest events are often affected by social control activities such as restrictive parade routes, permit denials, police provocation, and police failure to restrain those bent on attacking demonstrators. The government may pay and encourage counterdemonstrators, though only in a few recent cases have such actions been used. As one example, Bernard Barker and six other Cubans later to be involved in Watergate were flown in from Miami on White House orders to disrupt an antiwar demonstration on the Capitol steps. According to one of those involved, they were to punch Daniel Ellsberg, call him a traitor, and run. They did not succeed, but they did fight with some other demonstrators. Two of them were taken by police but were soon released (Wise, 1976, p. 174). The Secret Service roughed up and prevented demonstrators with antiwar and anti-Nixon signs from attending a Billy Graham rally in North Carolina. Demonstrators were told their admission tickets were counterfeit (*New York Times*, April 22, 1975).

In labor struggles, there have been many alliances between management and local and state authorities. In labor struggles up to the 1930s, goon squads and private police hired to break strikes and attack organizers sometimes avoided prosecution and were even deputized. Police and National Guard were also called out to break strikes.

Some of the actions taken or contemplated would be worthy of humorous appreciation for the imagination involved were they not on behalf of legally and morally questionable ends. The FBI in Newark suggested an action that would result in "confusion and suspicion" during a Black Panther party convention. The idea was to send a telegram warning that food donated to the convention contained poison and that one of its symptoms was stomach cramps. The FBI laboratory then planned to "treat fruit such as oranges with a mild laxative-type drug by hypodermic needle or other appropriate method." The oranges were apparently not injected because of the FBI's lack of control over the fruit during shipment, though Hoover felt that the idea "has merit" (Wise, 1976, pp. 318–19).

Efforts to Facilitate Social Movements

It appears that government actions aimed at damaging rather than facilitating movements have been much more formalized and prevalent. At least many more examples of the former have become public. It is hard to identify equivalent government agencies such as the police or FBI, or programs such as COINTELL, concerned with facilitating domestic social movements. The actions of nonpolice government agencies, courts, or legislators with implications for social movements are much more likely to be of a general and overt nature, rather than being at the specific micro-level in response to a given movement. When micro-level facilitative actions do occur, they are often indirect, and reactive; examples are courts' overturning, or inhibiting police efforts to damage a movement.

Many of the facilitative actions that police use are of a rather special nature. They may be part of an indirect strategy to strengthen or create (in order to control) a group that is the opponent, or rival, of the real target group. The government's aim is not to help the aided group obtain its goals as such. Or in the classic tradition of the provocateur, authorities may covertly encourage a group in order to sanction it later. A separate issue is that some actions by authorities inadvertently end up being facilitative.

It is easier to illustrate the right than the left side of table 1. Nevertheless there are some domestic examples of intended facilitation involving anti-Communists, the Klan, and the labor, civil rights, and women's movements. There are also many examples of facilitation in the activities of the CIA outside the United States.

Until the 1960s when the federal government legitimated the civil rights movement and put resources into voter registration and initiated the War on Poverty and community action, and the 1970s when women's rights gained considerable support, the major beneficiaries of facilitative efforts were right-wing, anti–civil rights, and management groups. Such groups have tended to involve countermovements and often vigilante-like action. The predominant forms of support were immunity and information. Periods of intense anticommunism—the red scare, the Palmer raids, and McCarthyism—have seen increased alliances and cooperative actions of government-investigating committees, police, and private groups, such as the American Protective League, the American Legion, and the American Security Council. Some retired FBI members or local police who have worked in intelligence units go to work for Americanism committees. Sometimes it appears that the social movement is primarily helping the government to a much greater extent than the reverse.

The granting of de facto legal immunity can be seen in some Latin American countries in attacks of the right on the left, which the government tends to ignore. Another example is the relation between the police and the Klan, where, in some parts of the South, the Klan was given what amounted to a license to break the law. Police in a sense delegated authority to Klansmen to carry out racial status quo–preserving activities that police could not legally carry out. Police behavior in many instances of earlier American racial violence has involved offering a de facto legal immunity to whites attacking blacks and some examples of the direct facilitation of particular actions by actually joining in the attacks (Marx, 1970).

The CIA gave large sums of money to domestic student, business, labor, church, and cultural groups. By strengthening moderate groups, such actions may have indirectly hurt more-radical groups. Although these moderate groups are not social movements as usually defined, they often give money and support to them. Ironically money given to the National Student Association may have helped build up an infrastructure and national student networks that were important to the later student movement.

A major way that government has aided recent movements such as those concerned with consumer and environmental issues has been through information leaks of various kinds. Groups such as Common Cause and Ralph Nader's consumer groups that seek to mobilize public opinion often appear to have allies within the government who pass on important technical and political information. Sometimes these efforts are part of a strategy by top administrators to build public support for goals shared with the movement. At other times, they stem from movement sympathizers within the government. As the cohort that reached adulthood during the late 1960s and early 1970s enters the government, this practice may become even more common. The Freedom of Information Act is likely to have important facilitative implications.

In a special category of pseudofacilitative activities, the government helps a movement (or segments of it) but not out of a desire to have it obtain its goals. Rather it can be a means of exercising partial control over it. Assumptions may be made about the extensiveness of mass anger and the predisposition to join a movement. A government-controlled movement able to obtain some concessions may be considered the best alternative.

The police-initiated Russian trade unions and some company unions are examples, as are the moderate Klan-type organizations created by the FBI. However hostile the FBI was to the Communist party, it took actions to keep it in its traditional form rather than to see it reorganized under a new label. Some observers would also place community action organizations created under the War on Poverty in this category.

EFFORTS BY OTHER GROUPS AND COUNTRIES

Recent congressional hearings offer much information on the extent to which the CIA has attempted to be a resource or a constraint for social movements in other countries (Commission on CIA, 1975; Select Committee, book I, 1976). Concomitantly many foreign countries have a strong interest in U.S. internal affairs.

A number of government investigations have been unable to find strong links between broad American movements such as the New Left, antiwar, and civil rights movements and the U.S.S.R., China, or Cuba. Yet it is unlikely that a lack of foreign intervention (in supportive or adversarial form) could be found for more narrowly based movements concerned with U.S. policy toward, and the nature of the government in, countries such as Cuba, Chile, Korea, Iran, Israel, and Yugoslavia and other countries of Eastern Europe. Such movements are often formed around a nucleus of immigrants. Depending on their orientation, they are likely to receive resources or face constraints from the country in question. We must ask questions about the Cuban government, as well as the CIA, in seeking to understand the Fair Play for Cuba Committee, or current struggles in Miami between groups with opposing views of Cuba. This also holds even for what appear to be strictly domestic issues—for example, the pro-Nixon demonstrations organized by Reverend Moon, who is apparently linked in complex ways to the Korean government.[8]

Another fascinating and almost completely unstudied source of external mobilization and constraint is the corporation. For example Samuel Zemurray, the man primarily responsible for building the United Fruit empire, created a 1910 revolution in Honduras. His hired bands swept through the country and established a puppet president sympathetic to the needs of United Fruit. Many years later, several United Fruit ships carried men and weapons to the Bay of Pigs (McCann, 1976). In the age of the multinational corporation, increased overt and covert intervention efforts may be expected.

QUESTIONS, PATTERNS, AND EXPLANATIONS
OF GOVERNMENT BEHAVIOR

In trying to account for the behavior of the government (rather than looking at what it tried to do or what the consequences were) a number of questions arise:

What are the historical roots of such behavior?

What conditions the decision to intervene?

What conditions the direction and form of the intervention—for example, whether it moves from information gathering to trying to affect outcomes; whether it aims to facilitate, redirect, or damage a movement; whether it is done overtly or covertly, legally or illegally, and directly on the group itself or indirectly on its environment?

How do officials justify and protect themselves with respect to actions they take?

Once government action has appeared, what factors affect its course and the frequent tendency for it to expand?

These are the kinds of questions that must be answered if we are to understand how external groups attempt to facilitate or damage a movement. Some of the answers may emerge after considering three empirical patterns of particular interest: (1) movements on the Left have received the most attention, followed by those on the Right, with relatively little attention being paid to movements or organizations in the center (except insofar as they were thought to be infiltrated by those from the Left or the Right); (2) efforts to damage social movements seem far more common than efforts to facilitate them; (3) the tendency for the government to intervene in social movement affairs has expanded over the last forty years.

The much greater emphasis on the Left than the Right may be explained by the fact that there are possibly more social movements on the Left than the Right; yet the imbalance of governmental attention appears to go far beyond this. For example, of the political cases in the Media, Pennsylvania, FBI files, more than two hundred involved Left and liberal groups, and only two involved right-wing groups. It could also be argued that the Left is more prone to illegal actions; yet the relative absence of successful prosecution of those on the Left would not support this theory. A General Services Administration audit of domestic intelligence investigations notes that only about 1 percent resulted in convictions. More likely, the pattern represents a carryover from a cold war ideology where the Left is defined as the enemy and the Right as the enemy of the enemy; it thus appears in a more benign light. In addition, the Left attacked J. Edgar Hoover while the Right praised him.

With his highly personalized style of directing the FBI, Hoover often used its resources against those he defined as enemies, whether or not they had broken laws or were clearly security threats. Authorities in general are closer in terms of social characteristics, ideology, and lifestyle to those on the Right. Cases where the government has intervened with right-wing groups have, in general, been more likely to involve manifest illegality that cannot be ignored, and often, as with Klan-type groups in the South, disagreements between local and national social-control agents. Cases where the Right turns on the government, as with Joseph McCarthy's attacks on the army or the John Birch Society's attacks on President Eisenhower, have also elicited responses.

The much greater emphasis on damage than facilitation (regardless of whether the Left or Right is involved) may be because social movements with their goals of change and their less institutionalized form are more likely to be seen as threats, rather than assets, by authorities tied to the status quo. Even where this is not the case, authorities may find it easier to justify illegal actions against those seen as subversive than to justify illegal actions on behalf of those seen as patriots. In addition, domestic social control agencies concerned with enforcing the criminal law have a conflict-apprehension ethos, that is probably more conducive to combative than facilitative forms of interaction.

In other countries, covert U.S. actions have involved facilitation to a much greater extent than has been the case domestically. For example, U.S. interests in Communist, Left-leaning, or anti-American countries are likely to be defined in opposition to the status quo. As such, the logic is to help elements wanting change, while in the United States (or in cases where its allies are weak or threatened) it has generally been the reverse: to damage social movements, some of which in a foreign context may themselves be facilitated by the Soviet Union or other countries.

The Expansion of Social Control

The government's ability and willingness to monitor and intervene in domestic social movement affairs has increased significantly in the last forty years.[9] According to the Select Committee, there has been "a relentless expansion of domestic intelligence activity beyond investigation of criminal conduct toward the collection of political intelligence and the launching of secret offensive actions against Americans" (Select Committee, book II, 1976, p. 21). There has been an expansion with respect to criteria for defining who is to become a target, the number of agencies involved, and the tactics used.

Those considered appropriate targets for FBI intelligence activities have expanded from Communist party members and groups, to those allegedly under Communist influence, to those taking positions supported by Communists, to those who might become subject to Communist influence. A wide range of domestic groups who broke no laws and had nothing to do with Communists, fascists, or foreign threats became subjects for intelligence activities and covert action. From a concern with Communists, government attention was broadened in the 1960s to include "racial matters," the "New Left," "student agitation," and alleged "foreign influence" on the antiwar movement. Counterintelligence activities and investigations were undertaken against "rabble-rousers," "agitators," "key activists," and "key black extremists." The women's liberation, gay, and ecology movements have also received attention, as have PTAs and religious groups.

Government intervention in social movements affairs spread from the FBI to the Internal Revenue Service, the National Security Administration, and military intelligence agencies. Local police have also become much more involved. Their activities are particularly relevant to understanding the struggles of blacks, students, and the peace movement during the 1960s and early 1970s. A significant expansion of political policing at the local level occurred, partly in response to encouragement and resources from the Justice Department. The IRS in response to White House pressure created a program to audit certain politically active persons and organizations. Army intelligence collected massive amounts of data and carried out surveillance on citizens. The CIA used its vague mandate to protect its intelligence sources and methods to set up Operation Chaos and to engage in electronic surveillance, break-ins, and the use of informers among domestic protest groups.

By 1975 this expansion had halted and, according to public accounts, was being reversed.[10] In the post-Watergate period and following the decline of mass demonstrations (and new austerity programs in many municipalities), authorities at both the local and national level have lessened, sometimes significantly, their efforts to monitor and intervene in social movement affairs in destructive ways. Formal policies were established and updated, dossiers destroyed, intelligence units reduced in size or disbanded, and new accountability measures created.

What best explains the general expansion of government intervention, particularly at the federal level, in social movement affairs since its revival in the late 1930s? Many different government agencies, different types of intervention, and thousands of different groups across the country expanded over almost four decades. The topic is highly complex and multifaceted. No single theory is sufficient. Yet the broad pattern indicates at least five types of explanations that may be relevant: (1) a reactive crisis-response model, (2) a pro-active anticipation-prevention model, (3) a bureaucratic and individual aggrandizement model, (4) a resource expansion-temptation model, and (5) a society-needs-devils model.

Crisis Response

This model assumes that systems operate to protect themselves and respond to threats to their equilibrium. Authorities are compelled to take the actions they do because of what the social movement does or claims it wants to do. As laws are broken, symbols attacked, and revolutionary rhetoric expressed, authorities respond in kind. They are seen (and publicly often see themselves) as reactive to subversive system-damaging social movements. Conditions for the emergence of such social control efforts and their expansion or contraction are found in the extent of the threat posed by a change-seeking social movement. If social control efforts have generally expanded over the last forty years, it is because the threats, or at least the perception of them, have also. As the threats decrease, so do social control activities.

To test this model, some objective means of threat assessment is needed, though it is likely to be difficult to get agreement on just who and what a threat is, particularly when laws have not been broken. A better measure might be authorities' perceptions of the extent of threat, though here one must be careful to separate actual from self-serving beliefs. National security and subversion offer easy rationalizations, as Watergate demonstrated. The threat-crisis argument seems consistent with the expansion of intelligence activities just prior to and during World War II; the creation of COINTELL programs against white hate groups, black nationalists, and the New Left, and the Huston plan, following the killing and intimidation of civil rights workers, civil disorders, and widespread antiwar and campus demonstrations; and the significant reduction in government efforts to damage social movements as relative calm returned in the mid-1970s.

Anticipation-Prevention and
Inherent Pressures in the Role

Tendencies to expand may be inherent in intelligence gathering and crime or subversion prevention roles. The role may be defined in such a way as to create an appetite that can never be satiated. Unlike the crisis-response model, the response here comes because a crisis is anticipated, or at least can be conceived of. This ability to imagine future threats calls forth action. The emphasis is put on offensive action. Factors conducive to this response are the vagueness of concepts like subversion and conspiracy, the absence of obvious states of goal achievement, and the fact that one can never be certain that an investigation has turned up all the relevant information. Those charged with such open-ended tasks may find it in their interest to cast the widest possible net and to operate as indiscriminate intelligence gatherers.

Officials can always imagine future scenarios that require new data-gathering tasks and preventive efforts (some of the actions directed against Martin Luther King, Jr. seem to have been of this sort). Proving hypotheses in intelligence work presents all the problems of data collection, interpretation, and validity found in proving them in a scientific inquiry. In addition, the subject may be consciously engaging in deceptive action. According to this rationale, an investigation that suggests minimal threat and no outside conspiracy may be part of a carefully designed trap to confuse the investigator, or the conclusion may stem from insufficient and careless investigation. Can you trust your own agents? Can one ever be too prepared in a context thought likely to become a war or when dealing with enemies that one's ideology may describe as utterly ruthless, cunning, and driven to subvert you?[11]

Recent government hearings offer abundant examples consistent with this model. In 1940 Hoover wrote that those advocating foreign "isms" "had succeeded in boring into every phase of American life, masquerading behind 'front' organizations" (Select Committee, book II, 1976, p. 31). The FBI's "theory of subversive infiltration" meant that Communists and other domestic enemies might be found anywhere. A belief that individuals are guilty until proven innocent calls for eternal vigilance. The FBI, with little statutory justification, came to define itself in a 1966 memo to all its field offices as an "intelligence agency . . . *expected to know what is going on or is likely to happen* [italics added]" (ibid., p. 70).

Vague, all-inclusive definitions became the rule. For example, the FBI manual stated that it was "not possible to formulate any hard-and-fast standards [for measuring] the dangerousness of individual members or affiliates of revolutionary organizations." The manual further stated, "Where there is doubt an individual may be a current threat to the internal security of the nation, the question should be resolved in the interest of security and investigation conducted" (ibid., p. 47). In the case of groups such as the New Left, efforts to define it were vague and were "expanded continually." The agent in charge of intelligence on the New Left stated, "It has never been strictly defined . . . it's more or less of an attitude" (ibid., p. 72). A memo to all FBI field offices noted that the term does not refer to "a definite organization" but a "loosely-bound, free-wheeling, college-oriented movement" and to the "more extreme and militant anti-Vietnam war and antidraft protest organizations" (ibid., p. 73).

There is always abundant room for ideological predispositions and/or contrary expectations on the part of supervisors to generate pressure for more information. In a large investigation of the civil rights movement, J. Edgar Hoover pressured one of his top assistants to keep investigating until he found the link between the civil rights movement and the Communist party that Hoover was convinced existed. His insistence came after an initial investigation found no such connection. President Johnson, unhappy over investigations concluding that there was almost no link between the antiwar movement and foreign countries, pressured for more vigorous and extensive investigations.

The source of this pro-active model may go beyond conspiratorial ideologies to a managerial model involving planning and the anticipation of demand (Graber, 1976). Galbraith's argument that the modern corporation has moved from passively being at the mercy of market forces of supply and demand to trying actively to affect those forces by intervention may apply here. Social control activities may also spiral because authorities increasingly feel a need to cover, protect, and justify their actions.[12]

Bureaucratic and Individual Aggrandizement

Factors that explain the origin of a phenomenon may not necessarily explain its continuance. Thus the origin of government programs for social movement intervention may generally lie in events that most members of a society would define as a crisis or a serious threat. However, the programs can take on a life of their own as vested interests develop around them, and new latent goals may emerge. Rather than social control as repression, deterrence, or punishment, it can become a vehicle for career advancement and organizational perpetuation and growth. The management and even creation of deviance, rather than its elimination, can become central. Intelligence and crime or subversion prevention roles offer rich possibilities to an entrepreneurial administrator or employee seeking to expand his or her domain. J. Edgar Hoover offers a clear example of this, but there are also many examples at the local level. The FBI increased from 500 to 4,000 employees by the end of World War II. Hoover, faced with the prospect of a greatly reduced agency with the end of the war effort, may have felt pressure to justify its size. The problem of Communist subversion offered a means of doing this. The bureau now has 25,000 employees.

Hoover skillfully manipulated the threat of domestic communism to gain continued support and increased resources from Congress, as his predecessors Attorney Generals Palmer and Dougherty had done with the red scare around World War I. Hoover was a moral entrepreneur with respect to both targets and tactics. He was a genius at using subtle language; he stressed "endeavors," "attempts," and "goals" of the target groups such as Communists, rather than their successes, because there were so few of the latter (Select Committee, book II, 1976, p. 49). Documents now available suggest that Hoover did not believe much of his own rhetoric and that he had accurate assessments of how weak and ineffective the Communist party was. When the size of the party began declining sharply, the FBI stopped reporting its strength and told inquirers that such information was classified (*Boston Globe*, November 19, 1975). Hoover also knew that whatever their rhetoric (which stopped short of incitement to violence), the Socialist Workers party did not engage in criminal acts over the thirty years that the FBI investigated it (Halperin et al., 1976, pp. 102–05).

Yet although this model fits some of the data, particularly J. Edgar Hoover's activities with respect to the Communist party, other data do not fit it. Thus Hoover appeared hesitant to move against the New Left, preferring to focus on the Old Left. When he finally did approve COINTELL operations, it was in response to a memo that rather than showing how the New Left was a threat to national security, argued that "the New Left has on many occasions viciously and scurrilously attacked the Director and the Bureau" (Select Committee, book II, 1976, p. 73). Vindictiveness rather than resource expansion seems the motive. However, an aggrandizement model would seem to fit the middle-management officials on the New Left desk who sought to extend COINTELL activities.

This model must also be tempered by noting that social control agencies operate within a broader political and social environment. Actions taken are partly in response to pressures perceived (both correctly and incorrectly) from this environment. Hoover, for example, was formally subordinate to the president and the attorney general, and he was very concerned with the public image of the bureau. His hand was not completely free. Some of the actions he took were in direct response to orders from superiors. In many of his actions, he may have anticipated what they wanted and not gone beyond that.

The bureau's reentry into political intelligence actions in the later 1930s was undertaken at the direction of President Roosevelt. The Johnson and Nixon administrations wanted information on and action against student, antiwar, and militant black protesters. Other actions that Hoover refrained from taking appear related to his concern with the public image of the FBI. His formal abolition of FBI break-ins, his reducing wiretaps by half in 1966, and his rejection of the Huston plan in 1970 are examples. With increased citizen and congressional concern, Hoover apparently believed such activities were too risky.

Yet to explain intervention in social movement affairs in light of the wishes of higher authorities has a question-begging potential.[13] The explanation is simply pushed up a level. We must then ask what conditions the behavior of higher authorities. Response to a perceived crisis and a desire to prevent a crisis are, of course, relevant. But as was the case with Richard Nixon and to a much lesser extent Lyndon Johnson and Franklin Roosevelt, a desire for the information gained from political intelligence and counterespionage, independent of any threats to national security, may also be involved. As the technology for these evolves, so too may the temptation to use it. Among the most interesting of questions are the links between having secret information and the desire to take covert action on the basis of it. Leaders, like the rest of us, may find that they can resist anything but temptation. An opportunity structure approach to deviance may apply to them as well as to more traditional deviants.

Governmental Expansion and New Resources

This century has seen a major expansion of government at all levels, and increased authority and centralization at the federal level. In this sense, increased government involvement—whether in health care, communications, or social movements—is part of a broader trend. But beyond this trend, the expansion of social control activities no doubt is also related to increased resources for doing this.

New opportunities and temptations have been created by ever more sophisticated technology for data gathering (bugging, electronic surveillance, and photography are examples), data storing, retrieving, and analyzing (computers as well as forms of analysis such as game theory or in-depth psychological profiles that call for data); and scientific developments permitting ever more subtle covert action.

An increasing pool of veterans of the cold war skilled in covert operations would also seem to be a factor. With respect to personnel, for example, all of those involved in the Watergate break-in were former CIA or FBI employees. John Caulfield and Anthony Ulasewitz, who did secret political investigations for the White House, were formerly of the New York City Police Department's Bureau of Special Services and Investigations. The absolute number of retired CIA, military intelligence agents, and local police increases each year. Thus in 1973, CIA director Schlesinger asked Congress to increase from 830 to 1,200 the number of CIA agents who could retire after twenty years of service at the age of fifty (*New York Times*, May 2, 1973). Lucrative pension plans at the municipal level also mean that an increasing number of local police are retiring at an early age after twenty or twenty-five years of service.

What line of work such retired agents choose, if any, is conditioned by many factors, but their availability offers new resources for covert social movement intervention and intelligence gathering on the part of government (which may choose to delegate out some of this work to its own private police, as Nixon did), private interest groups, or other social movements. Such former agents are in some ways the counterpart of the new group of social movement professionals noted by McCarthy and Zald (1973b). Both have specialized career skills independent of any specific social movement.

Society "Needs" Devils

This approach draws on a functionalist perspective on deviance from Durkheim (1960) and Erikson (1966). The creation of disvalued symbols is seen to help integrate a loosely organized society with considerable strain. Sanctioning of activists ("dangerous radicals," "subversives," "aliens," "reds," "hippies," "communists," "Klansmen," "militants," "fascists") who go too far from basic norms, even if they break no laws, can serve as a reminder to others to stay in line and can help bring a heterogeneous society together in shared condemnation of the outsiders.

Devil creation can also be seen as part of a scapegoating phenomenon wherein authorities' conscious manipulation of the threat of a social movement takes mass attention away from more basic sources of grievance, although with the increased education and sophistication of the American public and increased resources for mobilization, this becomes more difficult to do.

This model is the most difficult to test. It can involve teleological assumptions and the reification of the concept society. It is likely most useful for considering some of the consequences of government sanctioning of social movements rather than the expansion or contraction of such activities.

OUTCOMES: INTENDED AND UNINTENDED

I have noted ways in which authorities may seek to help or damage a movement and have offered examples to illustrate the relevant concepts. I have assumed authorities know what they wanted to do and were able to do it. Sometimes this is the case; often it is not. In considering efforts to damage or facilitate a movement, it is important to ask what the actual (rather than intended) consequences of such efforts are; whether the government achieves the result it seeks; if it does not, what factors prevent it; and what other results are possible.

Let us turn to some of the complicating factors that may result in consequences other than those intended by authorities. That there is frequently a gap between formal and informal factors and intended and actual consequences is not surprising. Indeed much sociological research is directed toward understanding this general issue. In this regard, it is necessary to inquire what is unique about the situation of authorities' responding to the social movements. At least six somewhat exceptional factors that increase the likelihood of the government's intervention having unintended consequences can be identified: the secrecy involved; the frequent illegality of the actions; the lack of effective intervention techniques in the face of the diffuse, noninstitutionalized collective-behavior character of much social movement activity; the need to establish credibility through seemingly loyal actions; and the reactive neutralization processes inherent in many social control efforts.

Secrecy has meant a lack of accountability and usual standards of performance evaluation. There are problems in controlling agents, and occasional scenarios take place in which secret agents (unbeknown to each other) engage in mutual intelligence gathering and provocation.

It is more difficult to damage social movements in a context with a tradition of civil liberties and with levels and branches of government that are not monolithic. Many of the actions taken by authorities have been illegal. When authorities take illegal or morally questionable actions in a nonconsensual context, they run the risk of helping the movement should they be exposed. The government's legitimacy and credibility may be damaged, and court cases may be filed because of illegal procedures.

But even if government actions are not exposed or there is widespread public support, the nature of the phenomenon and our lack of social engineering knowledge may result in effects on group processes, or individual motivation, that are quite different from those authorities sought. Attention directed toward a movement may convince activists that they are a genuine threat and that what they are doing is of vital importance. By clearly focusing external conflict for the movement, authorities may heighten the sense of group boundaries and increase internal solidarity. Surveillance may make participation more exciting. It may increase the will, resolve, and anger of some activists. It may call forth martyrs who become important rallying symbols. It may make activists more radical and push them away from the reformist belief that change within the system is possible.

Infiltrators may be an important resource for the movement. To establish and maintain credibility, they must take actions that help it. For example, FBI informant Robert Hardy provided leadership, training, and resources to those involved in the Camden draft board raid (*New York Times*, March 16, 1972). He stated, "I taught them everything they knew . . . how to cut glass and open windows without making any noise. . . . How to open file cabinets without a key. . . . How to climb ladders easily and walk on the edge of the roof without falling. . . . I began to feel like the Pied Piper" (*Washington Post*, November 19, 1975). A Klan informant has reported how while performing duties paid for by the government, he had "beaten people severely, had boarded buses and kicked people, had [gone] into restaurants and beaten them [blacks] with blackjacks, chairs, and pistols." FBI informants were formally told that they could not be involved in violence; nevertheless he understood that in the Klan "he couldn't be an angel and be a good informant" (Select Committee, book III, 1976, p. 13).

As a movement comes under increased attack, it may be able to obtain increased resources for defense or a counteroffensive from its mass constituency and other sympathetic audiences.[14] Rival groups may make covert attempts to neutralize and disrupt the activities of government agents. The conflict may escalate.

Recent social movement repression in the United States clearly has some unique elements. Judged in a historical and international context, much of it was relatively benign, particularly at the federal level. It is hard to imagine national police forces in most of the rest of the world today, let alone in the past, responding to opposition social movements by injecting oranges with a laxative, tattling about sexual affairs, or printing and circulating false offers of housing for demonstrators. If a group is judged worthy of attention, violence against activists, threats, and arrests are far more common and effective. For American police at the federal level (in the absence of legal violations), such actions were too risky and morally unacceptable to many agents in a domestic context. The lesser availability of these overtly repressive tactics helps explain the tactics that emerged and the receptivity to agents capable of provoking illegal actions to justify government intervention. Many of the FBI COINTELL actions are best seen as expressive and symbolic; they were a way of doing something when there was often little that could be done legally. The local, relatively spontaneous, mass-based, collective-behavior-like quality of much activism also made traditional social-movement monitoring and breaking tactics less applicable.

In broad outline, several conclusions can be made about the effect of government efforts to damage the social movements of the 1960s and early 1970s. Let us take goal attainment and organizational viability as our criteria and consider the movements that received the most attention from the FBI's COINTELL program. There is a varied pattern. In the case of the Klan, Communist party, Socialist Workers party, and more radical black groups like the Panthers, the evidence is consistent with the argument that social control efforts were effective. These groups did not obtain their goals and did not increase with respect to organizational viability; indeed most seemed to decrease. These groups tended to be ideologically extreme and to recruit from marginal sources. As a result, they may have been more vulnerable to government efforts to damage them because they could not draw on mass audiences for support and sympathy to the extent that the more moderate groups could. The Klan and more radical black groups also appear more likely to have been involved in felonious actions and to have used violent rhetoric, offering authorities greater possibilities for legal interventions. Relative to many of the other movements, they also seem to have in lesser abundance the organizational skills and sophistication needed to run a national movement.

Authorities appear to have been least successful against the antiwar, student, and moderate civil rights movements, groups that maintained, and even increased, strength until their major goals were obtained. In the case of the student and antiwar movements, this was in spite of massive efforts to damage them on a scale unprecedented in American history. With the exception of black groups, these movements have now declined, yet this is partly as a result of their very success.

In the case of the early civil rights movement, especially in the South, efforts by local authorities to damage the movement were more than matched by the facilitative efforts of the federal government (though efforts of nonsupport and even to damage can also be seen). The civil rights movement sought basic rights that had long been part of the American tradition for other groups, and it did so with nonviolent action in the name of Christianity. Its successes were the continuation of civil rights trends evident since before World War II. Only later, following the ghetto riots, did the federal government attempt covert action to damage the more radical black groups.

With the ending of the Vietnam war and the draft, greater flexibility and democratization on college campuses, and more sensitive college administrators who learned how not to be provoked and overreact to the small cadre of fully committed student radicals, the mass-based antiwar and more moderate student movements practically disappeared. They were at best heterogeneous and loosely held together by opposition to particular policies that were changed. They did not draw on shared interests growing out of historic or enduring cleavages and a culture of opposition within the society. As such, with victory came organizational defeat. Their large-scale, decentralized, participatory, fluid, shifting, and spontaneous collective behavior character did not lend itself well to the kinds of movement-damaging tactics the FBI had used against the bureaucratically organized Communist party. Yet even with better tactics, the level of mass support for stopping the war became so great and included so many powerful and respected business and political leaders that it is doubtful the movement could have been stopped within the traditional American framework. The same applies to the demands of the civil rights groups through 1964.

In response to the question of what happened to the student and antiwar movements, one is tempted to say they never really existed beyond the evening news and the immorality of the war or the incompetence of college administrators. They did not resolve the problems of structure noted by Jo Freeman (1977). At least they did not exist in the sense that the NAACP, Communist party, Socialist Workers party, Klan, and Black Panthers did. These groups had more ideological coherence and unity and a steadier organizational structure, and they were capable of mobilizing members and sympathizers in other than a reactive sense. They knew what they were for, as well as what they were against. Yet even in the case of those groups such as the Klan, radical blacks, and the Communist party, where the results desired by authorities appeared, can we conclude that authorities were responsible? Many factors beyond the efforts of external groups to facilitate or inhibit social movement processes affect them so there is a major difficulty in separating correlation from causation in natural field settings. Determining the effect of efforts at social control or facilitation on a given outcome is difficult. Where a major social change goal sought by a movement is obtained (and this is infrequent, particularly in the short run), it is difficult to tell how important the movement was to this end, what the causal link was, whether it occurred in spite of the movement's efforts, and whether the appearance of both the social change and the social movement were accounted for by some third set of factors.

Is the splintering of a sectarian group into two rival groups more a function of the efforts of authorities to create internal conflict, or of the seemingly endemic tendency of such groups to factionalism, even where no social control efforts are present? Is a high degree of turnover, sporadic participation, and ebbs and flows in mass participation more a function of authorities' ability to damage morale and create an unfavorable public image and the myth of surveillance and repression, or of the general problems involved in sustaining a mass movement, where many of the rewards for participation may be minimal and some may be available (if the movement succeeds) to nonparticipants as well?

With respect to the movements in question, it could be argued that government actions contributed to their failings but were not really decisive. The black power and black pride groups that grew out of the moderate civil rights groups failed when they opted for more radical goals and means. They moved from demands for inclusion and basic rights of a political and symbolic nature that could be granted without direct economic loss to whites (the right to vote, equal justice, nondiscrimination in hiring and public services, and racial dignity) to more controversial and zero-sum issues of an economic nature involving redistribution, retribution, quotas, nonachievement criteria, and, in many cases, racialism if not always racial separation. Matching the shift in goals were (primarily at the level of media rhetoric) calls for revolution, violence, and ties to the Third World. This shift in the nature of the black movement does not seem to be something directly initiated by agents of social control. It developed out of previous victories and defeats and the structure of American society. It had also occurred several times earlier in the history of the black movement. However, authorities were soon in the thick of it and no doubt encouraged (whether they intended to do so is less clear) through self-fulfilling effects the radicalism and violence of some groups such as the Black Panthers and the Student Nonviolent Coordinating Committee.

Like the more radical black groups, the Klan seemed on the wrong side of historical trends (something that was not always true). It failed to obtain its goals of halting civil rights gains for blacks, and its membership declined significantly. Once it became the subject of concentrated government attention, its well-documented pattern of criminal conspiracy and violence markedly declined. Government intervention efforts seem most successful here.[15] However, the same broad consequences might have been forthcoming, although they may have taken longer and at a greater toll of life, if the government had not been involved in preventive and disruptive efforts. The escalation of the conflict that characterized authorities' response to radical blacks did not seem to occur here, perhaps because the Klan started out violent and often correctly saw local authorities as their allies, or at least as being neutral.

In the case of groups such as the Communists and Socialist Workers party that sought radical economic change or black groups that sought separatism, one can argue that they would have failed anyway as their counterparts have throughout the twentieth century before efforts at social movement repression became so developed and commonplace.

The structure of American society and natural social movement processes seem to work toward the weakening of ideologically extreme movements and those not organized around fundamental societal cleavages. It is difficult to sustain less institutionalized collective behavior phenomena under the best of circumstances. This would seem to be even truer for movements resisting broad historical trends. External efforts seeking to facilitate such movements (and beyond local support for movements seeking to counter the civil rights movement, there was not much of this) would seem to have much more difficulty and would in general appear to be less effective than those seeking to destroy them. Many of the outcomes sought by authorities seeking to damage social movements were likely to happen anyway, though perhaps not as rapidly or to the same degree.

Some inferences might also be made from what happened between 1924 and 1936 when the FBI ceased domestic intelligence. There was not a sudden upsurge in movement effectiveness, although given the conditions of the depression, social movements proliferated. Movements such as those of Townsend, Long, Smith, and Coughlin gained in popularity and then almost disappeared for reasons that appear to have little to do with federal-level social control intervention (or its absence).

Nor in the period since 1975, when both the FBI and local police seem to have significantly reduced their policing of social movements, have movements suddenly flourished.

To be sure with respect to the local level and for particular people, groups, and events they were often decisive, though not always in ways that they hoped. Social control efforts certainly had some effect on the style and direction of many movements. The humanitarian community of love, trust, and openness sought by early student, pacifist, and civil rights groups becomes difficult to sustain in the milieu of paranoia, suspicion, and violence that authorities contributed to. Activists became more cautious in their dealings with strangers. The need to be suspicious of strangers is an obvious liability for a movement that seeks to build a mass base. But considering the broad national pattern, agents are only one among a variety of historical, cultural, social structural, and resource and grievance factors to be considered.

NOT BY RESOURCES ALONE

Just as there were clear limits to what social control agents could accomplish, there were limits to what the social movements could do. Both are bounded by historical, cultural, structural, and psychological factors that have not been well conceptualized.

Thus, the course of the Moon movement with millions of dollars, Madison Avenue techniques and superb organization was roughly parallel to that of other youth-oriented religious movements lacking their resources (Lofland, 1977). Such movements recruited poorly during the 1960s, significantly expanded during the early and mid-1970s as disillusionment with politics spread, and now are contracting. The availability of resources or social control does not help much in explaining this pattern, though it may be useful for intramovement comparisons.

A major future challenge for analysts of social movements lies in bringing together the resource mobilization perspective with its emphasis on organizational variables and rational self-interest, with the collective behavior perspective with its emphasis on emotion, expression, symbols, and the fluid nature of mass involvement.

I think the prime significance of government efforts to damage recent movements lies not in the all-too-easily-available conspiracy theories of social movement failure or success. Rather it lies in calling attention to an important and neglected variable, the increased ability of government to engage in practices that are abhorrent to a free society. Our liberties are fragile, and we must be prepared to ask with Yeats, "What if the Church and the State are the mob that howls at the door?"

ENDNOTES

1. I am thus taking prior structural conduciveness and strain (Smelser, 1963) or the kinds of social controls that may be operating through the culture, education, and "false" need creation noted by Gramsci (Genovese, 1967) and Marcuse (1964) as givens, even though these may be affected by those seeking to create or forestall the appearance of a social movement; they may have such effects.

2. This, of course, depends on how terms are defined and events assessed. What, for example, are we to make of the government's War on Poverty and community action programs? Were they an effort to facilitate poor people's movements by building alternative sources of local power that could fight city hall, or were they efforts to damage and defuse the civil rights movement through co-optation? I will start here with cases whose meaning is more manifest.

3. See, for example, work by Turner (1969), Morris (1973), Molotch and Lester (1974), and Estep and Lauderdale (1977).

4. In the investigation of the entertainment industry in the early 1950s, such activities went beyond merely releasing educational material to direct and indirect media censorship. Blacklisting, self-censorship, and anti-Communist crusades carried out through the media helped create an image of American society that was not conducive to left activism.

5. More than a million dollars had been spent by the CIA on its book development program by the mid-1960s. By 1967 the Senate Select Committee estimated that the CIA was responsible for "well over 1,000 books."

6. In part this may stem from undue reliance on an agitator theory of social movements: leaders and organizers, not social conditions, are seen as the key to movement unrest. In part it may stem from the inability of agents to do much else: leaders offer tangible specific targets for intervention in a way that mass sympathizers (many of whom are unknown to authorities) or broad social conditions do not.

7. For authorities, the power of such techniques lies in their self-perpetuating quality. Once the myth of the informer gains currency and seeds of doubt are planted, cooperation and trust are made more difficult, for anyone potentially could be one. The accusation of informer becomes available as a tool in intragroup struggle, and informers become an explanation for failures that may lie elsewhere.

8. With secret budgets, determining causal links is always difficult. According to some sources, money from Nixon in 1974 may have been channeled to Moon, who then provided pro-Nixon crowds, as at the White House Christmas tree lighting in 1974.

9. My concern is primarily with domestic affairs. However, a similar process of expansion occurred for the CIA. The CIA was created as an intelligence agency and not given clear authority or capability for covert action. Yet it quickly went beyond gathering intelligence to covert action. It moved from reporting on events to trying to influence them, at first abroad and later at home.

10. Not only may authorities on occasion be less than truthful, but given the context of secrecy and the morass of huge bureaucracies, they may find it difficult to know all that is going on in their own agencies, or whether policies are being followed. Note FBI Director Kelley's claim that FBI breaking and entering had stopped when it had not, or a CIA scientist's failure to destroy shellfish toxin after orders to do so from the president and the head of the CIA.

11. This voracious skepticism also applies to one's own efforts to maintain security. For example, the CIA was so concerned that someone might plant electronic surveillance devices in the walls of its new buildings in Langley, Virginia, that it developed a network of paid informers among construction workers on the job (Wise, 1976, p. 145).

12. Wilsnack (1977), in considering four information control processes (espionage, secrecy-security, persuasion, and evaluation), suggests the following hypothesis: "The more that a group or organization develops specialized, full-time roles for carrying out one process of information control, the more resources that group or organization will invest in each of the other control processes" (p. 14).

13. Empirically documenting this is also difficult. For example, the efforts of the Select Committee to find out who authorized CIA assassination attempts were, in the words of Senator Walter Mondale, "like trying to nail Jello to the wall." CIA agents spoke to each other in "riddles and circumlocutions." He continued, "I believe the system was intended to work that way: namely, things would be ordered to be done that should it be made public, no one could be held accountable" (Wise, 1976, pp. 214, 209).

14. In a nongovernmental context, Anita Bryant's campaign against homosexuals seems to have given the gay movement a significant boost. We can also wonder what such actions did to the self-image and work satisfaction of those in the FBI (many trained as accountants and lawyers) who carried them out.

15. Former Attorney General Nicholas deB. Katzenbach observed that following the killing of the three civil rights workers, "a full scale investigation of the Klan was mandated. Agents of the FBI interrogated and reinterrogated every known member of the Klan in Mississippi. Many were openly followed, using surveillance techniques that the bureau had developed in connection with organized crime cases. We learned more about the Klan activities in those months than we had known in years. I have no doubt that as an integral part of that investigation, members of the Klan on whom we were focusing our efforts became disoriented, distrustful of other members, and ultimately persuaded that cooperation with the ubiquitous FBI agents was the only safe recourse" (Select Committee, Hearings, 1976, 6:215). In 1976 an estimated 2,000 of 10,000 Klan members were paid FBI informants. Seventy percent of new Klan members that year were informants (ibid., p. 144).

Repertoires of Contention in America and Britain, 1750–1830

Charles Tilly

BOSTON IN 1773

"I wrote you the 8th instant and inform'd their Lordships of the Rebellious State of the People of this Town on Account of the Tea's exported by the East India Company subject to the Kings duty of three pence in the pound, which was resolved in the Town meeting should not be paid, and on that account an Arm'd Force was appointed to Parade the Wharf's where the Tea Ships lay to prevent its being Landed." The letter, dated 17 December 1773, came from the rear admiral Montagu at his base in Boston. He was reporting to the agent of the Lords of the Admiralty in London. "I am now to desire," Admiral Montagu continued,

> you will be pleased to inform their Lordships that last Evening between 6 & 7 O'clock, a large Mob assembled with Axes &c., encouraged by Mr. John Hancocke, Samuel Adams, and others; and marched in a Body to the Wharfs where the Tea Ships lay, and there destroyed the whole by starting it into the Sea.
>
> I must also desire you will be pleased to inform their Lordships, that during the whole of this transaction, neither the Governor, Magistrates, Owners, or the Revenue Officers of this place ever called for my assistance, if they had, I could easily have prevented the execution of this Plan, but must have endangered the Lives of many innocent people by Firing upon the Town. [Public Record Office, London, Colonial Office Papers, series 5, box 120, hereinafter cited C.O. 5/120.]

The National Science Foundation provided the financial support for the research behind this essay. I am grateful to R. A. Schweitzer, John Boyd, and Martha Guest for help in the research.

Collective Action and the Response of Authorities

The Boston Tea Party, as the events of that December evening came to be known, had been in preparation for about two months. The Northend Caucus had voted on 23 October to resist the landing of the dutied tea. Early in November handbills began to appear demanding that the tea consignees resign and send the tea back to England. Public meetings and anonymous notices both restated the demand that the consignees resign.

The meeting of 29 November, called by Boston's Committee of Correspondence, led to the posting of the "Arm'd Force" at Griffin's Wharf. As Governor Hutchinson described the gathering: "Altho' this Meeting or Assembly consisted principally of the Lower Ranks of the People, & even Journeymen Tradesmen were brought to increase the Number & the Rabble were not excluded yet there were divers Gentlemen of Good Fortune among them, & I can scarcely think they will prosecute their Mad Resolves" (Hutchinson to Dartmouth, 2 December 1773, quoted in Hoerder, 1971, p. 407). The tea consignees fled to the protection of the Castle. From there, after further meetings and additional threats, they eventually stated their willingness to store the tea unsold, but not to ship it back. Attention shifted to the shipowners, who were reluctant to carry the tea back to England, and unready to guarantee not to land it. The orderly destruction of their cargo on the evening of the 16 December decided the issue for them.

At the core of the tea-dumping crowd were two groups of activists who had gathered separately before walking to the wharf: seventeen members of the North End's Long Room Club, who were largely masters and shipbuilders; and a larger and more disparate group from the South End who had rallied at Liberty Tree, on the corner of Essex and Orange Streets (Hoerder, 1971, pp. 419–20). The preparation of the event drew on Boston's standard anti-British coalition. The coalition included skilled workers and masters from the North End; workers, masters, and merchants from the South End; professionals and merchants—Hutchinson's Gentlemen of Good Fortune—from the city as a whole. In the following years these three groups of activists played a major part in the widening campaign of noncooperation and resistance. They contributed to the erection of parallel institutions of government in Boston and in the rest of Massachusetts. They were the nucleus of a revolutionary coalition.

By December 1773, some version of the revolutionary coalition had been at work in Boston for eight years. The Stamp Act crisis of 1765 had brought it into being. From that point on, the allied craftsmen and merchants repeatedly attacked the local "placemen" whom they regarded as profiting from a willingness to favor the interests of the British crown over those of the American colonists.

Boston's activists stated their disapproval in more than one way. Over the decade from 1765 to 1775, we find them petitioning Parliament, sending delegates to England, organizing patriotic clubs, holding mock trials of their enemies, sacking the offices and houses of British agents, gathering for speeches at the Liberty Tree, marching through the streets to bonfires, tarring and feathering tea drinkers, and more. By 1774, much of the effort was going into two complementary sets of activities: destroying the effectiveness of the official British governmental apparatus and its personnel; and building a set of effective, autonomous, indigenous political institutions. In the first category fell the economic and social boycott of the British troops sent to occupy Boston after the resistance to the tea duty, the forced resignation of British commissioners and agents, the sabotaging of royal courts. In the second category came the organization of such revolutionary organizations as the Sons of Liberty, the addition of powers to the committees of correspondence, and the holding of people's courts and unauthorized town meetings. As Vice Admiral Graves wrote to the Admiralty on 23 September 1774, "They have obstructed, and are determined, let what will be the consequence, to oppose the Execution of the Laws, and to stunt, and destroy every Person, who will not take an active part against Government" (C.O. 5/120). By 1774 the people of Boston, and of all the American colonies, were creating an unauthorized but effective parallel government.

THE QUALITY OF COLONIAL CONTENTION

By the end of the year, indeed, colonists were not only boycotting and building, but attempting to seize control over portions of the existing British governmental structure. That emphatically included control of armed force. A letter from New Hampshire's Governor Wentworth, dated at Portsmouth on 14 December 1774, describes one such attempt:

> Yesterday in the afternoon one Paul Revere arrived in this Town Express from a Committee in Boston to another Committee in this Town, and delivered his dispatch to Mr. Saml. Cutts a Merchant of this Town who immediately convened a Committee of which he is one, & as I learn laid it before them.
> This day about noon before any suspicions could be had of their Instructions, about five hundred Men were collected together, who proceeded to His Majesty's Castle William and Mary at the Entrance of this Harbour and forcibly took Possession thereof, notwithstanding the best defence that could be made by Capt. Cochran & by violence carried away upwards of one hundred barrells of Powder belonging to the King deposited in the Castle. I am informed that expresses have been circulated throughout the neighbouring Towns to collect a number of People tomorrow or as soon

as possible to carry away all the Cannon & Arms belonging to the Castle, which they will undoubtedly effect unless assistance shoud arrive from Boston in time to prevent it. [C.O. 5/121.]

This action coincided with efforts, often unsuccessful, to seize cannons and rifles in other garrison towns along the American coast. It paralleled the effort to recruit British soldiers and sailors to the American cause. It supplemented the creation of groups of armed patriotic volunteers. A revolutionary situation was in the making.

A twentieth-century reader of the eighteenth-century reports from the colonies notices the wide, creative use of street theater: skits, tableaux, dumb shows, effigies, stylized symbols of the issues and antagonists. One example will give the flavor: the celebration of Guy Fawkes Day (known in the colonies as Pope's Day) of 1774 in Charles Town, South Carolina:

Saturday last, being the Anniversary of the Nation's happy deliverance from the infernal Popish POWDER-PLOT in 1605, and also of the glorious REVOLUTION by the Landing of King William in 1688, two Events which our Brethren in England seem of late to have too much overlooked, the Morning was ushered in with Ringing of Bells, and a MAGNIFICENT EXHIBITION of EFFIGIES, designed to represent Lord North, Gov. Hutchinson, the POPE, and the DEVIL, which were placed on a rolling Stage about eight Feet high and fifteen Feet long, near Mr. Ramadge's Tavern in Broad-Street, being the most frequented place in Town. The *Pope* was exhibited in a Chair of State, superbly drest in all his priestly Canonicals; Lord *North* (with his Star, Garter, &c. and shewing the Quebec Bill) on his right Hand; and Governor *Hutchinson* on his left, both chained to Stakes; the *Devil*, with extended Arms, behind the Three, and elevated above them, holding in one Hand a Javelin directed at the Head of Lord North, and in the other a Scroll, insrib'd "Rivington's New York Gazetteer;" on his Arm was suspended a large Lanthorn, in the shape of a Tea Canister, on the sides of which was writ in Capitals, "HYSON, GREEN, CONGON and BONZA TEAS." The Exhibition was constantly viewed by an incredible Number of Spectators, amongst whom were most of the Ladies and Gentlemen of the first Fortune and Fashion. The *Pope* and the *Devil*, were observed frequently to bow, in the most respectful complaisant Manner, to sundry Individuals, as if in grateful Acknowledgment for their past Services. About 8 O'clock, A.M. the whole was moved to the Square before the *State-House*, and back again to Mr. Ramadge's, when Divine Service began in St. Michael's Church; in which Situation it remained throughout the Day, without the least Appearance of Opposition, Tumult or Disorder. . . . In the Evening the whole Machinery was carried thro' the principal Streets, to the *Parade*, without the Town Gate, where a Pole 50 Feet high was erected, strung with and surrounded by a great Number of Tar Barrels. The TEA collected by the young Gentlemen the Tuesday before, being placed between the *Devil* and Lord *North*, was set on Fire, and brought on our Enemies in *Effigy*, that Ruin they had designed to bring on us in *Reality*. [*South Carolina Gazette*, 21 November 1774.]

The exhibit was complete with homiletic posters, such as:

ROBBERS AND WHITE-ROB'D SAINTS,
COMPARED TO TYRANTS.
MAGNA CHARTA, AND THE OATHS OF KINGS
ARE COBWEBS NOW;
WITNESS, THE VIOLATION OF THE BOSTON CHARTER.

Over Massachusetts Governor Hutchinson's head hung the words HIC VIR PATRIAM VENDITIT AURO: this man sold his country for gold. And on Hutchinson's breast were these lines:

Here in Boston,
Loaded with the undeserved Honours of my Country,
I chose to be her Curse;
I forg'd her Chains.
The World shall know me: Hutchinson my Name,
'Mongst Traytors damn'd to everlasting Shame.
Preferment comes neither from the East, nor from the
West, nor from the South; but from the North.
The Devil take *America*, if I can only get Preferment.

This was the texture of a routine patriotic celebration in the America of 1774. Despite the angry words, the festivities went off in calm, even in good humor. But the same iconography and the same rhetoric also appeared in many of the violent events of the time: forcible seizures of tea, attacks on agents of the crown, vigilante trials of transgressors against the rules of boycott and nonimportation, tarring and feathering of British sympathizers.

The forms of popular collective action in the prerevolutionary decade are not merely absorbing in themselves. They are relevant to major questions concerning the origins of the Revolution. Pauline Maier, for example, has used the character of popular action as evidence for her argument that the initial impulse of the prerevolutionary mobilization was *defensive*—an attempt to maintain liberties that the colonists regarded as embedded in the English constitution. Richard Maxwell Brown places the crowd of the 1760s and 1770s at the crossing-point of an indigenous colonial tradition of violent protest and the eighteenth-century British practice of bargaining by riot. Gary Nash offers an analysis of crowd action to support his portrayal of a well-developed popular radicalism among the colonists. Indeed, popular collective action such as the Stamp Act resistance is so visible and crucial in the history of the American Revolution that the advocate of any position whatsoever must fit an interpretation of that action into his general argument.

REPERTOIRES OF COLLECTIVE ACTION

My purpose here, however, is neither to infer an account of the American Revolution as a whole from the behavior of crowds nor to reinterpret crowd action in the light of a general thesis about the Revolution. I want instead to draw attention to some general features of popular collective action that take on a strong relief in the glare of a revolutionary situation. The main point is elementary: within any particular time and place, the array of collective actions that people employ is (1) well defined and (2) quite limited in comparison to the range of actions that are theoretically available to them. In that sense, particular times, places, and populations have their own repertoires of collective action. On the whole, the existing repertoire only changes slowly. At a given point in time, it significantly constrains the strategy and tactics of collective actors.

If the idea of a repertoire of collective action is plausible, it is not self-evident. It states a position rather different from two other competing ideas concerning popular collective action: (1) the notion of universal forms, such as quintessential crowd behavior or standard revolutionary actions; (2) the image of calculating tacticians who seize every opportunity to press their advantage and to fend off their disadvantage. In contrast with both these views, the idea of a repertoire implies that the standard forms are learned, limited in number and scope, slowly changing, and peculiarly adapted to their settings. Pressed by a grievance, interest, or aspiration and confronted with an opportunity to act, groups of people who have the capacity to act collectively choose among the forms of action in their limited repertoire. That choice is not always cool and premeditated; vigilantes sometimes grab their guns and march off on the spur of the moment, and angry women make food riots. Nor are the performances necessarily frozen, regimented, and stereotypical; demonstrators against the Stamp Act and the arrival of dutied tea often invented new ways of broadcasting their message and regularly responded to unanticipated contingencies by improvising. The repertoire is the repertoire of jazz or commedia dell'arte rather than of grand opera or Shakespearian drama. Nevertheless, a limited repertoire sets serious constraints on when, where, and how effectively a group of actors can act.

If the idea of a repertoire is more than a convenient metaphor, we should be able to compare the real world with the concept. Figure 1 sketches four possible relationships between the forms of action that are already familiar to a population and those it adopts when a new opportunity comes along. If there is no relationship between the probability of a given form of action and its similarity to the forms of action already known to the population, the idea of a repertoire is wrong. That could be true either because the forms of collective action were random and impulsive, or because actors generally chose the efficient means regardless of its familiarity. In the second case, familiar forms have an advantage for such reasons as the greater efficiency with which groups use them. To call the familiar forms in this case a "repertoire" is misleading. For the word to be useful, actors should display a preference for familiar forms that to some degree overrides questions of efficiency, which is not simply a function of the availability of information, and which leads them to choose differently from other actors elsewhere.

Sketches C and D portray cases in which the idea of a repertoire is useful. A *flexible repertoire* leaves some room for innovation and for the deliberate adoption of relatively unfamiliar means of action, but still cants the choice strongly toward familiar means, and sets some limit of unfamiliarity beyond which the actor will not go. A *rigid repertoire* confines the actor to already familiar performances: the actor does not innovate, and does not deliberately adopt unfamiliar forms of action—except, perhaps, in crises that alter the entire repertoire.

In his commentary on the initial presentation of this essay, Mancur Olson pointed out that the existence of a repertoire, in sense C or D of the word, rests on the presence of a tendency toward monopoly in the supply of new means of action. Otherwise, individual innovators who devised means of action that were more efficient or effective than those currently in use would be able to attract interested parties to their programs. Olson offered the observation as an objection to the idea of repertoire. (Indeed, he called it a "dangerous" idea.) But his observation is doubly useful. It brings out the fact that the implicit argument behind the notion of repertoire emphasizes the importance of constituted groups, rather than the ad hoc coalitions of interested parties, as collective actors. And it suggests the likelihood of a correlation between the extent to which constituted groups *are* the actors and the degree to which a standard repertoire constrains collective action.

One could, in fact, employ the four types or the continuum along which they fall as a taxonomy for real actors, and as the basis of speculation concerning the determinants of an actor's flexibility. It might be, for example, that the less specialized the group and the closer it comes to providing its members with a complete round of life, the more rigid is its repertoire. For the present, I have a simpler point in mind: the suggestion

Figure 1 *Alternative Portrayals of Collective Action Repertoires*

A. No Repertoire

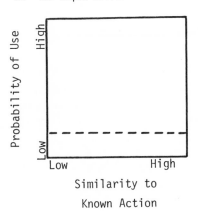

B. Advantage of Familiarity

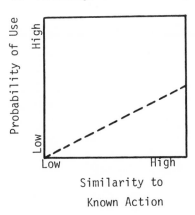

C. Flexible Repertoire

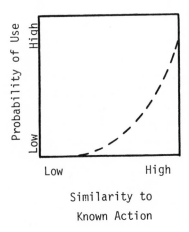

D. Rigid Repertoire

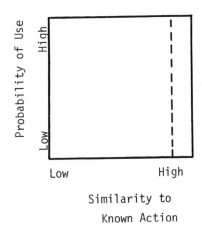

that for populations that have any significant capacity for collective action the flexible repertoire is the normal situation. Why? Because any particular actor's means grow out of the members' own previous experience with collective action and the actor's own specific relationship to other significant actors in its immediate environment.

DESCRIBING AND EXPLAINING REPERTOIRES

This particularism sets us two challenges. The first is basically empirical: to make a firm, reliable description of a particular actor's existing repertoire before attempting to explain its current action, or inaction. The second combines theory and observation: to account for change and variation in the repertoires of different sorts of actors. This essay makes a small response to the first challenge by sketching the varied repertoires of collective action in America and England between 1750 and 1830. As for the second, I have only preliminary suggestions to offer. A checklist of factors we must consider runs like this:

1. the pattern of repression in the world to which the actor belongs;
2. the relevant population's accumulated experience with prior collective action;
3. the daily routines and internal organization of the population in question;
4. the standards of rights and justice prevailing in the population.

The list is broad. Yet it excludes a number of factors various students have considered to be important: how angry or frustrated or deprived the population is, whether mobilization is proceeding rapidly or slowly, and so on.

Repression is probably the most underrated item on the list. Most observers concede some tendency for repression to lower the *level* of collective action. The controversy there turns on the strength, consistency, and contingency of the relationship: Do long-repressed populations eventually acquire the will to rebel? Does a rapid increase in repression tend to stimulate resistance before it has a depressing effect? We have less controversy, and fewer interesting speculations, about the effects of repression on the *form* of collective action. Yet we have reason to believe that those effects are considerable.

The first reason comes from the history of particular forms of collective action. Consider the strike: during the nineteenth century workers, employers and governments engaged in a continuing struggle; its general outcome was not only the legalization of some sort of strike activity but also the creation of shared understandings concerning the actions that *constituted* a strike. By no means all concerted withholding of labor qualified: the parties hammered out detailed rules excluding individual absenteeism, occupation of the premises, refusal to do particular jobs, and so forth. It is not simply that legislators made some forms of the strike legal and other forms of the strike illegal. That happened, too. But in the process the antagonists created—in practice as well as in theory—a sharper distinction between the strike and other forms of action with which it had previously often been associated: sabotage, slowdown, absenteeism, the demonstration. A narrowed, contained strike entered the repertoire of workers' collective action. Pressure from the authorities shaped the particular contours of the nineteenth-century strike.

The second reason for attributing importance to repression is the apparent success of authorities in channeling collective action from one form to another. In eighteenth-century Britain, the authorities tolerated or even encouraged assemblies for the purpose of preparing petitions for relief of the poor and the unemployed, but sent the militia against crowds that gathered at an employer's house to demand work or higher wages. In the short run, the pattern of repression channeled workers away from mobbing the employer and toward petitioning the magistrates. In the long run, a persistent choice of petitioning altered the organization of workers and diminished their capacity to mob when that might have been the most effective choice.

If the interplay between authorities and other actors significantly affects the collective-action repertoire, that fact makes it hard to amass independent evidence of the existence of a particular repertoire. If a group of Boston workers never sack the customhouse, is that because customhouse sacking has no place in their repertoire, or because they never have the opportunity and incentive to do so? We shall ultimately have to face the difficulty by thinking of all possible forms of action as falling into a long rank order of preference, the highly preferred forms constituting the repertoire. Compared with other groups, or with itself at another time, we will find a group employing a particular form of collective action when the expected costs of using that form are relatively high and the expected benefits of its use relatively low. Or, conversely, we will find the group failing to consider a course of action that otherwise comparable groups in similar circumstances have used effectively. Occasionally the sorts of documents with which this essay began give us evidence about the preference: let us in on the deliberations of a group on its way to action, show us reactions to the news that some other group has acted in a way that is foreign to the local group's repertoire, and so on.

Before we reach that point, however, we need to specify and to describe exactly what there is to explain: we need a thoughtful inventory of the means of collective action that different groups actually employ. A thoughtful inventory should lead to clearer ideas concerning the reasons behind the particular mix of actions observed, and perhaps to evidence confirming or denying the importance of a learned repertoire as a constraint on collective action. In the preliminary inventories that occupy the remainder of this essay, my hopes are modest. The range of collective action under consideration is narrow: it concentrates on forms of contention in which at least one party is making claims on another party—claims that would, if realized, require the second party to expend valuable resources. The empirical work I have done so far focuses, furthermore, on *gatherings* in which a number of people assemble in the same place and make such claims. The repertoires in question, then, are not really repertoires of collective action in general, but those portions of the repertoires that consist of contentious gatherings. If heavy repression, for example, encourages people to shift away from any gatherings at all toward the coordinated appeal to powerful patrons, that important relationship will tend to escape our attention. There is a final limitation to the evidence presented here: by and large, it does not attach the specific forms of contention to particular groups or follow the repertoires of particular groups over time; instead, it sums up the experiences of whole countries at different times. The evidence therefore bears only indirectly on the choice among the four models—no repertoire, advantage of familiarity, flexible repertoire, and rigid repertoire—which we reviewed earlier.

Rather than follow the technical and theoretical problems that face any student of repertoires, let us make four more quick stops in the available evidence: first, another look at America in the Revolutionary period, to gain a first impression of the effect of the political crisis on the repertoire of contention in the colonies; next, a glance at the United States fifty years later, to get some sense of longer-range changes; then, a return to the eighteenth century, but this time to Great Britain in the period of the American Revolution; finally, some observations on contentious gatherings in the Britain of the 1820s.

CHANGING REPERTOIRES IN AMERICA, 1750–1780

In the American colonies, the thirty years from 1750 to 1780 take us from a period of relative calm through the French and Indian War, through the Stamp Act crisis and further conflicts between the colonies and Britain, into the outbreak of open war with the mother country. Any inventory of contentious gatherings in the colonies registers those changes unmistakably. The Seven Years' War—known in America as the French and Indian War—began in 1756. During the years before the war, the most frequent contentions of any size were no doubt the meetings of local and provincial assemblies; among the most common actions, for example, were a town meeting's petitioning of a provincial legislature for protection on tax relief, and a provincial legislature's petitioning Parliament for the right to issue money or levy taxes. In those years, violent contention often took the forms of affrays between Indians and white settlers on the frontier; struggles between adjacent settlements for control of forests, fields, or water; resistance to impressment for naval service; resistance to the crown's commandeering of tall trees for masts; battles between customs men and colonists who wanted to evade the payment of duties; and the tracking down of runaway slaves. Public ceremonies such as Pope's Day were frequent occasions for the display of support for or opposition to officials and public policy.

With the arrival of 1756, Indian/settler battles and military engagements between French and British forces became much more prominent than before. Let us take, for example, the contentious gatherings reported during 1756 in two important weekly newspapers: the *Boston Gazette* and the *South Carolina Gazette*. From January through March, the fourteen reported events included eight violent encounters between Indians and white settlers in New York, New Jersey, and Pennsylvania; two gala greetings for famous generals in New York and Boston; two meetings of assemblies; and two escapes of prisoners. In the quarter from April through June, twenty-two events included another nine settler/Indian affrays; six relatively routine assemblies to transact public business and make demands on higher authorities; the welcoming of a general to New York and a governor to Charleston; two patriotic rites (one a day of fasting and prayer for the preservation of the government, the other a celebration of the king's birthday); a meeting of back-country Pennsylvanians demanding a militia; and the marching off of the governor and gentlemen of Maryland to build a new fort. July through September brought another twenty-two events: eight Indian/white battles, raids, or skirmishes; two assemblies of Indians; two conferences of colonial officials with Indians; six processions and receptions in honor of generals; Boston's public demonstration of support for the war; a meeting of the gentlemen of South Carolina for the purpose of forming an artillery company; the preparation of a petition for county courts in South Carolina; and but one routine assembly: to arrange the incorporation of Phillipstown, Massachusetts. The year's last quarter produced only fourteen accounts of contentious gatherings: seven instances of white/Indian violence, four patriotic celebrations, one conference between Indians and colonial officials, a meeting of the

Virginia legislature to raise money for the support of the Cherokee and Catawba participation in the war against the French, and a single meeting of the proprietors of Nottingham. Throughout the year come multiple accounts of troop movements and brushes and battles among the French, the British, and different groups of Indians.

If you automatically dismiss this catalogue as a biased enumeration of 1756's contentious gatherings, your impulse is absolutely right. The *Boston Gazette* and the *South Carolina Gazette* were surely more likely to learn of distant Indian raids than of distant town meetings; they were also undoubtedly more likely to print the news of the raids when they knew of them. Nonetheless, the list gives a sense of the texture of the more visible types of contentious gatherings in 1756 and can serve as a baseline for comparisons with other sources, periods, and places.

In 1756, acts of war dominated the list. In addition to acts of war, meetings of warriors and meetings with warriors stand out. War continued to loom large in American contentious gatherings for the next seven years. But the 1756 catalogue of events also brings out other issues, only indirectly related to the war, which became major bases of contention later on. In South Carolina and elsewhere, people at the frontier were making two strong demands on the officials in the coastal capitals: give us protection from Indians and outlaws; let us have our own courts, governments, and military units. The two demands were partly contradictory. Out of the contradiction grew the widespread vigilante and Regulator movements of the 1760s; local people took the law into their own hands. Other important issues shaping up in 1756 included the powers of the colonial legislatures to tax, regulate money, and control military activity. Those issues persisted to the Revolution.

Moving forward ten years to 1766 brings us into the midst of the Stamp Act crisis. That was the onset of determined colonial resistance to demands of the British crown. The war had ended in 1763. Britain had wrested Canada from the French at great expense and had built up its North American military establishments in order to protect its expanded empire. As the war ended, the British sought to help pay for the war and the expanded military expenses by increasing the return from old sources of revenue and by inventing new sources of revenue. A tightening of surveillance over customs was an important part of the first effort. It led to numerous clashes between coastal traders—smugglers, from the British point of view—and customs officers. The Stamp Act was a critical part of the effort to raise new revenue.

The Stamp Act required the use of expensive stamped paper for a variety of legal and commercial transactions. It went into effect in Britain months before its application in America; there it excited widespread grumbling and some localized resistance, but nothing like a national movement of protest. In the colonies, it brought a wide, determined coalition of patriots into being. By the start of 1766, the major cities had already been through four months of mobilization and conflict over the Stamp Act. By that time, organized groups of merchants, artisans, and other urbanites were actively and effectively blocking the application of the act anywhere in the colonies.

The action continued up to the repeal of the Stamp Act in 1766. There were public bonfires of stamps, mock trials, more public tableaux. Repeal itself was the occasion of major public celebrations with much of the same street theater. In Charleston, according to the *South Carolina Gazette* of 9 June:

> Wednesday last being the birth day of our most gracious and good Sovereign, King George III now in the 29th year of his age, the same was observed here with all possible demonstrations of affection, loyalty and joy; to the last of which the remarkable incident of the *repeal* of the stamp-act arriving that very day, added not a little. The morning was ushered in with ringing of bells, and a general display of colours on all the bastions and vessels. The Charles Town regiment of militia, commanded by the hon. Col. Othniel Beale, the artillery company commanded by Capt. Christopher Gadsden, and a new company, of light infantry, commanded by Capt. Thomas Savage, were all afterwards drawn up in Broad Street, and reviewed by his honours the Lieutenant governor, attended by his council, the members of assembly and public officers, who was pleased to express great satisfaction with the appearance and behaviour of the whole; and it must be particularly observed, to the honour of Capt. Savage's company, that they exceeded all expectation from the short time they had been formed. At noon royal salutes were fired from the forts, &c. and his honour gave a very elegant entertainment to the council, assembly, and public officers, at Mr. Dillon's, where many loyal and constitutional toasts were drank, amongst which the best friends to Britain and America were not omitted—The artillery and light infantry companies likewise had an entertainment in honour of the day at Mr. Dillon's.

In Massachusetts:

> On the first news of the repeal of the stamp act, in New England, the bells were set ringing at *Boston*, the ships in the harbour displayed their colours, guns were everywhere fired on all the batteries, and in the evening bonfires. At the same time a day of rejoicing was appointed; the morning of which was ushered in with music, the ringing of bells, and the discharge of cannons; the ships in the harbour displayed their colours, and on many of the houses were hoisted streamers. At one in the afternoon, the castle, and the batteries, and train artillery, discharged their ordnance; and at night the whole town was most beautifully illuminated. On

the common, a magnificent pyramid, illuminated with 280 (the number that voted for the repeal) lamps were erected, the four upper stories of which were ornamented with the figures of their Majesties, and fourteen of the worthy patriots who distinguished themselves by their love of liberty. [*Gentlemen's Magazine*, July 1766, p. 341.]

So it went throughout the colonies. The Stamp Act and its repeal were not the only objects of contentious gatherings in 1766, but they were the most visible. Otherwise, the pattern was much like that of 1756, minus the war.

By 1776, a new war had begun. Now the colonies were in more or less open rebellion against the crown, after several years of gradually detaching themselves from the effective control of the royal agents in America. In all the colonies outside Canada, full-fledged revolutionary committees and provisional governments completed the displacement of the old authorities. During the year, disciplined military forces pushed unsuccessfully into Quebec, then withdrew into England; another army evacuated the city of New York after a British landing on Staten Island. Meanwhile provincial legislatures and a Continental Congress deliberated, pronounced, declared independence, and made the provisions necessary for the support of the military operations and for the creation of new, independent instruments of government. These feverish activities absorbed or blunted almost all other interests and divisions. In one way or another, almost all of America's contentious gatherings linked directly to the revolutionary struggle for power. This state of affairs—a high level of mobilization, the dominance of military activity and state-making, the absorption of most local conflicts into one large conflict—continued for another six years.

This cursory review of American contentious gatherings in the thirty years after 1750 only hints at a significant change: the steadily increasing contact and coordination among the activists in different colonies. We noticed earlier the attention Charleston's patriots gave to Boston during their Pope's Day celebrations of 1774. As the front stage of confrontation with the British authorities, Boston generally attracted more attention than other colonies: news flowed, and so did rhetoric, symbols, the very form of gatherings. Liberty taxes, gallows, effigies, printed slogans, and bonfires became the standard accouterments of anti-British displays.

Throughout the period, three main classes of contentious gatherings prevailed: (1) acts of war, some of which consisted of attacks by armed forces on members of the general population; (2) resistance by well-defined groups, such as coastal traders, against the efforts of constituted authorities to control their regular activities or to take valued resources away from them; (3) assemblies authorized by law and public officials, in the course of which ordinary citizens often articulated grievances, demands, or political preferences; this third category included public holidays, ceremonial entries of dignitaries, markets, and the openings of courts and legislatures. From a twentieth-century point of view, it is surprising how much contention appeared in the midst of duly authorized gatherings and how little through *un*authorized efforts to assemble and make demands. Not that the Americans of the 1750s were servile or quiescent; their readiness to battle customs agents and the military recruiters shows the contrary. When faced with moral reprobates, furthermore, they were prepared to mock them in the streets, to burn them in effigy, to tar and feather them, to ride them out of town on rails. But when the ordinary Americans themselves directed a demand or complaint at holders of powers, they were very inclined to do so either through a display of sentiments at an already authorized public occasion or through the petition of a regularly constituted deliberative body.

In a time of considerable repression, authorized public occasions have some interesting advantages as the contexts of risky collective actions. In the form of spectators who have come to watch the fun, they provide potential participants who are already assembled. The participants in the public occasion always include elites and power holders. There they must make a publicly visible choice to side with the challenge or against it; if approached privately and individually, they might well be able to avoid committing themselves. Finally, the public ceremony gives a prima facie legality to the initial assembling of the collective actors—no small advantage if any group of a dozen or more that assembles on its own initiative is subject to dispersal or arrest under the riot act. In more abstract terms, the public occasion provides the means of (1) reducing costs of initiating the collective action and (2) spreading the costs of the collective action across many or all of its likely beneficiaries. Where the costs are high and the participation of others uncertain, reliance on public occasions is an especially attractive strategy for those who wish to initiate a collective action.

The American reliance on public occasions changed somewhat in the two decades after 1756. With the struggle over the Stamp Act we see a trio of related alterations in the pattern: an increasing readiness of ordinary citizens to organize their own ceremonies, symbolic displays, and demonstrations of sentiment without prior authorization; a rising importance of special-purpose associations such as the Sons of Liberty; an increasing employment of forms and symbols of moral reprobation in large-scale political conflicts. To be sure, elite organizers such as Samuel Adams and John Hancock often stood behind the scenes. To be sure, the coalition—implicit or explicit—between substantial merchants and established craftsmen frequently underlay the newly independent shows of force. That change in the structure of power lowered the likely cost of popular anti-British collective action. It helped transform the character of contentious gatherings.

AMERICA IN 1828

A half-century after the Revolution, the states were steadily filling up land from the Atlantic Coast to the Mississippi, and pushing on beyond. Although farming was the predominant economic activity, manufacturing was growing rapidly in the Northeast. The manufacturers of New England sought protection from foreign competition, whereas the cotton growers of the South prospered by shipping their product to the rival manufacturers of Great Britain. Regularly elected deliberative assemblies of various kinds—state legislatures, town councils, Congress, and others—were doing a major part of public business.

In that America, *Niles' Register* for 1828 reports a somewhat different mixture of contentious gatherings from the mixture we have noticed in the eighteenth-century papers. Of the ninety-three gatherings mentioned unambiguously in the 1828 *Niles'*, no less than seventy-two were deliberately called meetings. *Niles' Register* was strongly protectionist, its editor Ebenezer Niles a leading spokesman for the American System of protection for industry. We are therefore not surprised to find extensive discussions of the pending tariff legislation and the meetings surrounding it. It is nevertheless surprising to find that *Niles'* reported thirty antitariff meetings to only nineteen for the tariff. The wool growers and manufacturers of Massachusetts, for example, met in Boston to resolve protection. The acting committee of the New Jersey Society for protecting manufacturers and Mechanics Arts met in Paterson, likewise to plead for protection. So did a group of manufacturers in Philadelphia; the farmers and manufacturers of Dutchess County, New York; and fifteen other groups. The antitariff meetings concentrated in the southern Cotton Belt: Waterborough, Columbia, Colleton, Charleston, Beaufort, and elsewhere in South Carolina; Milledgeville, Athens, Montgomery City, Bowling Green, and elsewhere in Georgia. A number of these meetings honored individual legislators who had spoken up for the correct cause—whichever cause was correct in local eyes.

A closely related issue was the auction system, whose opponents argued that commodity bidding gave foreigners (read, especially, Englishmen) the advantage in controlling American trade. There were seven antiauction meetings to a single proauction gathering. With these thirty antitariff, nineteen protariff, seven antiauction, and one proauction meetings came another fifteen citizens' meetings on other matters, mainly of local concern. The remaining twenty-one events broke down as follows:

Two battles between groups of Indians;

Five battles and raids pitting Indians against whites;

Two burnings in effigy—one of a New York State senator who had voted against a local canal bill, another (in Columbia, S.C.) disposing of Henry Clay, Daniel Webster, and other supporters of the tariff, plus a facsimile of the tariff bill itself;

Six processions and public ceremonies, including the inauguration of the Baltimore and Ohio Railroad and the ground breaking for the Baltimore and Ohio Canal;

Two different occasions—one in Baltimore, the other in Cincinnati—on which a large crowd greeted Henry Clay on his arrival in town;

Four actions by workers: a turnout of laborers building a drydock in Charlestown, Massachusetts; an invasion of a Greenwich, Connecticut, cotton weaver's shop by journeymen who demanded that the master raise his workers' wages; an attack by riggers and stevedores against people who continued to work on vessels in New York harbor after a wage reduction; an attack by weavers of the Northern Liberties, Philadelphia, on the watch, in what appears to have been a struggle between Irishmen and Yankees.

As before, gatherings entered the tally only if the account gave evidence that at least one of the parties made a contentious claim. Most of the gatherings that did not quite make it into the enumeration were of the same general types; they, too, were mainly preplanned meetings over major issues of the day. Twenty-one of the marginal events were nominating conventions for the presidential election of 1828; one could easily argue that in those days before full-fledged political parties, such meetings should be added to the list of contentious gatherings. Doing so would simply increase the already impressive preponderance of regularly convened public meetings.

All these events had their eighteenth-century equivalents. Nevertheless, the reports in the 1828 *Niles'* bring us into a different world from the 1756 *Boston Gazette*. In the world of 1828, authorized public ceremonies play a diminished role as the settings for the statement of demands and grievances. Special-purpose associations appear to be important. And we have some signs that workers are pursuing their own collective interests as workers to a greater degree than in the eighteenth century.

In terms of repertoires of contention, the comparison between the eighteenth- and nineteenth-century sources hints at significant changes. All sorts of street theater appear to have declined. (Although these cursory compilations do not show it, the actions of night riders, vigilantes, and disguised avengers probably substituted to some degree for the actions of mocking crowds.) The disciplined meeting, previously announced, sponsored by a particular association or set of associations, organized around an announced agenda and presided over by a temporary or permanent set of officers, became a common vehicle for the statement of complaints and claims. The strike was on its way. The trend toward associations and meetings was already visible in the prerevolutionary mobilization. An observer of the two decades before the Revolution, on the other hand, would have had no good grounds for anticipating the decline of effigies, gallows, mock courts, and dumb shows as the paraphernalia of collective action.

A GLANCE AT EIGHTEENTH-CENTURY BRITAIN

On the other side of the Atlantic, some of the same transformations were occurring. The pattern of contentious gatherings in eighteenth-century Britain is better known than that of eighteenth-century America because George Rudé, E. P. Thompson, and other social historians have lavished attention on the British crowd and its context. As a result, my summary can be brief.

The eighteen contentious gatherings described in the 1756 *Gentlemen's Magazine* give us some flavor of the time. Eleven of them were food riots in which local people seized provisions from the stocks of bakers, grocers, or merchants. In two cases a crowd essentially took the law into its own hands: forcibly closing the shops that were illegally open, attacking two detested criminals while they were in the stocks. The remaining events were a mutiny, a battle between sailors and a press gang, the hanging of an unvictorious admiral in effigy, a miners' rising, and a celebration of Lord Mayor's Day in London.

Those few events of 1756 were characteristic of the time. When W. A. Smith enumerates "riots" (exact definition unspecified) from 1740 to 1775, 96 out of 159 events he finds are food riots, and another 20 are industrial disputes; most of the remainder consist of concerted resistance to some governmental action (Smith, 1965, pp 29–33). The food riot, apparently rare in eighteenth-century America, was a frequent occurrence in Britain. When prices rose, supplies dwindled, and local authorities did not themselves regulate the local food supply, crowds often did it for them. This substitution of a crowd for the authorities was a common pattern in eighteenth-century British contentious gatherings. Another common feature was the deliberate collective exercise of disputed rights —for example, in the events that the authorities called poaching in newly created hunts (see Thompson, 1975). The predominant orientation of the period's contentious gatherings was, in fact, defensive: groups of ordinary people resisted what they saw as other people's assaults on their rights, privileges, and possessions.

Two common characteristics of eighteenth-century British contentious gatherings we have already encountered in America. One of them is the use of pageantry and street theater to dramatize the conflicts at issue. Rituals, mocking songs, effigies, and dumb shows provided the texture of many a riotous assembly. The other was the prominence of sponsored public ceremonies: Guy Fawkes' Day, Lord Mayor's Day, the entries of dignitaries, public hangings. When it came to formulating new demands or complaints, it was rare—and dangerous—for ordinary people to assemble on their own initiative.

We must, however, separate the contentious gatherings of London from those of the rest of the country. The contentious gatherings of the capital were often large. They showed a level of preplanning that was rare elsewhere. The presence of Parliament and the court produced many events with significant links to national politics. London crowds had an unmatched reputation for independence and determination.

During the period from 1750 to 1780, London alone produced significant alterations in the repertoire of contention. A series of major political and economic movements stirred the capital. The Spitalfields silk weavers and other London crafts were organizing on an unprecedented scale. Sometimes they acted against particular masters. But in the 1760s they began a campaign of petitioning Parliament for such benefits as the exclusion of foreign silks. Petitioning itself was an old form, but when thousands of weavers marched through the streets to present a petition, it was a novelty.

At about the same time, gentleman-publisher John Wilkes was gaining a following through his attacks on the government. Wilkes himself first went to jail for his writings in 1763. He spent several years thereafter in exile, a popular hero. Whether Wilkes was in Britain or not, the Wilkites began developing tactics parallel to those of the craftsmen: showing up at trials and public punishments as an identifiable group, and in extraordinary numbers; and bending the long-established right of petition to include mass marches through the city. The tactics continued through Wilkes's campaigns for Parliament between 1768 and 1774. Wilkes continued to lead petition marches after becoming lord mayor in 1774. A new form of electoral politics and a new way of demonstrating a movement's strength were emerging. The Wilkites were coming close to creating the demonstration as a distinctive form of contention.

Wilkes had begun his public life as a critic of governmental incompetence, corruption, and tyranny. As the Stamp Act crisis and its aftermath made American policies salient issues in British politics, he became an advocate of American rights. Besides a series of proposals for increasing representative government within Britain, Wilkes's 1774 electoral program included a number of grievances that later appeared in the American Declaration of Independence.

The London Radical movement, with which the Wilkite movement overlapped, likewise developed a great sympathy for the American cause. The Radicals maintained contact with their American counterparts and attacked the government's arbitrary rule in the colonies as proxy and proof for its arbitrariness at home. Thomas Paine came from the London Radical milieu. Although the militant Radicals themselves were largely middle class, they included a number of radical craftsmen, and maintained a loose alliance with the organized workers of the city. They, too, took part in mass marches and shows of strength.

Finally, the popular anti-Catholicism of the later 1770s employed many of the same means. The anti-Catholic Lord George Gordon led huge marches to lay petitions before Parliament. His Protestant Association held mass meetings. In 1780, his followers went beyond marching, shouting, and meeting; they sacked the city's Catholic chapels. The causes, the targets, and—to some extent—the social bases were different, but the anti-Catholic forms of contention had a good deal in common with those of the Wilkites and the Radicals.

The Protestant Association was itself an important example of a major innovation: the deliberate formation of an association devoted to the pursuit of a single cause. The Americans, with their general Association to resist Britain, their Committees of Correspondence, and their local patriotic societies, became important models for the British. The Society for the Support of the Bill of Rights, formed in the 1760s, started with the patronage of great lords but foreshadowed the political parties and mass-membership pressure groups of subsequent centuries. Other associations proliferated. "By 1792," remarks Eugene Black, "political associations had arrived. The discerning read the future in organization. Even as association was the hallmark of growing national political maturity, the political expression of popular interests, so political association educated the public, both enfranchised and unenfranchised, on questions of moment. Mysteries of state became less mysterious. As the Commons slowly discovered its own potential power in Parliament, the public began to intervene in a manner which would prove decisive through political association" (Black, 1963, p. 279). The counterpart of the organizational change, as we have seen, was a shift in the repertoire of contention.

BRITAIN IN 1828

Even in 1792, however, a long road separated the British forms of contention from those of our own time. A move forward to the 1820s will help us detect the further changes that were in store. We arrive here at the first truly systematic enumeration of contentious gatherings reported in this paper. My research group is enumerating and describing a large set of events that occurred in Great Britain from 1828 through 1834. The period is interesting in its own right. It included the great mobilization and conflict surrounding the Reform Bill of 1832. During the same period, Britain experienced important struggles over Catholic Emancipation, parish representation, and the Corn Laws. The year 1830 brought the movement of landless laborers that we sometimes call the Swing Rebellion, as well as intense industrial conflict. It seems to have acted as gateway to the large-scale movements exemplified by Chartism and the Anti-Corn Law League. It also seems to have brought the last major round of older forms of contention, such as food riots and machine breaking. It is a promising period for the study of contention.

The events we are enumerating are occasions on which ten or more persons outside the government gathered in the same place and made a visible claim that, if realized, affected the interests of some specific person(s) or group(s) outside their own number. The sample includes all such events reported in the *London Times, Morning Chronicle, Hansard's Parliamentary Debates, Annual Register, Gentlemen's Magazine,* and the *Mirror of Parliament* that began anywhere in England, Scotland, or Wales on any date from 1 January 1828 through 31 December 1834. At this writing, it seems likely that the sample will include some twenty-five thousand entries.

The work is at an early stage. Here I can report only some fragmentary, preliminary impressions of 1828. Table 1 lays out a provisional count of qualifying events reported in our six sources for 1828. To get a sense of the table's meaning, let us first examine a list of the thirty-four events that occurred in May 1828, grouped according to the table's categories:

Violent encounters of poachers and gamekeepers, of smugglers and customs officers; brawls in drinking places: none;

Other violent gatherings: after a conviction for riot, a group of men from near Shrewsbury kindles a fire in front of the prosecutor's house and throws stones and brickbats at his house; a crowd in Stratford-upon-Avon attacks an inspector who attempts to keep a hawker from selling without a license; in the Hull barracks-yard soldiers attack civilian spectators at a parade and the constables sent to arrest some of the soldiers for a previous offense;

Other unplanned gatherings: Kidderminster weavers band together to block one of their number who applied for work at a blacklisted low-wage shop;

Authorized celebrations: none;

Delegations: a deputation from the general meeting of country bankers meets the Duke of Wellington at the Treasury, to take a stand on the renewal of the Bank Charter; a delegation of Haverhill weavers goes to their magistrate to complain of being obliged to buy inferior provisions from their masters;

Parades, demonstrations, and assemblies: none;

Strikes, turnouts: inmates of the House of Correction, Clerkenwell, refuse to do the work assigned to them;

Preplanned meetings of named associations: six different groups, including the United Committee for Conducting the Application to Parliament for the Repeal of the Test and Corporation Acts, the Protestant Society for the Protection of Religious Liberty, and the General Assembly of the Church of Scotland, meet to take positions on the repeal of the Test and Corporation Acts; other meetings on other issues involve the Anti-Slavery Society, the Pitt Clubb, the Society for Superseding the Necessity of Climbing Boys in Sweeping Chimneys, the Chamber of Commerce, and two Friendly Societies;

Preplanned meetings of public assemblies: the mayor, aldermen, council, and livery of Nottingham meet in Guildhall to thank Parliament for the repeal of the Test and Corporation Acts;

Other preplanned meetings: two different Catholic parishes in Norwich meet to petition Parliament for political rights; a group of Irish Catholics meet in London to vote thanks to those who have supported their cause; a congregation of London Protestant Dissenters petition Parliament for no more concessions to the Catholics; licensed victuallers meet at the London Tavern to act against unacceptable government regulation of their trade; South American bondholders meet at the City of London Tavern to promote their claims on the new trans-Atlantic states; journeymen dyers of Manchester meet to seek an advance in wages; parishioners of St. Giles', London, meet to launch an inquiry into wasteful expenditure of their funds; the inhabitants of Bridge Ward, London, meet to take a position on the plans for the new London Bridge; a general meeting of the weavers' trade in London supports the striking weavers of Kidderminster; delegates of Friendly Societies meet to take a position on the pending Friendly Societies Bill; the electors of Aylesbury meet to celebrate the election of Lord Nugent "on independent principles"; a public meeting in Liverpool petitions Parliament to request measures to prevent the burning of Indian widows on the funeral pyres of their husbands.

Regardless of the group's title or professed aims, none of these gatherings entered the sample unless the accounts contained some evidence that the group had made claims of some sort at this specific meeting. (The weakest evidence of a claim we allowed was the appearance in Parliament of a petition from the meeting in question; most of the "preplanned meetings of named associations" entered the sample via that route.) Hundreds of additional meetings, and some other kinds of gatherings, failed to qualify on this ground.

The catalogue itself gives a sense of the texture of contention in that time. We see the importance of taverns and coffeehouses as meeting places, the proliferation of special-purpose associations, the frequent confrontations of journeymen and masters. The events also provide a rough inventory of the day's major public issues. In 1828 as a whole, the standard issues were the political rights of Dissenters and Roman Catholics, the proper organization of parish government (especially the use of elite Select Vestries), the regulation of Friendly Societies, and the wage demands of industrial workers. All of them show up somehow in May's contentious gatherings.

The categories of table 1 result from a compromise between the demands of analysis and the needs of our initial enumeration. "Other violent gatherings," for example, include the confrontations in Shrews-bury, Stratford, and Hull described earlier; attacks on tollkeepers; and a variety of other events. Preplanned meetings, on the other hand, usually took place in an enclosed space under the sponsorship of a pre-viously organized body. They typically had announced agendas. At that time, indeed, it was common practice to use a small newspaper advertise-ment to announce a forthcoming meeting and state its purpose.

The large number of meetings in the provisional sample, however, does not result from the practice of advertising meetings in advance; we do not include an announced meeting unless we find evidence that it actually took place. There is, nevertheless, an unresolved problem in the enumeration of meetings. The great majority of preplanned meetings of named associations enter the sample from reports of parliamentary proceedings. The usual circumstance is the reading of a petition to Parliament from a meeting of the Association. Accounts of meetings in regular news reports, on the other hand, normally say what interest the participants in a meeting represent, but rarely give it a specific associa-tional name. As the list of events from May 1828 showed, the partici-pants are usually described as "licensed victuallers," "South American bondholders," "journeymen dyers," and so on. This is even true of meetings that send petitions to Parliament. Thus, it is not yet clear whether we are dealing with two different kinds of meeting or two different ways of describing the participants in the same kind of meeting. My provisional conclusion from the evidence comes closer to the second view: it is that a formally constituted committee or association ordinarily called the meeting and issued the petition (if there was one) in its name, although the public meeting was open to all who shared the same interest.

The number of meetings is impressive. The 281 meetings reported in table 1 amount to two-thirds of all the year's contentious gatherings. Even if our enumeration procedure overrepresents meetings (which is quite possible), the evidence remains persuasive. By the 1820s a standard way—probably *the* standard way—of acting together on a grievance or an unrealized interest was to form some sort of association, to assemble under its auspices, and to issue demands and complaints in its name. We saw this form of action emerging in the 1760s. It regularized and routinized only later. The rise of the meeting, the rise of the association, and the rise of electoral politics occurred in tandem. One plausible interpretation is this: the eighteenth-century invention of the association as a device for conducting electoral campaigns proved successful and invited emulation. The association became a standard part of British electoral custom and law. The toleration of associations for electoral purposes then provided a model and a legal precedent for the creation of associations in pursuit of other ends, especially ends that had some connection with electoral campaigns. The gathering both of electoral associations and of regular public assemblies such as the vestry provided a model and a warrant for the preplanned meeting as a device for contention. Once the electoral campaign, the association, and the public meeting were established elements of the repertoire, they reinforced one another. It remains to be seen, of course, whether this plausible reconstruction fits the fine historical details. One of the objects of our inquiry into British contention from 1828 to 1834 is to see whether such an interpretation will hold up to close historical scrutiny.

By contrast, both unplanned gatherings and authorized celebrations appear to have declined in importance as the origins of contentious gatherings. The decline varies with the year, the group, and the issue. For example, our first explorations of 1830 suggest that routine markets produced a good deal of that year's contention. Nevertheless, the assembly of the general population patronized by the elite and authorized by local officials seems to have been much less important in the 1820s than it had been a half-century earlier. Strikes, too, varied considerably in prominence from one year to the next. Yet it is clear that in the 1820s they had not acquired anything like the salience they would have in the decades to come.

Most puzzling is the paucity of parades, demonstrations, and assemblies. Given the near-creation of the demonstration toward the end of the eighteenth century, we might have expected it to be a prominent form of action by the 1820s. Because the Reform and election campaigns of 1831 did include a number of parades, demonstrations, and assemblies, it is possible that 1828 is simply an exceptional year in that regard. For such refinements, we shall have to await further evidence.

Within the currently available body of evidence, the differences among areas of Great Britain are intriguing. As table 1 shows, more than half the contentious gatherings enumerated for 1828 occurred in London and three nearby counties: Dorset, Hampshire, and Kent. No doubt that finding is partly due to the Londonward bias of our six sources. However, such verification as we have obtained so far via *The Scotsman*, the *Lancaster Gazette*, and other sources outside London indicate that the contention of 1828 did, indeed, concentrate heavily in and around

Table 1 *Percentage Distribution of Contentious Gatherings in Great Britain, 1828, by Type and Area*

Type of Gathering	London	Dorset	Hampshire	Kent	Lanca-shire	Other England	Wales	Scotland	Total	N
Poachers vs. gameskeepers	0	0	0	0	0	12.7	0	5.9	5.1	21
Smugglers vs. customs	0	0	0	0	0	0.6	0	0	0.2	1
Brawls in drinking places	1.9	0	0	0	0	1.9	0	0	1.5	6
Other violent gatherings	11.7	8.3	10.0	4.0	12.0	12.1	20.0	11.8	11.4	47
Market conflicts	0.6	0	0	0 *	0	1.9	0	0	1.0	4
Other unplanned gatherings	0	0	0	4.0	0	0.6	0	0	0.5	2
Authorized celebrations	1.9	0	0	0	0	0	0	0	0.7	3
Delegations	1.9	0	0	0	0	1.3	0	0	1.2	5
Parades, demonstrations, rallies	9.9	41.7	0	12.0	12.0	7.0	20.0	11.8	9.9	41
Strikes, turnouts	0.6	0	0	0	4.0	0	0	0	0.5	2
Preplanned meetings of named associations	38.3	25.0	70.0	16.0	24.0	33.8	20.0	41.2	34.6	143
Preplanned meetings of public assemblies	10.5	8.3	10.0	8.0	4.0	1.3	0	5.9	6.1	25
Other preplanned meetings	22.8	16.7	10.0	56.0	44.0	26.8	40.0	23.5	27.4	113
Total	100.1	100.0	100.0	100.0	100.0	100.0	100.0	100.1	100.1	—
N	162	12	10	25	25	157	5	17	413	413

London. Lancashire was the only county outside the London region to contribute more than nine gatherings to the sample. At that time, the workers of Manchester and nearby industrial areas of Lancashire were organized, active, and vociferous.

The differences in pattern among areas are not huge, but they are reassuring. Struggles over poaching and smuggling occurred entirely outside the high-contention counties. The miscellaneous "other violent gatherings" spread obligingly across all areas in roughly the same proportion—on the average, 11 percent—of all events in the area. On the whole, meetings did more of the work of contention in London and nearby areas than in the rest of Great Britain. Yet meetings were so dominant in all areas as to give a final picture not of diversity but of uniformity throughout Great Britain.

CONCLUSIONS

As for the validity of one model or another of repertoires, the evidence is (as promised) indeterminate. The comparison between eighteenth- and nineteenth-century patterns of contention in America and Britain provides encouragement in its evidence that people on both sides of the Atlantic adapted the available forms of action to new problems as the problems came along. The comparison indicates a parallel movement away from the patronized public occasion toward the preplanned meeting of people organized around a particular interest. The great prominence of the preplanned meeting and the special-purpose association in American and British contention of 1828 suggests a standardization of the repertoire of collective action.

On the other hand, the crude categories and high levels of aggregation in these descriptions diminish their value. For the choice among models of repertoires, the questions that count most are (1) whether particular groups made deliberate choices among a few well-defined courses of action; (2) whether they strongly preferred forms of action that were already familiar to them; and (3) whether they tended to adapt existing forms of action to new interests and opportunities rather than inventing new forms that might be more effective in the circumstances. The crudity and aggregate character of the comparisons offered in this paper forbid any confident conclusions on these questions. To get at conclusions, we need more refined portrayals of the particular forms of contention, and we must follow the action of the same groups through time.

The point of this preliminary survey, then, is to clarify what has to be explained, and to reflect on the possibility that one model of repertoires or another might help explain it. In the cases of eighteenth- and nineteenth-century Britain and America, we have a number of different features of contention to explain. There are the apparently declining significance of sponsored public celebrations and ceremonies as the occasions for contention, the standardization of symbols and routines in the struggle for American independence, the rise of preplanned meetings devoted to particular interests, and a series of other changes in the form of contention. There is also the fact that each time and place has its own dominant means of contention.

In all these regards, the central problem is to place the actions of the groups involved somewhere on the continuum from pure efficiency (and therefore no useful application of the idea of repertoire) to rigid repertoire (and therefore little or no scope for adaptive efficiency). My own provisional conclusion runs like this: the instances we have been examining come close sometimes to the flexible-repertoire model, sometimes to the advantages-of-familiarity model, but never approach the no-repertoire extreme and rarely approach the rigid-repertoire extreme; one possible factor determining the position of a set of contenders on the continuum is the extent to which they form a coherent group outside the arena of contention.

If that is the case, this preliminary survey of forms of contention provides strong reasons for distrusting two standard accounts of conflict, protest, and collective action. The first sort of account reasons directly from some sort of strain, malaise, dissatisfaction, or individual attitude prevailing in a particular population to that population's involvement in contention. The second reasons directly from the population's *interest* to its action. The line of analysis we have been pursuing here does not deny the relevance of interests or dissatisfactions to a population's action. But it insists on the importance of mediating factors: the internal organization of groups, the current opportunities to act effectively, the available repertoires of contention. It suggests, furthermore, that changing interests and dissatisfactions account for little of the short-run variation in contention, whereas changing opportunities and internal organization account for a great deal of it. The line of analysis argues, finally, that opportunities and organization interact to produce an available repertoire of contention, which then constrains the actions of contending parties.

This essay has resembled an archeologist's reconstruction of an ancient pot, using a few shards, some previous experience, and a great deal of imagination. If the archeologist is clever and has happened on the right fragments, he may produce a good fit. More often, the reconstruction is erroneous: the model is the wrong shape, the fragments really came from two different pots, or they came from no pot at all. Yet even an inaccurate reconstruction is helpful. It invites comparison, inspires alternative sketches, and lends itself to refutation or improvement when the next shard appears.

We have actually been attempting two reconstructions at once: of this particular pot, and of all pots. In reconstructing this particular pot, we have examined the prevailing repertoires of contention in England and America during the century after 1750. The examination, to be sure, has been cursory and provisional; it has concentrated on contentious gatherings to the neglect of less visible forms of contention and has drawn on limited sources for selected periods.

The provisional examination has, however, yielded interesting conclusions. It points to a significant relationship between the forms of contention that flourished in the nineteenth century—the demonstration, the strike, the meeting, and so on—and two changes that were under way in the later eighteenth century: the growth of special-purpose associations and the rise of electoral politics. It gives us indications of a common Anglo-American heritage affecting the forms of contention. In both countries we witness a decline of street theater as a tool of contention, and an associated dwindling of the relative importance of authorized public ceremonies as the settings for the statements of claims and grievances. The material suggests that the pattern of government and the associated structure of power in the two areas shaped the entire pattern of contention, whether or not it had to do specifically with influencing the government. It gives us some reason to believe that major mobilizations and conflicts such as those preceding the American Revolution on both sides of the Atlantic themselves reshaped the patterns of collective contention in Britain and America; Samuel Adams and John Wilkes helped invent forms of action that subsequently altered the choices available to aggrieved or ambitious groups of citizens. Finally, although we have barely discussed governmental repression, it looks as though the differential response of authorities to the various forms of contention significantly affected the prevailing repertoires.

In reconstructing all pots, we have also been reflecting on the nature of repertoires of contention in general. The fragmentary evidence on Britain and America gives some encouragement to the idea of a flexible repertoire, with room for innovation and the occasional deliberate adoption of unfamiliar means of action. After the fact, it is not difficult to see the recurrence of a limited number of slowly changing forms of action in British and American contentious gatherings. We see Englishmen innovating within the limits set by the petition march, Americans adapting the devices of moral reprobation such as tarring and feathering or the mocking serenade to political ends. That is the easy part of the job.

The hard part has two phases. The first is to establish whether the existing repertoire itself constrains the pattern of collective action; after all, whatever recurrence of contentious forms exists could well result from the recurrence of the interests, organizations, and opportunities that produce contention. The second part is to explain the variation and change. What are the relative contributions of repression, tactical experience, and organizational changes? How do they interact? These questions, fortunately, drive us back from the analysis of repertoires for their own sake to the analysis of contention as a whole.

II

MOBILIZATION AND TACTICS
IN CONTEMPORARY MOVEMENTS

OVERVIEW

The modern feminist movement and millenarian movements vary enormously in ideology and in tactics and breadth of mobilization. Yet both face problems of mobilizing constituents and encouraging movement commitment and effort toward accomplishing movement goals.

In "White-Hot Mobilization" John Lofland presents a brief description and contrast of a millenarian sect in a dormant first period and a period of extensive mobilization. The detailed case materials for many of his conclusions can be found in Lofland (1977a). He shows how a small social movement organization can manufacture the image of itself as a widespread and vital force. Lofland chronicles a wide array of techniques used by this social movement organization, operating with few ideological constraints or constituent constraints upon tactical choice, to develop additional resources, mobilize sympathizers, create constituents, and gain widespread publicity.

Jo Freeman in "Resource Mobilization and Strategy" utilizes case material from the feminist movement and feminist organizations to attempt to develop an approach to understanding how the strategy and tactics used by social movement organizations are shaped and constrained by the opportunities available to them and by the nature of their constituencies. Premovement experiences and preferences and the personal situations of constituents shape tactical choice. The kinds of resources that are readily at hand in the daily rounds of constituents may offer tactical opportunities to one movement organization that are not available to another.

White-Hot Mobilization:
Strategies of a Millenarian Movement

John Lofland

Social movements differ in the level at which they are mobilized at any given moment, at various periods of their careers, and over their life histories taken as a whole. Mobilization thus viewed as a variable rather than a dichotomy encourages us to think in more detail about elements and degrees of mobilization and the factors upon which these in turn depend (cf. McCarthy and Zald, 1973b).

If we orient ourselves to conceiving the most extreme possibilities of movement mobilization, we may envision a pure, or "white-hot," state of maximum mobilization, which has such features as:

1. the active pursuit of a program of publicity, missionizing, migration, colonization, warfare, or other effort openly, dramatically, and substantially to alter the movement's relation to its host society. In purest form, the effort is to capture the host society;
2. the fielding of a significant full-time corps of totally dedicated members who constitute a major portion of the movement's adherents;
3. the investment of a significant portion of the movement's resources in expanding the number of totally dedicated members;
4. the expenditure of large sums of money ("large" as defined by any given social context) in pursuing and supporting the three lines of activity and arrangements just mentioned and the evolution of devices to generate continual supplies of large-scale funds.

The image, then, is one of well-funded and undivided dedication to altering the movement's position, a dedication that is carried on by an expanding body of true believers. Of course, most movements come nowhere near such a white-hot level of mobilization. Most often, few members are especially dedicated; funding is slim; the program is timid and unacted on; recruitment is haphazard and sparse. But some few movements are, at least for a time, able to achieve white-hot mobilization. By examining such statistically infrequent but contrasting cases we can perhaps learn something about the factors that keep most movements so relatively tame, so lukewarmly mobilized.

I will here examine a single instance of white-hot mobilization, asking: By means of what strategies was it possible to turn a warm into a white-hot mobilized movement? The movement to be analyzed—here called "the DPs"—is the American wing of a Korean-spawned millenarian religion. Followers believe that their leader, a Rev. Soon Sun Chang, is the new Christ who will shortly (by 1981, it is hoped) restore the world to an earthly and perfect Garden of Eden. Chang and the believers will preside over an earthly theocracy.[1]

WARM MOBILIZATION

The first DP missionaries arrived in America in 1959 and achieved only a few dozen converts over the first several years. But by continuous, amoebalike division of each budding communal center, by the end of thirteen years (in 1971), they had grown to about five hundred members spread among about fifty far-flung centers. Headed by a Ms. Yoon Sook Lee, the movement existed at a relatively modest level of mobilization. At that time:

1. It lacked a program to alter the movement's position aggressively and dramatically. Mostly, members rather timidly and covertly strove to make converts (Lofland, 1966; Bookin, 1973–76). Each center had a relatively great amount of autonomy regarding programs of activity and each was directly responsible to the national office.
2. Members lived communally at centers, but most held conventional jobs and practiced their religion during nonworking hours.
3. Recruitment efforts centered on enticing people to attend lectures at the center.
4. Members contributed their incomes to the movement, and these funds supported centers, missionizing activity, and an array of front organizations (Lofland, 1977a), but no large-scale organizations geared specifically to conversion were mounted.

WHITE-HOT MOBILIZATION

Having grown wealthy on the Korean and Japanese branches of his movement, Chang himself took up residence in the United States in late 1971. He was appalled by the modest mobilization he found and set immediately about whipping more movement out of the American movement by initiating simultaneous changes virtually across the board. The logic of exposition forces a serial accounting of these, but it should be kept constantly in mind that each separate strategy I describe has a mutual dependence on each of the others: they formed a "systematic package" of changes that supported and enhanced one another.

First, he established a set of grandiose and proximate goals the movement had to achieve. He hammered away that there were three seven-year periods on the road to the restored and perfect world to be ruled by DPs: 1960–67; 1968–74; 1975–81. They were then in the crucial last three years of the second seven-year period. They had to give all to achieve a powerful and famous movement in America. New-member and dollar-raising quotas became omnipresent, and eight elaborate publicity-garnering campaigns and events were staged between 1972 and 1976: an early 1972 seven-city speaking tour; a twenty-one-city speaking tour in 1973–74 (starting at Carnegie Hall, with each of the twenty-one stops costing about a third of a million dollars); a thirty-two-city tour in early 1974; a ten-city tour in mid-1974; an eight-city tour in late 1974 (starting at Madison Square Garden, with each stop costing from a third to half a million dollars); a rally for "new hope" in late 1975; a rally at Yankee Stadium in mid-1976; and a rally at the Washington Monument in late 1976.

These and several other events and operations were occasions of maximum movement goal-direction and involvement; each was public, challenging, and exciting. Each provided opportunities for taking initiative in planning, doing huge amounts of publicity, enticing people to attend, staging and managing the events themselves and the expensive dinners that went with each, and so on. The movement was *happening*. (Greater detail on the astonishing array of what was happening is reported in Lofland, 1977a).

Each effort was defined as a huge success, of course, and the morale of believers was kept up by those signals of progress and the other devices found commonly in social movements (and all of social life, for that matter, as explained in Blumer, 1969; Lofland, 1966, part 3).

Second, a program of the complexity and expense Chang projected and actually brought off clearly required a reasonably large and well-organized apparatus. He did not have one at the end of 1971, and in order to create it he first purchased an estate at "Tinkertown," near New York City, and set it up as a national training center. Selected members from the dispersed centers were ordered there for training, and they were joined by leaders drawn from foreign wings of the movement, primarily Japan. (They entered the United States on missionary training visas; by 1973 there would be some six hundred foreign members in America, many of whom did not speak English.)

In fullest form, this training consisted of several dozen believers undergoing forty days of lectures and lecturing, thirty days of witnessing in New York City, and thirty days of flower and candle selling (discussed in a moment). They heard and lectured on the complex DP doctrines at least three times and were given three chances to pass an apparently difficult written examination.

By such a means, Chang "called out," educated, and increased the commitment of the already most committed DPs. He was creating an elite corps. By mid-1974 perhaps a thousand people had received the Tinker-town training. But more: he did not send them back to their centers. He formed them into bus- and van-going mobile teams. At its height in 1974, there may have been almost a thousand people (about half of whom were foreign members) organized into about three dozen teams evangelizing from state to state, street peddling, and doing advance work and staging chores for Chang's speaking tours and other activities. The centers became "crash pads," of a sort, out of which teams worked in a given area before moving on, although teams often slept in the van, a campground, or a cheap motel. These teams were, in effect, a new organization, a floating and literally deployable corps directly responsible to Chang.

The centers were organized into their own new system. The country was divided into ten regions headed by a regional director, under whom were several state directors, who were in turn over center directors. Within centers, members were organized into "trinities," groups of eight or so people under a powerful "trinity leader." Paralleling the traditional U.S. army squad, the trinity leader supervised almost all member action. In order to maximize time for leadership, center directors were ordered not to hold outside employment.

The language of this new organization interlaced military and business terminology. Heads of the mobile teams were "commanders"; there was a "chain of command"; and they had tough "production goals," such as "earn one member per month." In the quest for maximum productivity, the less than properly productive were rotated into different jobs. Their coordinating newsletter reports a vast number of assignments, reassignments, and rotations in this period, suggesting a frantic effort to match job and person to the best effect.[2] Members were organized into various kinds of teams and pitted against one another in productivity contests: Americans against foreigners, centers against mobile teams, new members against old, and so on.

An observer of the early phases of this change in 1972 characterized the shift in this manner: "There was no more activity that was not church-related and organized. The whole operation got much tighter, more goal directed, and local leaders had less freedom. They also seemed to be doing better in terms of getting more recruits to come to lectures and in giving better organized and presented lectures" (Bookin, 1976). As Chang summed it up in early 1973: "We must purge your old concepts of the American movement under the Divine Precepts."

Third, all of these and many activities I have not mentioned were very expensive: white-hot mobilization is expensive. By what devices can a movement generate the fifteen or so million dollars a year that this one was now spending?

1. An unknown amount came from the Korean and Japanese branches of the movement. In Korea, a significant portion of believers worked in Chang-owned factories, lived in close-by dormitories, and were paid only token wages. Chang was personally a multimillionaire, and he likely at least primed the pump of the American movement (as he did also in England and elsewhere, it is reported).

2. It has often been alleged that some money came from the South Korean Central Intelligence Agency and/or the American CIA. Personal interconnections among these three have definitely been established, but the flow of money has not.

3. These two sources were popular explanations of their wealth at the time the DPs became famous, I believe, because one of their more likely sources of major income was so ingenious, novel, and fantastic: street peddling by a large portion of a rapidly growing number of true believers, previously used with great success in Japan. Items such as flowers, candles, candy, and dried flower arrangements were purchased cheaply in bulk and sold on streets, in bars, and in other public places for one or a few dollars. Hard workers could gross 80 to 150 dollars a day, clearing at least 60 percent, as all the peddlers had to be self-supporting. On the basis of a very conservative estimate, it can be seen that five hundred people netting one hundred dollars a day for three hundred days a year can produce fifteen million dollars a year for a movement! And that is a very conservative calculation. There is no doubt that street peddling produced money of at least this magnitude, and likely more, in every year of this period.

This success on the streets was importantly facilitated by Chang's early edict that all members must wear close-cropped hair and neat and conservative attire. Looking rather like the more familiar Mormon male missionaries of America (with the addition of "blissed out" smiles), and presenting themselves as raising funds for noncontroversial programs, they gained the attention of ordinary citizens, who were quite responsive to their proffered wares. (Innocuous peddling covers included work on a "drug program" or a "youth program.")

4. Many local groups operated their own economic enterprises: a few hotel-apartment housecleaning and janitorial services, gas stations, and restaurants. All the enterprises were labor intensive; the labor was essentially free, and the returns were reasonable.

5. Least significant, converts gave all their possessions. Parents were sometimes milked for more money by such devices as long-distance pleas for funds to pay nonexistent auto repair or medical bills.

The mystery of the movement's wealth is less a mystery when we begin to comprehend the possibilities of selfless and fanatical levels of dedication on the part of even a few hundred educated young people. By giving their all in the public places of a permissive and free society, they could generate astounding resources for the leaders of the movement and for their own local activities. By purchasing slow-moving country estates and other such "prestige" property, on which they made minimum down payments,[3] and by mounting flashy publicity campaigns, the DPs could by 1974 appear to be a formidable and large social force. Outsiders beholding this display gauged its substance in the terms with which they were familiar: normal investments, normal returns, paid employees with fringe benefits, and all the rest. People therefore assumed Chang must have vast resources and wealth. Outsiders did not appreciate that fanatical dedication along certain lines could (for a time, at least) leapfrog the ordinary laws of investments, wages, returns, and social display. (Such leapfrogging has, however, its own large price, as we shall see.)

Fourth, recruitment efforts were reorganized in a way that helped to produce a marked increase in membership. The five hundred of 1971 jumped to something over two thousand in 1974 (augmented by about six hundred foreign members).

The new mode of making converts brought prospects along through three stages. Focusing on its operation in and out of "State U City" and "Bay City" on the West Coast—the major producers of new converts—a prospect was, first and commonly, literally picked up hitchhiking or approached on the street and invited to dinner with "the Family" at a commune and/or to hear a lecture on some noncontroversial topic such as "world peace." Once at a DP center, most commonly for a free dinner, he or she was assigned the "buddy" who had been the initial contact and treated with extreme solicitude and "loving" support by the dozens of DPs assembled for the meal. After eating, an entertaining and unoffensive lecture was given on the principles that bound the Family, stressing sharing, loving one another, community activity, and other abstract ideals to which virtually anyone could subscribe. Chang and his movement were never mentioned and even religion per se was de-emphasized. Then prospects were invited to a weekend workshop at the Farm, a several-hundred-acre retreat some fifty miles north of Bay and State U cities.

The second phase began with arrival at the Farm. Details of its operation are available elsewhere (Lofland, 1977a, and 1977b); it will suffice to say here that prospects were effectively encapsulated in a physically exhausting, emotionally arousing, and intellectually reorienting round. A signal feature of DP effort at the weekend workshop is captured in their concept of "love bombing"—intense effort to make prospects feel they were overwhelmingly loved by DPs and to give them a desire to "melt together" (another DP term) with the embracing collective. General DP, unexceptional ideas were stressed in lectures (e.g., the "principle of give and take," Lofland, 1966, pp. 14–23), but many specific, heterodox doctrines, aims, and programs were not.

Prospects who responded favorably (and hundreds apparently did in the early seventies) were invited to stay on at the Farm for various periods. It was in the third phase, if there, that the more specific and "objectionable" doctrines were revealed, in the context of waxing love and commitment. One important step in the process of increasing commitment was going into a nearby city to street peddle; the fact that one could make a hundred dollars a day or so at it was "mind-blowing" and rewarding for many.

It is of course difficult to separate the power of the conversion organization from the effects of the social trends and changing definitions of discontent that were also occurring between 1972 and 1974. I think we can say, though, that this new conversion organization would not have been as effective had the American mood about public affairs also not changed. It is a fact of fundamental import, I believe, that all during the turbulent social optimism of the sixties, the DPs did not do well at converting. Politics, disorders, communes, drugs, hippie driftings, and Woodstock celebrations framed the imaginations of young people. Despite its dark and violent side, the sixties were an affluent and creative era. Conservatism and social-cultural sterility reasserted themselves, of course, and the sixties literally and socially ended in the Cambodia invasion of 1970. The killings at Kent State and the closing of college campuses closed a period in American life. And as has been documented across numerous societies and historical periods, when avenues of political activity and this-worldly optimism are thwarted, the political impulse is disguised as religion and reasserts itself as a religious ferment (Smelser, 1963, chap. 10). This is precisely the direction that the eternal discontents of youth began dominantly to take in the early seventies: Jesus freaks and East-West mutant religions abounded. It is in this now-shifted context of fashion in defining discontent that the DPs thrived. Their religious motif—indeed, their *conservative* religious motif—fit into the new ideas of plausible public definitions of private stresses.

THE COOLING OF WHITE-HOT MOBILIZATION

White-hot mobilization would appear to be an enormously difficult achievement and an even more precarious state to sustain. Chang stoked up the movement in 1972 and 1973, reaching a peak heat in late 1974 during the eight-city tour starting at Madison Square Garden. He seemed to have extended the movement to about its limits by 1975, for the stresses of its taut stretching began to show.

1. On the program and goal front, evangelical campaigns were abandoned and resources husbanded for the Yankee Stadium and Washington Monument events that were over a year away. DP strategists openly acknowledged they might not have sufficient resources or membership even to stage the Yankee Stadium rally successfully.

2. Weariness became visible in the ranks, and members began to defect in 1975 and 1976.

3. The conversion organizations were decreasingly productive. Newer converts were defecting at a higher rate than previously, but new converts tended to balance defectors, keeping the total membership approximately stable, but far below the goal of constant and rapid growth. An emergency missionizing program conducted in early 1975 failed to increase converts.

4. Funding apparently continued to be no large problem.

In 1975, moreover, a new set of factors began to enter the picture. White-hot mobilization had been achieved in a socially benign context. DPs were unknown; they claimed to be and were publicly thought to be ordinary fundamentalist and evangelical Christians. As time went on, their millenarian, "fanatical," "bizarre," and "cultish" beliefs, aims, and practices became known. Social criticism started and reached a crescendo in mid-1976, embodied in a wide variety of local and federal investigations, convert-parent lawsuits and other actions, and uniformly negative and extensive media coverage (see Lofland, 1977a).

In the face of all this, Chang announced an end to the current period of his American ministry and left for Europe, aparently aiming to fan those parts of his movement into white-hot mobilization. The American movement began to cool down to something closer to its previous level of warm mobilization.

GENERALIZATIONS

What might we learn from this case about high levels of movement mobilization? Allow me some unfortunately obvious but I think still worth stating generalizations of a tentative character:

1. White-hot mobilization is rare and a function of a rather peculiar conjunction of being able to (a) pose for members a belief in pressing and exciting objectives and achievements that can be attained if they are striven for with all one's effort; (b) deploy members in an elite, indoctrinated, mobile corps; (c) generate large-scale funding; and (d) do the preceding things in an auspicious social context with a conversion organization that can furnish a rapidly expanding membership.

2. White-hot mobilization is self-terminating. Members grow weary. The host society is likely to react negatively and begin to thwart the movement's programs.

3. The recruitment and training of a mobile, elite corps is an important mechanism for redirecting a movement through giving it a "split-level" organization.

4. Irrespective of the effects of the machinations of movement-manipulable factors (funding, conversion organization, split-level organization, etc.), I am impressed with the crucial role of larger social trends and contexts in movement mobilization—and movement fate in general. Chang initiated changes in organization, conversion and funding at precisely the time (1971–72) when American youth were the most enthusiastic about communal, East-West mutant, fundamentalist Christian, and other such religious views of reality. Significant numbers of youth were still posturing in alienated wanderings about the country. The DP organization was only one of dozens of religious groups that prospered between 1971 and 1974. Good organization, conversion technique, and large funding help, certainly, but only this more fundamental matter of auspicious social context made it possible for these movement-manipulable factors to be effective. We see the importance of context clearly in the fact that, by 1975, fashions in defining discontent had already begun to shift again. The DPs, along with dozens of other religious groups, had to cool down, redirect, and retrench.

ENDNOTES

1. Background detail on the DPs is available in Lofland, 1966, 1977a, 1977b, and in several other sources I cannot cite because they do not accord the movement anonymity. The sources of my data are described in Lofland,

1977a, n. 2. The indispensable help of Andrew Ross, Michael Greany, David Taylor, and Hedy Bookin is gratefully acknowledged.

2. Rotation was also, however, spurred by a desire to put as many people as possible through the Tinkertown training.

3. A 1976 estimate of central movement real estate reported equity of about ten million dollars in thirty-five million dollars' worth of property.

Resource Mobilization and Strategy: A Model for Analyzing Social Movement Organization Actions

Jo Freeman

It is a common assumption among students of social movements that a movement's strategy is largely determined by its ideology. That is, a movement first analyzes its situation and decides on its goals, then fashions an appropriate strategy for obtaining them. Yet new movements often arise in response to a crisis situation or a long history of more subtle grievances, and find themselves embroiled in action long before they develop elaborate concepts of where they want to go, let alone how to get there. Once an ideology begins to form, it may redirect the group's strategy, or it may merely confirm it. In either case there is not the simple linear relationship between ideology and strategy that is so often assumed; rather, there is a dynamic one in which it is not always clear which is the chicken and which is the egg.

What is clear is that whatever strategy a group desires, it must be developed within certain confines. The group can do no more than its resources and its environment permit, and if these are inadequate to meet the dictates of its ideology, it is usually doomed to inefficacy. Weatherman proclaimed itself the Revolutionary Vanguard of the 1960s. Yet its efforts to act out its ideology quickly destroyed the organization as any kind of a political force, by condemning most of its members to withdraw from public activity as fugitives. The Socialist Workers Party has also claimed revolution as its ultimate goal. Its realization of the limits of its resources and of how to use the available opportunities for action within our political system has not brought about revolution. But it has given the SWP a voice in places where Weatherman is only a macabre joke.

A structuralist approach to social movements would look at the confines within which a movement's strategy develops, the resources it can realistically mobilize, the limits on the uses of these resources, and the environment that molds the possibilities for effective action. Ideology might or might not be a significant factor, but at best it would be only one factor. This essay attempts such an approach, drawing upon the author's familiarity with contemporary social movements in general and the women's liberation movement in particular. It is hoped that what we have learned from the most recent wave of social movements can be translated into some conceptual frameworks that can be used to understand the next wave—with a better success rate than that of the pre-sixties' literature.

Because I will illustrate my points primarily from the women's movement, I want first to review the origins and structure of the women's liberation movement for those who are not already familiar with the literature on it. The major writers in the field agree that there were two distinct origins of the movement, on either side of the "generation gap" of the sixties (Freeman, 1975; Hole and Levine, 1971; Carden, 1974). Although the participants in both branches were largely white, middleclass, and college-educated, there was a distinct age difference among the founders, who represented different political generations.[1]

The first origin was the formation of the National Organization for Women (NOW) in 1966 by women associated with the president's and state commissions on the status of women. The second origin was the formation of loose associations of young women—usually non-students—involved in the movements of the sixties.

The two branches that resulted are structured in distinctly different ways. The "older branch" possesses several prominent and numerous minor core organizations. The structure of such groups as NOW, the Women's Equity Action League (WEAL), Federally Employed Women (FEW), and some fifty different organizations and caucuses of professional women has tended to be traditionally formal, usually containing local chapters and national governing bodies with elected officers, boards of directors, bylaws, and the other trappings of democratic procedure. All started as top-down national organizations lacking a mass base. Some have subsequently developed mass bases, some have not yet done so, and others do not want to.

The structure of the "younger branch," on the other hand, can best be thought of as a decentralized, segmented network of autonomous groups.[2] Its basic unit is the small group of from five to thirty women held together by an often tenuous network of personal contacts and feminist publications. These groups have a variety of functions but a very consistent style. Their common characteristics are a conscious lack of formal organization, an emphasis on participation by everyone, a sharing of tasks, and the exclusion of men. The thousands of sister chapters around the country are virtually independent of one another, linked only by numerous publications, personal correspondence, and cross-country travelers. They form and dissolve at such a rate that no one can keep track of them. With time and growth, the informal communications networks have partially stratified along functional lines, so that, within a single city, participants in, say, a feminist health clinic will know less of different groups in their own area than of other health clinics in different cities. A few cities, primarily smaller ones, have coordinating committees that try to maintain communication among local groups and to channel newcomers into appropriate ones, but none of these committees has any power over the activities, let alone the ideas, of any of the groups it serves.

This conscious lack of hierarchy means that the groups share a common culture but are politically autonomous. Even within the groups, the lines of authority and the process of decision making are often diffuse and hard to discern. The groups are not purely democratic, and there is usually a power structure, but only occasionally is it an overt one with elections, voting, and designated authoritative positions.

The difference in the structure of the two branches corresponds very closely to the traditional dichotomy between communal and associational organizations. Communal organizations are small, local, and functionally undifferentiated, whereas associational organizations are large, geographically extensive, and complex, with a well-defined division of labor. As Tilly has pointed out, a "group's organizational structure limits the means of mobilization" (1975, p. 505). Because these two different styles of organizations functioned as the mobilizing units that deployed the resources of the movement, they make the women's movement a natural laboratory for comparing the effects of structure on strategy.

RESOURCE MOBILIZATION PERSPECTIVE

The resource mobilization perspective on social movements that has developed in the last few years has been extraordinarily valuable in throwing light on important aspects of social movements that had been previously ignored. But the time has come for a more systematic consideration of the many new questions that have been raised. One of these is "the question of how a movement acts upon the larger society to promote changes with which it is identified" (Turner, 1972, p. 146). Decisions about how a movement will act are not always made by a leader or even a small committee of strategic experts, as many movements are not subject to that kind of hierarchical control. Often, major strategic decisions will flow from circumstances or be made and executed by an otherwise insignificant group of protestors whose success is then emulated by others.

For example, the first sit-in of the sixties was accomplished by some college students in North Carolina; it was not decided upon by the leaders of the major civil rights organizations of that year. Although these leaders were quick to see its uses, the idea of sitting-in spread largely through the media and informal communications networks of students. On the other hand, the earlier Montgomery bus boycott was a decision made by the black community leaders of that city and organized through the churches. Many other examples could be given. What is needed is a model within which strategic considerations, both planned and spontaneous, leader-directed and grassroots, can be analyzed. I would like to offer such a model. This model will highlight the resources available to a social movement organization at a given time, the limitations on use of these resources, and the ways they can potentially be deployed.

My model of strategic decision making by social movement organizations (SMOs) has four major elements, which have many components. These elements are mobilizable resources, constraints on these resources, SMO structure and internal environment, and expectations about potential targets. Figure 1 graphically illustrates the process by which the elements affect strategic decision making. Each of these elements is deserving of a paper in its own right. Because this is not feasible, only the major points of each will be touched on, and less attention will be paid to those questions or typologies that are adequately covered by other authors. This model should be viewed as an exploratory one, not as a definitive analysis.

MOBILIZATION RESOURCES

The most obvious distinction among the varieties of resources available to organizers is that between the tangible and the intangible. Virtually every social movement must have some tangible resources, primarily money, space, and a means of publicizing the movement's existence and ideas. These are interchangeable, but only up to a point. Money can buy space, but not always vice versa. On the other hand, money can be used to publicize the movement most of the time, and publicizing the movement can also be used to raise money.

It is a mistake to judge the affluence of a movement from its monetary contributions. A primary reason many new movements emerge out of older ones is that the older movement provides not only a cooptable communications network (Freeman, 1975, chap. 2) but also some very

Figure 1 *The Components of the Model of Strategic Decision Making*

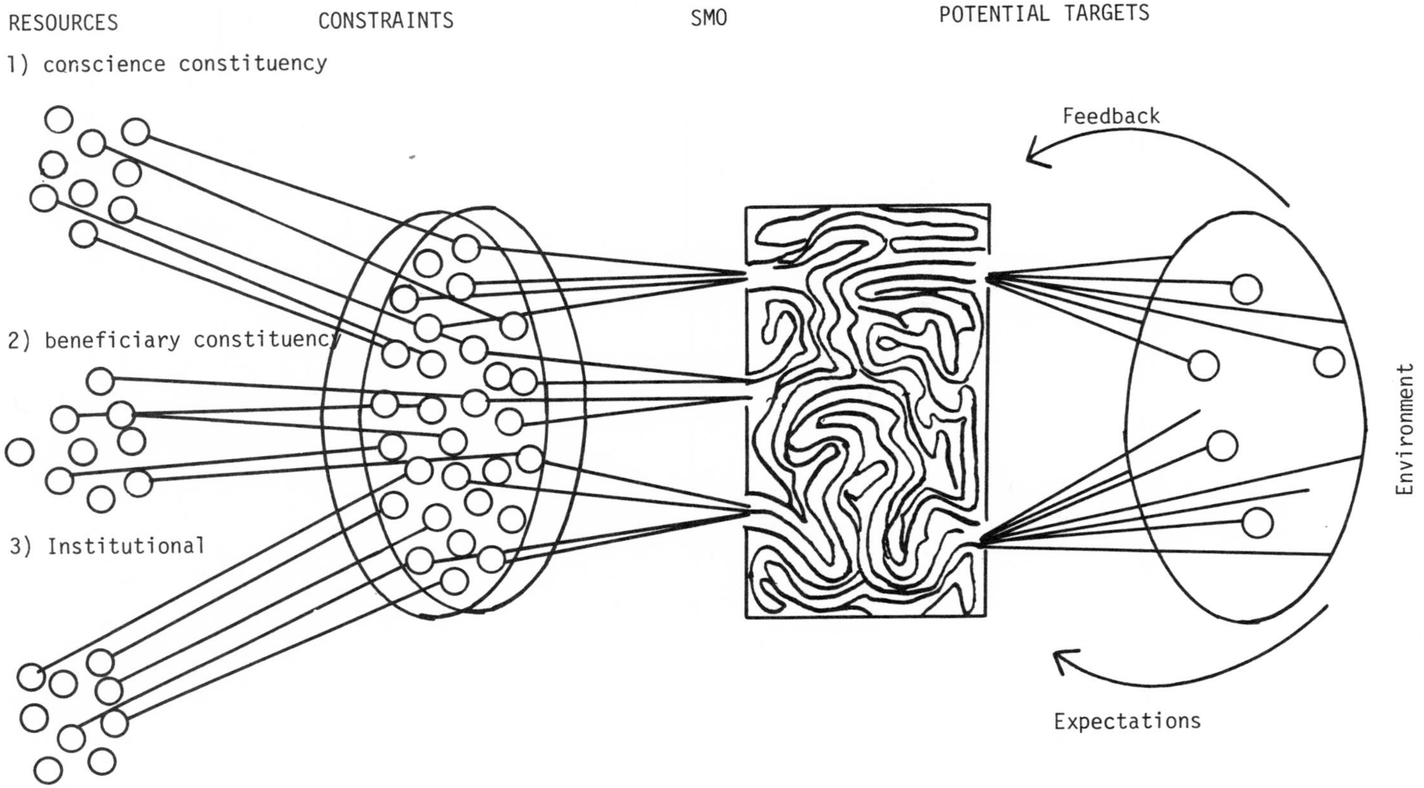

RESOURCES   CONSTRAINTS   SMO   POTENTIAL TARGETS

1) conscience constituency

2) beneficiary constituency

3) Institutional

Feedback

Expectations

Environment

valuable resources that would be at best expensive and at worst un-attainable if the older movement did not exist.

Both branches of the women's movement relied on space donated by others during their early days. The younger branch used a room and mimeograph temporarily contributed by the radical Institute for Policy Studies in Washington, D.C., to organize its first national conference in 1968. NOW was organized initially out of the Extension Division of the University of Wisconsin and then out of the United Auto Workers Women's Committee office in Detroit. When this space was lost in 1967, due to the UAW's dismay at NOW support of the ERA, NOW was forced to divert precious funds to renting an office in Washington, D.C., which it had trouble womanning.

The younger branch had access to something more important than space—the network of underground newspapers and numerous New Left conferences held every year. Had this branch of the movement emerged five years earlier—or later—when such resources were minimal, it would have had a much harder time getting off the ground. The value of this particular resource for publicizing the new movement among potential adherents was so great that it is practically impossible to trans-late it into monetary terms. NOW did not have access to such a resource, and though it had more money than the younger branch, it did not have the enormous amount that would have been necessary to achieve the equivalent amount of press coverage. Thus, it took NOW years longer to achieve the numbers of the younger branch. This difference points out that movements that appear to be poor, that draw from seriously deprived constituencies, may in fact be rich in some less obvious, but still tangible, resources.

People are the primary intangible resource of a movement, and movements rely very heavily upon them. In fact, one could say that a major distinguishing factor between a social movement and an organizing interest group is the particular mix of resources each relies on. Interest groups tend to mobilize tangible resources, some of which are used to hire professional staff to translate the rest of the resources into political pressure. Social movements are low in tangible resources, especially money, but high in people resources. Such resources are harder to convert into political pressure, let alone social change, in part because they are not very liquid, but for many activities they are more valuable. The civil rights movement recruited many young people to spend dangerous summers in the South registering blacks to vote. Even had enough money been available, it is dubious that this resource could have been bought. It is also questionable whether hired personnel would have been as effective. An analysis of the Southern Christian Leadership Conference's summer 1965 voter registration projects showed that those which registered the most voters tended to have the least money. In effect, lack of money forced the "outside agitators" to live in and depend on the local community, and this dependency in turn facilitated registration.

However, not all people can make the same contribution to a movement. The many different resources people can contribute can be divided into three categories. The first I will call "specialized" resources. Their essential characteristic is that they are possessed by only a few participants—and only a few really need to possess them, as the point of diminishing return is reached very quickly. These resources include expertise of various sorts; access to networks through which other resources can be mobilized; access to decision makers relevant to the movement; and status, whether within the movement's constituencies or within the polity the movement is trying to influence.

The other two categories are unspecialized, in that any participant could contribute them if so inclined. These are time, primarily to perform necessary labor and/or sit through meetings, and commitment. Commitment is not dedication. Commitment is the willingness to take risks or entertain inconvenience. Whenever a deprived group triumphs over a more privileged one without major outside interference, it is because the deprived group's constituencies have compensated with a great deal of time and commitment. As a member of President Ford's staff told me during the Republican convention, when I asked her why the Reagan supporters were so close to victory when they started so far behind, "They're willing to get up at 6:00 A.M. to go to a delegate caucus; we aren't." [3]

Because a movement relies so heavily on people resources, most activities involve their deployment. If a great deal of time is demanded to attend meetings, there may be much less available to do work. If the standard of commitment requires acts subject to felony arrest, movement resources may be quickly diverted to fighting legal battles. Groups with little access to specialized resources through their own constituencies must frequently spend other resources developing conscience constituencies to supply their specialized needs. Even this strategy can backfire. The southern civil rights movement effectively mobilized young white students to supply specialized resources—especially northern public attention. But within two years, the movement decided that the whites' value had been expended and that their presence interfered with local people's developing organizing skills.

I have prepared a table (table 1) comparing the resources available to the younger and older branches of the women's movement at the time of their initiations (of course, this pattern has changed over time), so I will not explore these comparisons here. But having categorized resources, we are still not finished with them. We next have to ask where they come from and what are the costs of mobilizing them.

Table 1 *Resources Mobilized by the Early Feminist Movement*

RESOURCES	YOUNGER BRANCH	OLDER BRANCH
Tangible		
Money	Little	Some
Space	People's homes, IPS	Various offices
Publicity	Underground papers, New Left conferences	Committees on the status of women lists, limited access to establishment papers
Specialized		
Expertise	Community organizing, Pamphleteering	Public relations, lobbying
Access to networks	"Radical community," Students	CSWs, Professional groups
Access to decision makers	None	Some in government, media, and unions
Status		
In polity	None	Little
In group	Only in the "movement"	Little
Unspecialized		
Time	Much	Little
Commitment	Much	Some

There are three major sources of mobilizable resources: the beneficiary constituency, any conscience constituencies, and nonconstituency institutions. As defined by McCarthy and Zald, the beneficiary constituency consists of political beneficiaries of the movement who also supply it with resources, and the conscience constituency of those sympathizers who provide resources "but are not part of the beneficiary base."[4] Institutional resources are those available independently of the movement's existence that can potentially be coopted by it. For example, if a law exists prohibiting discrimination, the power of the state to enforce this law can theoretically be coopted to help a movement eradicate discrimination.

Before Title VII of the 1964 civil rights act was passed, the civil rights movement occasionally employed sit-ins to force employers to hire more blacks. Afterwards, the movement encouraged individuals to file complaints with the relevant government agency and helped many to go to court to compel employers to end discrimination. By coopting the institutional resource of the court, through the passage of Title VII, the civil rights movement acquired legitimacy for its fight against employment discrimination and was able to have an impact on far more employers and far more jobs than could otherwise have been affected.

The primary distinction between a conscience constituency and a coopted institution is that one has a theoretical *right* to the resources of the latter. That is, access is *institutionalized*. The most obvious source of cooptable institutional resources is the government, but it is not the only one. When the YWCA made the ending of racism its "one imperative," it was in effect saying that the black movement had a *right* to the Y's resources for that end.

Regardless of their origins or natures, resources are not just there for the asking. They have to be mobilized, and this activity in turn takes resources—which a particular SMO may not always have in abundance. Before Title VII, the major resource the civil rights movement used to attack discrimination in employment was large numbers of individuals sufficiently committed to risk arrest in a sit-in. This resource was most frequently supplied by CORE, whose history of nonviolent action had attracted to it large numbers of individuals—black and white—willing to engage in these tactics. After Title VII the major resource the civil rights movement needed was lawyers to argue cases in court. CORE had few of these, and its role in ending employment discrimination dissolved. Fortunately, the civil rights movement had another organization, the NAACP, well endowed with lawyers who could provide this now necessary resource.

Sometimes not having the resources necessary to take advantage of a particular opportunity can be disabling. The women's movement did not use court action as readily as the civil rights movement did—even though many of the same laws proscribed sex discrimination—because it had never organized legal resources adequately. Yet it could not use the sit-in against employment discrimination because the mere existence of a legal channel undermined the legitimacy of such a disruptive tactic. Fortunately, the independent development of a "Title VII bar" has provided that resource, even though it is not one under movement control. Similarly, the ACLU Women's Rights Project now provides most of the legal planning and talent for the women's movement that the NAACP Inc. Fund provided for the black movement. To a certain extent one could say that the women's movement coopted the resources of the ACLU to its ends.

Resource Mobilization and Strategy   **175**

A major factor affecting the costs of mobilizing resources is their density. Because campuses attract young people in large numbers, an SMO seeking to reach them can efficiently do so by going to the campus. Women, however, are rather dispersed, so that even with a mailing list of potential supporters, greater amounts of time and money must be spent to mobilize women for a particular activity than students. Without such a list, the costs escalate.

Enormous resources are required to reach, let alone mobilize, aggrieved groups that are atomized and scattered throughout the population. Those that are concentrated can be mobilized fairly easily, which is one reason why students are so readily available to so many movements. Scattered groups can be concentrated by being drawn together as part of the mobilization process of another movement or some other agency. For example, the Community Action Programs set up under the War on Poverty became fertile grounds for welfare rights movement organizers. Without the government, the movement might not have been able to develop.

The reason many different movements tend to appear during the same historical period is not that different groups just happen to discover their grievances at the same time, or even that the example of one group alerts others to opportunities to alleviate their own grievances. Rather, it is that the resources one movement generates can be used for cognate movements. Organizing or publicizing skills gained in one movement are readily transferable. One movement's conscience constituency can become the next movement's beneficiary constituency. The civil rights movement contributed significantly to the emergence of many other movements for just this reason.

CONSTRAINTS

It is easy to think of resources as abstract entities that, like money, can be used for almost anything if enough is available. Unfortunately for most movement organizers, they are not. Instead, all resources—even money—have constraints on their uses. These constraints differ, depending on the source, but their existence acts as a kind of filter between resources and SMOs. These filters are so important that they can totally redirect the resources of a movement, much as a prism does a beam of light. And it is these filtered resources that an SMO has to work with, not the raw product.

The two branches of the women's movement drew upon similar if not identical resources in comparable if not identical amounts, from people with close class and educational backgrounds. Yet one branch formed numerous national associations, many of which opened Washington offices to lobby the government, whereas the other organized numerous small groups whose primary tasks were education, personal conversion, and service projects. The younger branch of the movement *could* have formed a national organization at its 1968 conference yet did not even make plans for an annual conference. It *could* have used the IPS office in Washington as a base from which to put pressure on the government but never even discussed such a possibility. It *could* have organized mass demonstrations, as NOW did in 1970, but took to WITCH hexes instead. Such divergence of energies cannot be explained unless one looks at the constraints, conscious and unconscious, on the resources available for action.

I have identified five different categories of constraints, and more no doubt could be found. Mine are values, past experiences, reference groups, expectations, and relations with target groups. The first and the last in the list have been identified by other authors (Turner, 1970); the other three have either been overlooked or only mentioned vaguely.

Because these terms do not really require definitions, their filtering function can best be explored by applying them to the two branches of the women's liberation movement. Both the age differences and the political networks from which the two branches emerged provided their members with different values, experiences, reference groups, expectations, and relations with target groups. These differences strongly influenced the kinds of SMOs that were created, and the SMO structure in turn joined with these filters in a synergistic effect that molded the strategic possibilities.

The early participants of the younger branch came largely from the radical community, and their values reflected that community's interpretation of basic American concerns (Kramer, 1972). The radical movement's concepts of participatory democracy, equality, liberty, and community emphasized that all people should participate in the decisions affecting their lives and that all contributions were equally valid (Lewis and Baideme, 1972, p. 83). These values led easily to the idea that all hierarchy is bad because it gives some people power over others and does not allow everyone's talents to develop. The belief was that all people should be able to share, criticize, and learn from one another's ideas, equally. Any kind of structure or any kind of leader who might influence this equal sharing was automatically bad (Shelly, 1970, p. 7). The logical conclusion of this train of thought—that all structure and all forms of leadership are intrinsically wrong—was not initially articulated. But the potential was clearly there, and it did not take long for the idea of leaderless, structureless groups to emerge and eventually dominate this branch of the movement.

The adherence to these values was premised on the assumption that all women were equally capable of making decisions, carrying out actions, performing tasks, and forming policy (Lewis and Baideme, 1972, p. 87). These assumptions could be made because the women involved had little experience in democratic organizations other than those of the New Left, where they saw dominance for its own sake, competition for positions in the leadership hierarchy, and "male ego-tripping" ruling the day (Piercy, 1970; Morgan, 1970). They had felt similar domination and control for its own sake in the social structures—primarily school and family—of which they had been part. The idea that there was some relationship between authority and responsibility, between organization and equal participation, and between leadership and self-government was not within their realm of experience.

The founders and early activists of NOW, however, had gained their political experience in party politics, various bureaucracies, and the civil rights movement. They considered structure in organizations a help, not a hindrance; were highly task oriented; found parliamentary procedure a convenience; were trained in public relations; and did not feel it necessary to live out egalitarian ideals in their own organization. Getting equality was more important than living it. Their concept of a well-run organization was not one in which everyone participated, but one in which everyone contributed to the tasks of the movement. Their concept of democracy was not one in which everyone had a say in all decisions, but one in which any who wanted could have a say. Equality meant equal respect, not equal influence. Leadership was good, not bad.

The more immediate experience of the early participants in the two branches also had effects on their initial choices of tactics. Both had had experience with mass demonstrations, and both had had experience with the press. But radical women shared with radical men a certain jadedness about the value of mass demonstrations. They certainly had not ended the war and appeared to absorb enormous amounts of time and energy to proclaim messages that fell on deaf ears. Instead, what was needed was actions that would catch people's attention by challenging old ideas and raising new ones. Younger-branch women did this creatively with WITCH hexes, zap actions, and a "freedom trash can" at the 1968 Miss America contest in which "instruments of female oppression" were tossed. Ironically, while women used these tactics to catch the eye of the public and press, they didn't want to talk to the press. Quite frankly, they were afraid of the press; and because they had access to the underground press, they did not feel an acute need to appear in the established press. They had participated in so many demonstrations that were reported so inaccurately that they did not think their words would be reported the way they wanted them to be.

NOW women would have felt much too inhibited to engage in WITCH hexes (which they thought were silly) but felt no inhibitions about the press. Many were PR professionals and knew how to present their case, as well as not to expect too much. They were also quite willing to demonstrate, even though many knew the days of mass action were probably over. The first contemporary feminist picket line was organized by NOW in December 1967 to protest EEOC inaction on rewriting its want-ad guidelines.[5] NOW members had learned the uses of pickets and parades from the civil rights and union activities that most had engaged in. They did not give them up even when some of their "more respectable" members left in disgust to form another organization (WEAL).

These direct action tactics and NOW's other activities were aimed not merely at catching the public eye but specifically at pressuring the government. These tactics were merely part of an overall campaign that also used letter writing, court suits, and meetings with government officials. Many early NOW members had engaged in lobbying for other groups, and it seemed perfectly logical to continue their activities for a new movement. Besides, the initial impetus for NOW's formation had come from the EEOC's reluctance to enforce the anti–sex-discrimination provision of Title VII; so pressuring for equal enforcement clearly had to be a priority.

Another major difference between the women of the younger and those of the older branch was their reference groups. Although a reference group is not always a group, it is a standard against which people compare themselves in order to judge their own behavior and attitudes.[6] This well-established concept from social psychology is not one that has been used to analyze social movements, but it has a great deal of explanatory power. When I first watched and read about Weatherman's "Days of Rage" and other low-key terrorist tactics, I found myself quite puzzled by what appeared to be a totally unrealistic assessment of potential support from the American public. It was only after reading extensively about the Weathermen (Jacobs, 1971) and in their literature that they began to make sense. I realized that many had spent the preceding years visiting international revolutionaries—largely Cubans and North Vietnamese—outside the United States or had talked to those who had. These revolutionaries, in effect, became their reference group. From them they acquired the idea that the true revolutionary is one who is not afraid to strike a blow in "the belly of the monster" (i.e., the United States), even if it meant his or her own suicide. I suspect that what Weatherman's tactics were calculated to gain was not support or even attention from the American public but a sense of having met revolutionary standards.

The standards new feminists wanted to meet were very different for the two branches. Younger-branch women first and foremost considered themselves *radical women*. Though women of both branches wanted to "start a mass movement of women to put an end to the barriers of segregation and discrimination based on sex (Sarachild, 1975, p. 131)," younger-branch women felt this could be done only through "radical action and radical thinking." The desire to be radical virtually precluded any pressure activities. The greatest fear of radicals in the late sixties was that they would be coopted by the system into helping improve it through reform rather than destroying it through revolution. The idea that they could instead coopt institutional resources to their own aims was totally alien. "Our role was not to be . . . a large 'membership organization.' What we were talking about being was . . . a 'zap' action, political agitation and education group something like what the Student Non-Violent Coordinating Committee (S.N.C.C.) had been. We would be the first to dare to say and do the undareable, what women really felt and wanted" (Sarachild, 1975, p. 132). This kind of thinking meant that actions that "blew people's minds" were OK, but picketing the EEOC to change its guidelines was not.

The movement's most prevalent activity and organization, the consciousness-raising rap group, also grew from this radical orientation. The women who developed this tactic felt that

> the first job now was to raise awareness and understanding, our own and others'—awareness that would prompt people to organize and to act on a mass scale. . . .
> Consciousness-raising—studying the whole gamut of women's lives, starting with the full reality of one's own—would also be a way of keeping the movement radical by preventing it from getting sidetracked into single issue reforms and single issue organizing. It would be a way of carrying theory about women further than it had ever been carried before, as the groundwork for achieving a radical solution for women as yet attained nowhere. [Sarachild, 1975, p. 132.]

Although C-R, as it came to be called, started with one group, it quickly spread throughout the movement for two reasons. The first was that many groups of women who met to discuss women's oppression and to develop strategies for changing it found themselves talking more and more about their own personal experiences. This was an activity for which they had ample resources. For those who had strong ties with the New Left, personal discussion was not an acceptable occupation because it was not "political." When the women of New York presented consciousness raising as a form of radical action at the 1968 conference, it gave them a rationalization for what they were doing anyway. The second reason was the extraordinary hostility and resistance of the radical men to women's simply discussing their situation. Men dismissed the topics as petty and the process as therapy. The radical women took this resistance as a sign that they were on the right track. "In the beginning

personal changes in orientation and attitude through recruitment and conversion in which organizational survival is a dominant concern.

The centralized movement devotes minimal resources to group maintenance needs, focusing them instead on goal attainment. However, this choice is somewhat movement reinforcing, as short-range goal attainment in turn becomes a means of maintaining group cohesion.[8] The decentralized movement, on the other hand, is compelled to devote major resources to group maintenance. As long as it defines its major task as "people changing," this activity, too, is group reinforcing, because maintaining a strong sense of group solidarity is the means through which personal changes are accomplished. These simple, heuristic relationships work well as long as a movement group is conscious of the way in which its structure limits its strategic possibilities. A source of problems for many movements is the attempt to pursue strategies for which their structures are inappropriate.

As Zald and Ash (1966), among others, have pointed out, the most viable movement is one with several organizations that can play different roles and pursue different strategic possibilities. Thus, the growth, development, and demise of a movement is not the same as that of the individual organizations within it. Most contemporary movements in this country have had complex structures and consequently fit both heuristic models. For example, the younger branch of the women's liberation movement is almost a paradigmatic example of the decentralized model, as it has no national organizations and has consciously rejected hierarchy and a division of labor. The older branch has several national organizations that reticulate only slightly with one another. None fit the classic hierarchical model perfectly, but they are close enough for analytic purposes.

Neither branch of the movement deliberately created a structure specifically geared to accomplish its desired goals. Instead, the founders of both branches drew upon their previous political experience. Women of the older branch had been trained in and used the traditional forms of political action. National associations were what they were familiar with and therefore what they created. Women of the younger branch inherited the loose, flexible, person-oriented attitude of the youth and student movements, as well as these movements' disillusionment with traditional politics and traditional forms of political action. They strove for something new—and radical.

Once these different structures were created, they in turn molded the strategic possibilities—occasionally contrary to the professed desires of at least some of their members. Both branches have made some efforts to change their structures, yet these structures have remained essentially the same as what they begin with. Organizational structure cannot be changed at will. What arises in response to one set of concerns in effect sets the agenda for what the movement can do next.

The younger branch provides an excellent example of this molding effect, as the original intentions of its founders were not consciousness raising, but radical action. C-R was supposed to be a means to an end— not the major task of the movement. Nonetheless, the loose, fluid, supportive C-R group was so successful that it became the model for all other groups. People resisted the idea that different movement tasks required different structure, or for that matter any structure at all. Instead, they elevated the operating principles of the small group to the status of feminist ideology, making it virtually impossible to adopt any other structure.

I have discussed the problems derived from "the tyranny of structurelessness" elsewhere (Freeman, 1973) and will not go into them here. Suffice it to say that the activities that could be developed by this branch of the movement were limited to those that could be performed by small, homogeneous groups without major divisions of labor. These activities were primarily educational or service projects that could be set up on a local level. Consequently, the younger branch of the movement set up numerous women's centers, abortion-counseling services, bookstores, liberation schools, day care centers, film and tape production units, research projects, and rock-and-roll bands. Production of a feminist publication was one of the most feasible projects for a small group to handle, and hundreds were developed. But there was never any national coordination of these projects; many were repetitive or competitive; and they frequently became closed, encapsulated units whose primary purpose was to provide a reason for their members to stay together.

The molding effect is less obvious with older-branch organizations because there was a greater congruence between strategic intentions and organizational structure, but it is there nonetheless. NOW and the National Women's Political Caucus provide an interesting study in contrasting problems. NOW was created to be a national lobbying organization, and initially that is what it was. From the beginning it required that national dues be paid by all members, whether they were members of chapters or not. Chapters, in turn, were largely autonomous units. After passage of the Equal Rights Amendment in 1972, it gradually became apparent that a mid-level structure of state organizations was necessary to press for ratification in the states. Neither individual chapters nor the national organization was capable of being effective on the state level. The creation of these state organizations has proved to be a difficult, time-consuming task that is still continuing.

The NWPC was created in 1972 in order to elect more women to office. Modeled on the American political party, it created state organizations from the beginning but did not require national dues. This structure hampered NWPC effectiveness on the national level, and it, too, has gone through a difficult period of trying to establish national dues and collect them from recalcitrant chapters who prefer to concentrate their resources on state legislatures and local elections.

Ironically, a third organization, the Women's Equity Action League, has changed its strategy to fit its organization instead of attempting the opposite. It was founded in Ohio as a splinter group from NOW in 1968 and was intended to be a small, powerful organization for professional, executive, and influential women around the country. It discovered over time that a significant percentage of its membership was in Washington, D.C., and that its members elsewhere had some influence on Washington politicians. Therefore, it came to redefine itself as primarily a national lobbying organization whose primary resource was not numbers but expertise.

EXPECTATIONS ABOUT POTENTIAL TARGETS

As an SMO searches for effective actions, there are three factors it must consider about potential targets and the external environment: (1) the structure of available opportunities for action, (2) social control measures that might be taken, and (3) the effect on bystander publics.

As Schattschneider (1960, p. 72) has pointed out, "The function of institutions is to channel conflict; institutions do not treat all forms of conflict impartially, just as football rules do not treat all forms of violence with indiscriminate equality." Nor do political institutions treat all demands from all groups impartially; instead, institutions and the "rules of the game" operate as filters to eliminate some and redirect others. Because SMOs are generally dissident groups, they frequently lack the resources to exploit the "usual" opportunities for action. Thus, the success of such a movement is often determined by its ingenuity at finding less obvious leverage points from which to pressure its targets, creating new avenues for action, and/or effectively substituting resources it has in abundance for those it does not have.

Finding leverage points within the political system generally requires some intimate knowledge of its workings and so is an alternative available only to those not totally alienated from it. Ralph Nader's "Raiders" have been very effective at finding leverage points. Affirmative Action in higher education became a public issue when a faculty woman sought a remedy for her failure to get a particular job for which she was qualified and found that none of the antidiscrimination laws covered her situation (Freeman, 1975, pp. 191–209). Her discovery of Executive Order 11357, which required affirmative action for sex as well as race, illustrates the fact that such leverage points are found as much through luck as through knowledge.

Creating new avenues is a far more common form of action for dissident movements, especially when they have minimal knowledge of or access to the political system. The civil rights and student movements very effectively attracted public attention to their causes through non-violent demonstrations that prevented people from engaging in "business as usual" without so flagrantly violating norms of behavior that the demonstrators could be dismissed as pathological deviants. Unfortunately, such tactics are "creative" only when they are new; thus, their effects wear off over time. Sometimes such tactics become institutionalized, as did the strike and boycott originally developed by the labor movement. Other times they simply lose their impact. The recent arrest of over one thousand people protesting at a nuclear plant at Seabrook, New Hampshire, made much less of a public impression than the "Freedom Ride" busses of the fifties or the campus arrests of the sixties.

Resource substitution is a particularly common strategy for social movements that want to utilize institutional channels but do not possess the normal resources for their utilization. Groups that cannot command large voting blocs to elect favorable candidates can achieve equivalent access by supplying the time and commitment of their members as campaign workers. This has been successfully done by the Gay Rights movement to gain support from local politicians, as well as other groups.

Not infrequently, the structure of available opportunities for action presents no feasible alternatives. This may be because a particular SMO constituency is too alienated or too ignorant to take advantage of what is available, as is the case with movements of the seriously deprived. It may also be because the particular resources of a movement do not fit the channels available for action, because the SMO's structure or values do not allow it to participate in those channels, or because the available channels are not capable of dealing with a movement's demands. In theory, the younger branch of the women's liberation movement was just as capable as the older one of mobilizing its supporters for lobbying activities, but the constraints on the uses of its people resources, as well as its small group structure, made this opportunity for action an unfeasible one.

When there are no feasible opportunities, movements do not simply go away; instead, discontent takes forms other than political action. Many riots are now seen as a form of political activity. Withdrawal movements of varying types are quite common when dissident groups feel highly alienated. These withdrawal movements may be "apolitical" in the sense that their members identify their activities as spiritual or cultural. Many, however, are quite political but redefine their politics in "alternative" forms. When the New Left turned to "alternative institutions," it saw these as a new means of pursuing its politics, not a rejection of politics. However, as has happened with communes and some other leftist activities, it is not uncommon for what began as an alternative political institution to become an apolitical one. In this way some movements can be "cooled out" so that what began as a means of making public demands becomes a refuge for seeking personal solutions.

When a movement does appear to find successful avenues for action, it generally encounters social control measures of one sort or other. Gamson (1968, chap. 6) has analyzed "the management of discontent," and therefore I will not do so here. But it should be pointed out that direct opposition is a two-edged sword. As Gurr (1970) and Gerlach and Hine (1970) have illustrated, some opposition is necessary to maintain movement viability. A solid opponent can do more to unify a group and heal its splits than any other factor. Many of the student sit-ins of the sixties would never have amounted to anything if the university authorities hadn't brought in the police. But even if the enemy is not so blatant, it is the perceived and not the real opposition that is important. Movements that neither perceive nor experience opposition find it difficult to maintain the degree of commitment necessary for a viable, active organization. Often opposition will be blown up larger than life because it serves the needs of group cohesion.

However, the relationship between opposition (real or perceived) and movement strength is not linear. Effective application of social control measures can kill a movement, as can completely ignoring it. Similarly, a perceived opposition of great strength can effectively destroy a movement by convincing people that their actions are futile. For example, the many infiltration and conspiracy theories that Left and feminist groups have developed to explain their internal problems have an initial effect of heightening commitment against a pernicious enemy. But if carried too far or too long, they can serve to undermine the mutual trust necessary for movement survival. Thus, an opposition that contributes to trust and commitment in the short range can kill it in the long.

The degree and success of opposition affects not only the movement but also the relevant bystander publics. Bystander publics are not direct targets of a movement's actions, but they can affect the outcome of these actions. As a general rule, movements try to turn bystander publics into conscience constituencies who will supply the movement with additional resources, and try to prevent them from becoming antagonists who will discourage targets from responding to movement demands (Turner, 1970; McCarthy and Zald, 1973b). Movements that cannot find leverage points are very dependent on the reactions of bystander publics, and it is not uncommon for demonstrations to be used not to affect a particular target directly but to gain sympathy and support from other parties. The southern civil rights movement's primary strategy was to use nonviolent demonstrations, in expectation that an overly violent social control response would attract third-party support. When it brought these same tactics to the North, where the bystander publics were the targets, they largely failed.

The civil rights movement's failure to appreciate that tactics viable in one arena would not work in another is a very common one. SMOs plan their actions on the basis of expectations about potential target and bystander public response. These expectations are initially derived from premovement experience or from that of cognate groups. Once actions are initiated, direct feedback becomes relevant. When an activity proves successful, it is generally repeated without analysis of the context that permitted that success.

For reasons already discussed, the younger branch of the women's liberation movement was not interested in ordinary pressure tactics aimed at political institutions. Even if it had been, none of its participants had the necessary experience in this kind of action to provide a model of how to do it. They did have experience with zap actions, and several of these were executed during the first years of the movement's existence. Although the actions were approved by other movement participants, they did not receive favorable feedback from the general public at which they were aimed. Usually they were ignored, and when not ignored, ridiculed. But had this been the only available outlet for their energies, zap actions might have continued.

In the meantime, consciousness raising had been systematized and spread widely. Feedback from this process was immediate and favorable. Women recruited into the C-R groups spoke frequently of the emotional release the groups sustained, and they kept coming back. Though not all women liked C-R, most did, and it became the prevalent activity. Because it was so successful, the movement's immediate target changed from the general public to the women in the C-R groups, with other younger-branch activities serving less as a means of direct impact on the public than as a magnet by which to attract new recruits into C-R groups.

In the meantime, the older branch maintained its basic, successful strategy of institutional pressure, though it expanded its repertoire beyond the initial activity of lobbying. Although some organizations within the older branch, such as NOW, added C-R activities, they did so as a membership service, not as a basic strategic device. This branch of the movement has been very attuned to the structure of available opportunities for action. It has paid much less attention to actual and potential social control measures and to bystander publics. Nonetheless, it is still affected by both these factors: its leaders are merely unaware of how it is affected.

In conclusion, some flaws in the model just presented should be pointed out. The most glaring one is that it is not a dynamic model. It does not explain changes over time in any of its components or in strategic outcomes. Rather, it enables one to look at an SMO at one point in time to determine the resources available for mobilization and the potential ways in which these resources can be deployed. In addition, the model ignores fortuitous circumstances that might benefit a particular movement's goals and the accidents of history that are often so crucial in a movement's success or failure. Fortuitous resources, as well as accidents, certainly have an effect on final outcome, but unless their availability can be reasonably predicted or controlled by an SMO, they play little part in strategic decision making.

Despite these flaws, I think use of this model could help SMO leaders to analyze their strategic options and help outside observers to explain why certain actions are chosen. Needless to say, the real world is far more complex than the simplified version presented here. The relevant question is whether this model provides a skeleton on which that complexity can be usefully displayed.

ENDNOTES

1. Rudolph Heberle provides one of the best discussions of the importance of political generations in his classic book *Social Movements* (1951). He defines a political generation as consisting of "those individuals of approximately the same age who have shared, at the same age, certain politically relevant experiences" (pp. 119–20).
2. This description of movement structure and its ramifications is thoroughly developed by Gerlach and Hine (1970).
3. Interview with Bobbie Kilbourg, August 1976.
4. I have borrowed the ideas of beneficiary and conscience constituencies from McCarthy and Zald (1973b), who in turn borrowed the latter from Michael Harrington (1968).
5. The EEOC had initially ruled that separate want-ad columns with racial labels were a violation of Title VII but that those with sex labels were not. NOW wanted the EEOC to "de-sexigate" the want ads by ruling that all labels were illegal.
6. This term was first used in 1942 by H. H. Hyman, but the idea goes back much farther.
7. William Gamson (1975, p. 197) most explicitly discusses the strategic possibilities of this model.
8. See Freeman (1975, pp. 100–102, 145–46) for further discussion of this point.

III

THE COURSE AND OUTCOMES
OF SOCIAL MOVEMENTS

OVERVIEW

A particularly knotty problem in the study of social movements is how to assess their impact. One solution is to examine their institutionalization. The two papers in this section focus upon the broader question of social movement impact on society, though in quite different ways. Charles Perrow attempts a sweeping look at the social movement activity of the 1960s, asking how the surge of activity can be explained and, ultimately, what difference it all made. Snyder and Kelly note the lack of attention to the empirical outcomes of social movement activity and attempt to specify a theoretical and methodological approach to the investigation of such outcomes.

Perrow's many comments about starting and ending dates of movements are gleaned from his systematic look at coverage of various issues in the *New York Times* over the last several decades. Presenting a series of competing explanations (e.g., changed consciousness, neo-Marxist, resource mobilization, and random process) of the rise and decline of social movements, Perrow attempts to evaluate the various positions with the data set at his command. He concludes that none of the perspectives does an adequate job of accounting for all the movements at which he looks, and he attempts to specify the strengths and weaknesses of each. Rather than viewing his conclusions as evidence for the inexplicable nature of social movement phenomena, however, we would view them as a spur to more and better attempts to develop an integrated theoretical approach.

Snyder and Kelly, using urban violence as their major example, attempt to develop an analytic methodology for investigating the effects of violence upon the achievement of various social movement goals. They are correct that a process approach and attention to feedback mechanisms are crucial to the understanding of shifts in tactics over time. They also present a methodology for appropriate time-series analysis utilizing comparative case material.

The Sixties Observed

Charles Perrow

Interpreting the 1960s is likely to become a minor industry for social scientists in the next few years. The turbulence of the decade was both unanticipated and unprecedented. Following the announcement of the "end of ideology" we had nothing but ideologies; following descriptions of massification and one-dimensional humanity, we had a multicolored dreamcoat of diverse causes and selfless and courageous youths risking lives and careers; in the midst of the longest sustained period of prosperity in recent history, we had hunger marches, riots, bombings, and official murders in extravagant numbers.

Explanations are only slowly beginning to take shape, and they inevitably reproduce the categories of mainstream social science ideologies and the few radical channels dug to divert those flows. We have or will soon have psychodynamic analysis of youth, demographic-generational accounts, traditional collective behavior explanations, rapid cultural and social change accounts, and neo-Marxist interpretations. One distinctively new approach, that of resource mobilization, threatens to supplant traditional collective behavior accounts, but I think it has

This essay has benefited from the research of the following members of the project team, and I am very indebted to them, and to our indefatigable project secretary, Mary Luyster: Mitchel Abolafia, ecology; Peter Freitag, peace; J. Craig Jenkins, farm workers; *Douglas McAdam, blacks; *David McCaffrey, medical care; *Michael Mart, teachers; James Olsen, Indians, Puerto Ricans; *Michael Ryan, welfare rights; David Uglow, women. In addition, shorter projects were conducted by Ellen Sensat (Students), Peter Lanciano (Catholic Church), and Mark Wernow (Radical Left). Asterisks indicate that drafts of their projects are or shortly will be ready for circulation.

The research was supported primarily by a grant from the National Institute of Mental Health, 5 RO1 MH20006-04 SSR; additional support came from a National Science Foundation dissertation grant to Jenkins and from the Center for Policy Research.

immediately split into two wings, though this judgment may be premature and inaccurate. Part of the difficulty of sorting out the area as it is developing is that different things are being explained. Is the focus the 1960s themselves, or social movements in general; the dynamics of movement organization, or the background and context of the movements; the specific ideological content, or the process of social movements regardless of ideology?

This contribution will be very modest in view of these enormous questions and disparate foci, and rather inchoate in view of the state of the field and the quite preliminary state of analysis of data from a project I am directing. I will ignore the psychodynamic and collective behavior interpretations entirely; express abrupt doubts about the demographic generational and cohort theories; single out the most succinct and striking formulation of resource mobilization for extensive criticism; discuss two synthetic formulations, greening and graying; and conclude with a suggestion for a mottled theory.

First, a brief word about my own data, which occasionally figure in this essay. A group of students and I have been coding the abstracts of news stories that appear in the *New York Times Annual Index* in order to understand the dynamics of several movements or issues from, roughly, 1950 through 1972. The movements or issues I am drawing on for this essay are: civil rights and black power; the various student movements; the peace movements; the issue of medical care; the issue (it was not a movement) of reform of the Catholic church; the farm worker, Puerto Rican, welfare rights, ecology, women's, and American Indian movements; and militant strike activity by teachers. The range of variables used, analysis techniques, reliability problems, and an example of what an individual project looks like can be found in a recent publication (Jenkins and Perrow, 1977).

CONCLUSIONS

First, some general conclusions and speculations. The civil rights and student movements started in 1956 and 1958 and had uninterrupted histories (though changing issues and fortunes) through 1972, setting them apart from the others. Thus, an explanation of the 1960s cannot cite the youth culture, swollen college populations, prosperity, or the war in explaining the origins of these two seminal movements. Nor will an "issue cycle" approach (Downs, 1972) illuminate movements that last from fourteen to sixteen years. Nor is the explanation of "exhaustion" compelling, as activists did not drop out of these movements in 1960 or 1964 (nor did sophomores have much occasion for being exhausted in 1972, after one year of protest).

Many of these movements had existed before, and there was militant activity in the 1950s for the farm workers, teachers, Indians, and the disarmament and testing aspects of the peace movement. Indeed, even at the height of Joseph McCarthy's popular acclaim, some of these were active. Thus, there is need for an explanation of why they tried and failed in the 1950s and succeeded in the 1960s, but as noted above, college populations and prosperity are not sufficient arguments, as the civil rights and student movements started before these phenomena.

Aside from civil rights and the multi-issue student movement, the other movements started or were reactivated within a three-year period: farm workers and peace in 1965, Puerto Ricans and welfare rights (and black power) in 1966; ecology and the militant phase of the women's movement in 1967; teachers' militancy and the militant phase of the continuing American Indian movement in 1968. This is an incredibly crowded time. But though it corresponds to the escalation of the Vietnam war, which started in February 1965, the issues are not directly connected to the war. Indeed, the issues are extremely diverse. This may be an artifact of our selection procedure (we picked the prominent ones that could be researched through the *Times Index*), but we think not. We studied some other issues (not discussed here), and they, too, appeared after 1964 (prison riots, the drug "crisis," the radical Right, and the birth control controversy). Something other than a war was going on, and though wars affect everything, the war provides little illumination of teacher militancy, welfare rights, ecology, women's liberation, prison riots, American Indian protests, and so on. Everyone agrees that this was a special time, but what made it special was the diversity of issues that were subject to protest. Therefore, explanations must detail the connection between the presumed conditions or events that occasioned the protest and the wide variety of protests.

As extensive as the diversity was, protests did not reach every group "at risk." Many groups that did not differ markedly from one or more of those that protested had failed to form sustained movements that were nationally visible and/or disorderly—the aged, poor southern whites, blue-collar workers, Vietnam veterans, and many disadvantaged ethnic groups. Grievances and mobilizable resources were there for all of these. Just as the conditions or factors that explain wars that did happen usually existed when wars did not happen, so do we have a problem of explaining why some movements never materialized. There is also the distressing problem of why some of those that did appear did so in, say, 1966 rather than 1958, or 1962.

One of the best explanations for the concurrence of movements (though not why these but not other groups mobilized) is suggested by Jo Freeman in this volume. Rather than relying upon a "climate of the times," or contagion, or a notion of an oversupply of professional reformers looking for real or imaginary issues, she argues that once some movements got going (for whatever reasons), they created resources and dislodged resources for other groups, enabling them to start movements. Thus, one might argue, though the war was not connected to farm worker militancy, it did mobilize students who could be used once the boycotts began, illustrated that there was a public that would respond to direct mail appeals, or indicated that for a time at least the federal government was too preoccupied with other matters to allow, for example, the U.S. Employment Service to bring in strikebreakers by helicopters. In this fashion, it is not necessary to provide a single explanation for all movements nor for the birth, maturity, and decline of particular movements.

However, there is a requirement that explanations for the birth, maturity, and decline of movements be examined for consistency. If a rising tolerance of militancy helps explain teachers' strikes, it is hard to cite a declining tolerance of militancy to explain the demise of black movements. The explanation is more likely to have something to do with the differences between white teachers and militant blacks. More important, if movements free and create resources, we need an explanation of why the first movements could occur, and it must be cast in terms of the conditions that allow resources to become available. I will argue later that elite disunity, indifference, or tolerance is an important factor. But some explanation must be provided of why it was once not possible to mobilize resources, if the mobilization of resources becomes an explanation for the activism of diverse groups at a later period. Finally, and most important, when movements decline, as most of them did in the early 1970s, the cause of the decline must be at least *consistent* with the cause attributed to the rise and maturity. If rising prosperity led to movements, but many died before the prosperity declined significantly, there must be an important additional factor that explains movement origins.

The demise of many of the movements proves to be the most difficult problem theorists will have to contend with. An exhaustion or cyclical theory will have to be very elastic to cover all movements, and thus it becomes suspect. The cohort-generational theories are clearly inapplicable here, as I shall argue. "Repression" is always a popular explanation with some (and I lean heavily toward it), but Gary Marx in his essay in this volume, is not at all sure of it. Even "success" has to be taken seriously, after the very thoughtful and provocative piece by Anthony Oberschall (1977). And, of course, it is possible to believe that some died by their own bungling hands.

I tend to discount the last explanation. SDS spawned Weatherman, and it was a sad day for the movement. But had there been a viable movement, the excesses of the Far Left—inevitable in the normal-curve distribution of ideology and tactics in any large movement, I would think—would not have had their impact. It is probably more accurate to say that the student movement was dying, and thus the Weathermen appeared and loomed large. Was it dying because of its inefficiency and bungling? Judging from the evidence in Kirkpatrick Sale's excellent book (1973) (and disregarding his occasional quite conventional interpretations), it was inefficient and bungling almost from the start, but that made no difference. Again, in the case of civil rights, I do not think that black power, fratricide, and cop-baiting were the consequence of organizational ineffectiveness or tactical bungling, but I do think that the civil rights movement just might have gone on to bigger and better things if the liberals in the Democratic party had not rejected it in the 1964 convention. Except for very limited-purpose political movements, such as the Temperance movement, social movements cannot be expected to be orderly, judicious, and businesslike. They succeed or fail for reasons other than the ability of their leaders, their federated or centralized structure, their use or rejection of violence.

Here I seem to be clearly at odds with Gamson's impressive work (1975). But I would suggest that because violence only *tends* to pay, for example, we are free to say that violence is not a key variable. The associations he reports are too weak for explaining the 1960s; they suggest that a larger context is much more important. What that larger context might be in the case of the United States from 1956 to 1972 is beyond me at the present, but there follow four suggestions.

DEMOGRAPHIC-GENERATIONAL FACTORS

It is widely accepted that the occurrence of disorder must be connected with the bulge in the youth population and the location of that population in age-segregated institutions (colleges). Norman Ryder, an influential proponent of cohort analysis and a formal demographer, offers the most succinct statement of this view. Writing in 1972 with protesting youth in mind, he says "We would do well to consider the extent to which current discontent with the process by which children are turned into adults is attributable less to systemic flaws than to engulfment by numbers" (Ryder, 1974, p. 46). The numbers show a 52 percent jump in the size of the youth population (aged fourteen to twenty-four) between 1960 and 1970; in absolute terms, from 26.7 to 40.5 million. The decade was "statistically unique," because it is the only one in the one-hundred-year period from 1890 to 1990 to register an increase in the ratio of young people to those older people (aged twenty-five to sixty-four) "who provide the time and energy and skill required for socialization of youth, and pay the required taxes" (p. 47). In fact, the ratio increased by 39 percent in this period. There were, accordingly, proportionally fewer parents to socialize these youth, and proportionally fewer teachers (it is assumed) to educate them. If, in addition, there is rapid social change (he casually mentions the shift from rural to urban occupations and locations, and the increase in education), "the problem of transmission of culture is exacerbated" (p. 52). "Society at large is faced perennially with an invasion of barbarians. Somehow they must be civilized and turned into contributors of fulfillment of the various functions requisite to societal survival" (p. 45). The process is "painful" and made more so if there is rapid social change. In conclusion, then, "the increase in the magnitude of the socialization task in the United States during the past decade was completely outside the bounds of previous and prospective experience" (p. 45).

In addition to sheer numbers, there is the location of the barbarians—they are segregated in schools, and in the eighteen-to-twenty-four-year-old group, in colleges. There was a striking increase in the number and proportion of young people attending some sort of institution of higher education between 1960 and 1970. As the resource mobilization view will note, they had flexible schedules, leisure time, no family responsibilities, and pocket money. As the proponents of generational conflict argue, their values differed from those of their elders.

It was an explosive mixture, one in which "systemic flaws," such as racial discrimination or any ugly war, need not have played a dominant role. Presumably, some sort of protest about something or other was very likely under these circumstances. One variant of the resource mobilization thesis I will consider is also "structural" and also refuses comment on the content of the protests or their political direction, a matter I shall return to. (Cultural change theories, such as those of Richard Flacks or Theodore Roszak, also emphasize the demographic and educational changes, but attribute specific ideologies and values to the youth.)

The changes did take place, but it is striking how gradual they were and how long a time period they covered. The much-discussed youth bulge and college bulge are exaggerated by the universal practice of citing decade changes rather than yearly changes. The size of the fourteen to twenty-four-year-old cohort certainly increased in the decade by 52 percent, as Ryder notes, but the rise started in 1953, and though it picked up somewhat by 1960, it was still very steady through 1972. There was no sudden influx of youth in 1958 when the student movement started, or in 1965 when many other movements began to take off. The socialization burden could hardly have been greatly increased, as the youth cohort as a percentage of the total population was actually lower in 1960 than it was in 1950, and rose very little by 1970. Any socialization problem was probably slight, because it was spread over the decade; all parents "at risk" did not suddenly find themselves with one extra teenager in 1965, as one might infer from the usual statements.

The college enrollment data also present problems. The increase actually started in 1955 and was quite steady and hardly dramatic until about 1963 and 1964, when it did take a more dramatic rise until 1968; then the rate of increase slowed. The sharp increase did correspond with the increase in insurgency, but these figures included all higher education enrollments. Because junior colleges are more vocationally oriented and were not involved in protest until quite late in the sixties, and then not heavily, we might exclude them from the figures. When we do, the rate of growth slows considerably; in fact, the rate was considerably higher in 1956 than at any subsequent time. Student protest correlates much more highly with the escalation of the Vietnam war than it does with any rise in enrollment, reminding us that systemic flaws might be more significant than engulfment by numbers.

Furthermore, though students were involved in many movements, they were not the backbone of most movements, nor the initiators, nor in any other sense crucial to their successes. The teachers, farm workers, Indians, Puerto Ricans, welfare mothers, and those involved in women's rights (as distinct from women's liberation) were not college youth with idle time on their hands and a higher score on the liberalism scale than their parents. Of course, no one attempts to explain all the stormy sixties in terms of the youth bulge, college bulge, and generational conflict. But it is quite conceivable that little of it, even those parts where the students were very active, as in the civil rights and peace movements, might be so explained.

Finally, the students, the youth, and the generation gap did not go away about 1972, but remained as high as ever. Yet most movements did go away. Only a judgment that the movements succeeded would be consistent with this finding, unless we add to the explanation of the source of the disorder other variables, which then changed to bring about the demise.

For example, we might say that repression worked. If so, then elite tolerance, disunity, or inattention, along with the demographic bulges (such as they were), must be cited when explaining the beginnings of the movements. To add a political variable significantly changes the nature of these more structural interpretations. And to make a previous point once again, an exhaustion explanation is hardly convincing, as new hordes of barbarians are produced every day, ready to take the place of the fallen, if generational conflict is indeed important.

We might say that the war was a significant variable, which heated up at the beginning of most of the insurgencies and was winding down at the end. But the blacks and the students started protesting long before the war, and it is hard to link the war to teacher militancy, farm worker protest, welfare rights, and so on (though the militancy of the war protests, or more likely the earlier civil rights movement, could have stimulated these to some extent). A good part of the student protest was over the war, but again we must be careful and bring ideological content in the picture.

There were two issues: the war itself and the draft. Of course, the student movement started well before the war, and more important, though it often focused upon the war from 1965 on, it was certainly not limited to the war. Figures on the draft do not provide much support for the view that it fueled the movement—that is, the issue might make it a self-regarding movement rather than an other-regarding movement. Draft induction levels were considerably *higher* during the Korean War years of 1951, 1952, and 1953 than they were at any time during the Vietnam war. There was little or no opposition to the draft during the Korean War on the campuses. There was an antinuclear bomb and testing movement well before the war came along (e.g., the peace vigils). Draft figures actually declined sharply after 1968, but campus protest increased. Most college students were not at risk, and opposition to the war was more dramatic after the reinstatement of the 2S college deferment and introducing the lottery system than before. The antiwar movement was, finally and obviously, co-ed on the campuses.

Thus, to state a very obvious point, the war was probably an issue with youth because it was seen as immoral. An explanation for the protest that cites demographic changes or self-protective behavior (or, as we shall see, affluence, leisure time, movement professionals, and organizational resources) is surely quite incomplete. For all their flaws, the older views of social movements did manage to emphasize specific grievances and ideologies. Further, if there had been no Vietnam war, and no (gradual) rise in the youth and college population, I would argue that the 1960s still would have been stormy. As we shall see, there was too much going on in the late 1950s and early 1960s before the reputed bulge and the war.

RESOURCE MOBILIZATION

There are two variants of this perspective. RM I, as I will call it, was formulated chiefly by Oberschall, Tilly, and Gamson. It is Clausewitzian in character; protest is the continuation of orderly politics by other (disorderly) means. Because protest grows out of the ongoing political process and is a part of it, it need not be irrational nor discontinuous, as older theories might suggest. It is a commodious view of social movements—all kinds of things can become resources for movements, and there are all kinds of ways to mobilize them. Especially in

Oberschall's quite catholic formulation, a large variety of social-psychological, sociological, political science, and economic theories find their place (Oberschall, 1973).

The RM II version, formulated by McCarthy and Zald (1973b), building on the insights of the politician and social scientist Daniel Moynihan, is a good deal narrower in scope and is only applied to the 1960s (though its generality is, of course, asserted). Politics play a minor role in it; instead, it finds its agreeable imagery in economic theory. It is industrial capitalism in the political arena. It is more rationalistic than RM I, is indifferent to ideology, and has little, even at times no, dependence upon grievances. Ideology, grievances, and political power are the coin of RM I, but an economic-organizational, input-output model informs RM II. RM II is a very striking formulation and constitutes a genuine insight, in my estimation. But I think it works for only a small number of movements in the 1960s, and a more serious drawback is that it takes us away from the central puzzle of the period—the emergence and diversity of risky, even at times exciting, other-regarding behavior.

This resource mobilization II view is consistent with the generational view, but much more elaborate. It has an interesting history. This view was first formulated in a remarkably prescient piece published in the fall of 1965 in the *Public Interest*, titled "The Professionalization of Reform," by Daniel P. Moynihan. Moynihan expanded his ideas in his 1968 book, *Maximum Feasible Misunderstanding*, which attracted enraged reviews from liberals. In 1973 John McCarthy and Mayer Zald put out their very influential and quite remarkable piece "The Trend of Social Movements in America: Professionalization and Resource Mobilization." This developed, extended, and, where the limited available data permitted, supported the argument Moynihan had made. It has been succinctly restated in a recent article (McCarthy and Zald, 1977).

In the hands of Moynihan, it was an insightful bit of debunking, arguing that the white middle class, quite unbidden, took up the cause of the poor. In particular, professional reformers with social science backgrounds created new careers out of a mixture of surplus funds in the federal budget and a conviction that they could solve intractable social problems. Promise much and deliver little was the recipe for the disorder that followed. Good Catholic that he is, Moynihan is skeptical of promises for the here and now; and good politician that he is, he understands the necessity of delivering little to the poor and the danger of maximum feasible participation. This cynical tone pervades the elaboration of McCarthy and Zald.

In contrast to RM I, group solidarity is virtually dropped as a variable, along with grievances (which can be manufactured by issue-entrepreneurs if they do not exist and thus are not only secondary but, on occasion, unnecessary). In RM I, an increase in deprivations does not necessarily mean an increase in protest; political resources are better predictors (including the resource of solidarity). In the McCarthy and Zald formulation the abandonment of collective behavior premises does not lead to the unrestrained embracement of a political process model. Instead, we have an economic model. Political factors are present, of course, even as they are in traditional collective behavior interpretations; but they are there as limits, not as engines. Of course, they write, other things than discretionary resources are important, such as "means of communication, transportation, political freedoms, and the extent of repression by agents of social control," as these enter into a cost-benefit calculation (McCarthy and Zald, 1977). But the bulk of the discussion concerns, to use their terms, issue elasticity, substitutability of products, competition for resources, demand curves, advertising, vicarious consumption, product switching (brand changing) and product loyalty, product evaluation, product arousal value, slick packaging, entry costs into a social movement "industry," and so on.

As an antidote to an unrestrained and romantic "hearts and minds" approach, such talk is salutory. But the striking thing about the movements of the 1950s and 1960s (and social movements in general) is that they were not business organizations and industries. I suppose that the murder of civil rights activists, unarmed students, and sleeping Panthers could be treated as industrial accidents, and police and vigilantes as examples of hazardous working conditions, but do we not thereby lose a degree of distinctiveness? "Conscience constituents"—supporters of a movement who do not stand to benefit directly from it—are even denied the dignity of believing in the goals of a movement or of being appalled at the conditions that brought it forth. I rather think that Jane Fonda is sincere in her opposition to the Indo-China war, and Robert Redford sincere in his support of the environmental movement, and such sincerity would make a difference. This is where social movements differ from capitalism; Joe Namath is not expected to be sincere in his endorsement of products. Yet our two social scientists would deny the distinction. Speaking of the use of names, they remark, "Jane Fonda and Dr. Spock were to the peace movement and Robert Redford is to the environmental movement what Joe Namath is to panty hose and what William Miller is to American Express Company credit cards" (McCarthy and Zald, 1977).

Thus, this startling offshoot of resource mobilization theory has two characteristics. First, solidarity, guts, and even praxis, if you will, become irrelevant. Second, political factors are only weak constraints, rather than possibly central factors. RM I is a political process model; that is the central insight that distinguishes it from the traditional collective behavior and social movement literature. McCarthy and Zald removed Freud but replaced him not with Marx or Lenin but with Milton Friedman.

The data we have fail to support RM II in several respects. At issue are two central mechanisms of their model: leadership that comes from outside the aggrieved collectivity and makes a profession of leading dissident groups; and the rise in discretionary income, some part of which is given to social movements, providing employment for the professional leaders. The civil rights movement emerged, of course, before any rise in prosperity and without any increase in activity from the churches and foundations. Indeed, it appears that the bus boycott in Montgomery and the student sit-ins in Greensborough stimulated the foundations and churches, rather than the other way around, as Douglas McAdam argues in his work on our project. Furthermore, the leadership of both of these key initial phases of the movement was black and was created in the process of these two movements. The remarkably rapid spread of the sit-ins and the forbearance and discipline of the Montgomery boycotters would suggest, contrary to RM II, that the aggrieved population played an immense role itself. I will not go into the matter here, but McAdam stresses the political realignments at the federal level as an explanation of the movement, and the *Times* data show a considerable change in this respect from 1948 to 1954. (A similar change appears in the women's movement, according to *Times* data analyzed by David Uglow.)

The RM II model fares no better with the student movement. It is true that students have more loose change, time, mobility, and perhaps leadership skills than most parts of the population, and both RM II and the cohort theories make much of this. But they have always had these resources; there was no change in 1958, when this movement might be said to start. Nor do I think the students were led by organizers from the old Left. This is the red diaper baby theory, which is consistent with RM II and the youth culture interpretations (e.g., Kenneth Keniston, 1968). In this view, radicals of the late 1930s were diverted or silenced by World War II, the internal security issue following it, and by the Korean War; but their offspring appeared on the campuses in the late 1950s with a radical ideology, organizing skills, and access to bail money. Many of those who were active at the time and had radical parents have told me of the concrete contributions they made to the early movements. But though the pacifist Bayard Rustin (three years in the federal penitentiary during World War II) and others helped Martin Luther King, Jr., during and after the bus boycott, and Michael Harrington (a Shachtmanite socialist who wrote *The Other America*) left his dismal Y.P.S.L. loft in New York City to work with the civil rights movement and speak at colleges, it can be argued that the black and the student movements *drew* these people in, provided them with their first opportunity to play out their ideologies on a large stage, and *ran over them* in a few years. As Harrington says in his very candid autobiography, *Fragments of a Century*, speaking of the student New Left, "We of the fifties Left were simply too weak to serve as a point of departure for the New Left of the sixties" (1973, p. 149).

We think of the student movement as emerging with the Vietnam war, but listing a few events from the early years indicates what must be explained (these come from the chronologies in Massimo Teodori, 1969, and Sale, 1973):

1957–58 Progressive student parties start on campuses—SLATE at Berkeley, others at Chicago, Oberlin, Michigan, Columbia

1958 3,000 student-power demonstration at Cornell

1958–59 School desegregation marches in Washington—10,000 in 1958 and 30,000 in 1959 (organized by Rustin, but all organizers were surprised by the turnout)

1959 The pacifist Student Peace Movement founded

Studies on the Left appears

1960 Sit-ins, marches, and demonstrations, largely locally initiated, in support of the southern sit-ins in some northern and western campuses

Large march in San Francisco, mostly students, to protest the death penalty for Caryl Chessman

Fair Play for Cuba committee formed

Student Nonviolent Coordinating Committee formed

68 students arrested in protest demonstrations against the House Un-American Activities Committee in San Francisco. The next year competing film versions of the event by HUAC and the students toured the campuses.

Thousands of students visit Castro's Cuba

Nineteen sixty-one had the Freedom Rides, campus demonstrations against the invasion of Cuba, protests against the bomb shelter program and then peace vigils against atomic testing, the first assassination of a civil rights worker, the first dramatic increase in SDS membership, and much, much more. Something had happened to college students, and it wasn't that they had increased in number (the first eighteen year olds of the baby boom hit the campuses in 1963) or that they feared being drafted. Nor had crucial outside funds or professional movement organizers appeared. Their leaders were consistently rejected by the movement base and pushed in directions they did not intend to follow. The country was in the grip of a recession, so that affluence is hardly an apt explanation. The movement embraced student power, humanitarian-

The Sixties Observed   **203**

ism (the Chessman example), civil rights, radical analysis, national self-determination, anti-anti-Communism, and peace.

The best evidence for RM II is the concurrence of prosperity and the emergence of several movements from 1965 on. The data are striking. The 1960s experienced the longest period of unbroken prosperity in recent decades. Unemployment fell from 1961 to 1969; strike activity, as measured by Hibbs's three-factor index, was at its lowest level from 1960 to 1965 since 1950 (Hibbs, 1975); even 1968 was much lower than the peak years of 1952 and 1959. Inflation increased as the war heated up, but in the percentage of change in the consumer price index, the rises did not become steep until 1967–68, peaking in 1969–70. Finally, the proportion of poor people fell steadily from 1959 to 1972. One is tempted to say that protest appeared in times of plenty.

Private philanthropy has been rising steadily throughout the century, and its rise from 1950 to 1970 was dramatic, from under $5 billion to $19.2 billion. But the curve is fairly steady; only after 1967 does it become quite steep. Foundation contributions are a small part of the total figure, but their rise is substantial. This would be the figure most relevant to the RM II view. Breaking private philanthropy down into the most relevant subcategory, allocations to race relations, youth services, and welfare, we find the figure almost doubling from 1960 to 1970, though the rise is quite steady. The biggest change is a sharp increase in the rate of change from 1965 to 1966, and it continues to increase at somewhat more than 10 percent a year until 1969, when it is halved. Thus, there is support for this part of the resource mobilization viewpoint; prosperity gave rise to increased funding of social causes, presumably liberal ones. There remains, however, the serious question of which came first, the social movements and protests or the funding. It seems possible that the foundations, churches, and liberal unions were pulled into the action by the movement. Perhaps their resources were necessary but not sufficient. Perhaps a general liberal drift coincided with prosperity. Whatever the explanation, the data are clearly consistent with RM II.

But unfortunately, the movements level off and decline, for the most part, starting about 1970. Affluence, though cut somewhat by inflation and declining stock prices later on, still remains very high compared to the early 1960s. Congress put restrictions on foundations in the late 1960s, but presumably the movements had other sources of funds by then. I do not know how serious these restrictions were, but foundations were not the only source of funds for the movements. Public opinion polls certainly show an increasing perception of social problems and increasing degrees of delegitimization, so direct mail appeals should have been quite successful unless something else would explain the decline in donations. Professional reformers still exist in large numbers; in view of movement declines, there is certainly a substantial surplus of trained manpower here, but they are unable to keep their "industry" alive. RM II seems unable to explain the demise of these movements unless they are all counted as being successful, which is hardly the case; and even if they were, there are many other groups that could be mobilized with all the leaders and the funds. To explain the demise, the economic model must be significantly broadened to include political variables.

THE GREENING OF AMERICA

A serious case can be made that the United States experienced a rapid and deep-seated liberalization starting from the mid 1950s (in the next section I will make a good case that things got worse in the same period). The cultural revolution approaches (Flacks, 1967; Reich, 1970; Keniston, 1968) are consistent with this argument, as would be RM II if the other-regarding motives of the middle class who donated time and money to the movements were mentioned. In the case of the civil rights movement, the process starts much, much earlier, of course. There is an unbroken series of favorable federal civil rights legislation reaching back to the early part of the century, and increasing in volume from the 1930s. Basic social legislation was enacted in the last years of the Eisenhower administration, which presaged the War on Poverty, such as it was. This is not the place to detail these changes, but it is well to be reminded of them when we speak of the "explosive" sixties.

None of the cultural revolution theorists make much of an effort to explain why it came about, other than the youth bulge, prosperity, and disenchantment with the cold war. These are hardly satisfactory, but I have nothing to offer in their place. A larger theory of history is required, and those sociologists who consider the 1960s have not come up with one, though historians may have.

I must admit to a strong field-experimental bias in favor of the greening view. In every issue we considered, the contrast between the early 1950s and the late 1960s in our data source is extraordinary. It is an incredibly enlightening experience to read thousands of abstracts of news stories from the 1950s in these areas (for some issues there were no stories at all, which is even more telling). No one on the project team has failed to be astounded by the climate of the 1950s and the sharp contrast with the late 1960s. In the field work for the project, we deal with what Richard Hamilton (1972) labels the "concerns and issues of the day," as they were presented in that day, unretouched by the curve-smoothing interpretations of the historian, unmystified and abstracted by the sociologist, unsanitized by the trend-seeker. Naked, bare, specific, daily, concrete events and utterances go by with rapidity, producing a profound sense of discontinuity with the present. In just one glance we see that at the opening of the decade the American Legion could receive the blessings of all political and cultural leaders of New York City and stage an Americanism parade in Harlem led by marching columns of black children protesting the evils of Communism and the joys of Americanism. Even in the last years of the Nixon administration, the green fields sodden with presidential rain and gloom, the feminist, the gay liberationists, Chavez, Mario Savio, Berrigan, Abernathy, Shanker, and so on could recall the dramatic change that took place in the sixties. What happened to America in such a short time, according to this view?

First, affluence arrived for a substantial middle and upper middle class. Living standards for all increased. Contributions poured into public-regarding activities. The preoccupation with subversion and thus with conformity declined dramatically. The cold war seemed unnecessary; test ban treaties worked. There was something being done about civil rights and poverty. Lifestyles changed as youth took over. All authority was subject to delegitimization. More youth went through the liberalizing process of higher education, and lower education itself changed. Money and reform swept into the ghettos. True, a war crept up and then burst forth in 1965, but the citizenry finally made its prosecution intolerable and the start of new ones difficult.

The beginning, not the end of ideology, is found in affluence. But if so, where did it all go? It is possible to argue that it all more or less succeeded, as Oberschall (1977) has suggested. Every issue-area we considered has seen some reforms, and some of the movements have clearly moved into more respectable, institutional, and moderately successful phases—farm workers, American Indians, women's rights, collective bargaining for teachers, and perhaps the low-keyed but persistent ecology movement. I am told by Ronald Lawson of Hunter College that there is now more activity in the area of tenant organizing than at any time in the past. I am told by radical feminists that there is significant activity in thousands of small groups across the country, providing the base building that the 1960s only began. Many university reforms are slipping back into the educational philosophy of the 1950s and earlier, and ROTC has crept back to the campus, but perhaps these reforms were inadvisable after all, and ROTC is an important subsidy for students in a recession. Meanwhile, we have radical textbooks that never existed before, students on committees, teaching evaluation exercises, serious radical journals and several "radicals in the professions" groups, and a respectable audience for such previously outlandish terms as imperialism. (I reached this optimistic outlook in a 1972 volume called *The Radical Attack on Business;* see especially pp. 265–68.) In these respects I think there is no doubt that things have changed greatly in the last twenty to twenty-five years.

Perhaps only the longing for the excitement of the late 1960s is a legitimate source of disillusionment.

"THE GRAYING OF AMERICA"

Manuel Castell's phrase, from a work in progress of that title, sums up the alternative, radical view. People are always speaking for the radicals, and it is a difficult task, as they come in almost as many shapes and sizes as the liberals or the conservatives. I can claim only to be interested and sympathetic, not to be radical. So the following account must be received with caution.

This view would not necessarily deny that there was more affluence in the 1960s than in previous decades, more political activity, and more cultural diversification. However, the affluence was no substitute for authenticity for the middle class and did not reach many exploited or cast-off pockets of the lower class. The political activism was largely ineffectual and a result of worsening contradictions in the system, not a freeing of energies for change. Cultural experimentation and diversification existed but were a desperate and largely negative reaction to oppressive homogeneity.

At the center of such a thesis are the contradictions of advanced capitalism. First, capitalism resists a widespread redistribution of wealth or even income (we had more prosperity but no redistribution of income or wealth in the 1960s). This resistance imperils production and thus private sector employment, so that the state must make work, leading to a fiscal crisis that becomes apparent to middle classes and frightens them. Second, capitalism thrives on huge organizations, private and public, that increase the alienation of both blue- and white-collar workers. The declining ability of home markets to absorb surplus production requires imperialism (as does the ravage of natural resources), which guarantees an arms race and a war economy even in peacetime. At home, there is production for waste, rather than use, and in time this means increased manipulation and then alienation of the people. A massive legitimization crisis occurs, as a result not of increasing education, sophistication, and autonomy, but of increasing manipulation and economic crises.

For the greening theory, each social movement is a testimony to the ability of groups to thrust themselves into the decision-making process more effectively than before, and some for the first time. For the graying perspective, each is a testimony to the inability of world capitalism to handle its contradictions. It is hardly much consolation that things become so bad that insurgent movements appear and then must be put down at considerable public expense. Let us examine the dark side of several of the movements that we have considered, remembering that for the greening perspective, their very existence was cause for celebration and does not need this baleful interpretation.

The centerpiece of the greening theory would probably be the heroic struggle of the blacks, first in the civil rights movement, then in demands for political and economic power. But the wary support of the initial movement (or the failure to suppress it ruthlessly) resulted from a cool calculation of the increasing role of blacks in the presidential elections and their value as a surplus labor pool. Encouraged, middle-class blacks fought discrimination in public places but then went on to the economic and political issues, where the leadership of the Democratic party forthrightly blocked their aspirations in 1964. The black power movement was a backlash from this blocking and produced a backlash from the whites. Symbolic and inexpensive gains were achieved by the civil rights movement, but economic gains are at the mercy of the forces of capitalism, and politically the blacks inherit only the nonviable urban cores, just as the government inherits the nonviable industries, such as some sectors of defense, the railroads, and bus and subway lines.

Students sensed that the educational factories were training them for conformity and dependence in the bureaufactories they would gradu-ate to, and under the tutelage of an increasingly sophisticated New Left they fought the war, even when they were not subject to draft, and confronted the political machines, racists, agribusiness, and so on. Ha-rassed and shot at, they sought succor in the counterculture. Educational reforms are now being eroded, and the recession encourages conformity. The whole increase in college attendance was necessary to delay entry into a labor market that was virtually frozen on the private side, with new jobs coming largely from government and war. The increase in colleges meant that virtually all the middle class could go to college, while the proportion of the working class going to four-year institutions actually remained stable. Junior colleges toilet trained the lower middle class and parts of the working class for an antiseptic world of meaning-less work. Their eruption, joining the elite universities in protest at the end of the decade, was quite unanticipated and forcefully put down.

The War on Poverty, poorly funded and largely rhetorical, was abandoned after 1969. The government had fumbled at first with its "maximum feasible participation of the poor," but funds were soon channeled through compliant local politicians. Income inequality in-creased in the second half of the 1960s.

Middle-class movements were well controlled, though some sur-prises occurred. The women's movement started in the federal bureauc-racy and was still safe with the educated and professional women in National Organization of Women; but the women's liberation movement (as distinct from the NAACP-like women's rights movement) was an unanticipated offshoot of the radical student and radical civil rights groups. It tapped a powerful well of resentment and even reached into the working class (where both liberation and rights were desperately needed, in contrast to, say, the universities). These groups continue to be harassed by the authorities today and can be considered a genuine success that evaded the twin weapons of the state—repression and recession.

Each social movement started out on a safe program; the 1962 version of graying was the SDS *Port Huron Statement*, reading now as a mild and safe denouncement of America. Many movements were supported by liberal staffers in the bowels of the giant foundations who shunted off a tiny proportion of the funds to medical research and education into radical groups, until Congress put a stop to such activity. Once alienation was made manifest and disaffection unloosed, each movement escalated to radical and even hysterical demands, to the surprise of elites. By 1967 the costs had risen sufficiently for the Johnson administration to commence repressive action, but the effect seemed only to inflame and mobilize the disaffected. The Nixon administration, playing on the fears of the public that the discontent could not be contained, stepped up the repression, and the arrest and death figures mounted. A "fat-squeezing" recession aided the effort and brought back the sullen order and docility we see today, something the greening theory could never have predicted.

Only a few sanitized movements remain. It was necessary to prepare the public for the need to tax them to pay for the costs of cleaning up industrial pollution, and thus the environmental movement was endorsed and even financed by government, business, and those foundations tied to business. Distracted by the collection of soft drink cans, the public avoided any serious consideration of requiring that business and industry pay for their externalities out of dividends or out of funds reinvested for the great god Growth. Large producers fuss about the continuing environmental movement, but as long as it consists of legal regulations, they can be assured that small competitors cannot have an advantage, and indeed are disadvantaged by most of the requirements.

The medical care crisis resulted in an extraordinary surge of profitability for the health industry—drug firms, medical equipment firms, medical supply firms, proprietary hospitals, research institutes, medical schools, and, of course, doctors and all those who benefit from Medicaid and Medicare. Tax moneys poured into their coffers through government programs, and the number of maldistributed hospitals and physicians soared. There is nothing like a crisis to spur profits in the short run, as medical care, Sputnik, Vietnam, and now energy all illustrate.

With the mechanization of Texas agriculture, it was possible to eliminate the bracero program (which supplied strikebreakers) and allow the unionization of farm workers. The move to have the Teamsters Union control them appears to have failed, but mechanization has been stepped up in California. Gains were made by the farm workers, but only when the cost to agribusiness had dropped considerably. The cost of collective bargaining by teachers is not a problem for elites, as it is met from regressive state and local tax revenues. Finally, the war proved too costly, financially and socially; provoked increasing elite disunity; and thus had to be ended.

Today, in this view, we emerge from the decade with few losses for the elites but still no solution to the worldwide problem of a declining rate of return for capital. There will be greening. There is likely to be another round of insurgency in a few years as monopoly capital fails to solve the fiscal crisis of the state, but scenarios for the collapse of world capitalism and the West may intervene and bring fascism.

Of course, one may be eclectic. One may mix judicious portions of both greening and graying, use RM II where it seems appropriate, and argue that the cohort and college bulge must have had some effect and could have heightened the generational conflict to some degree. But more important than this eclecticism is a mottled view that is skeptical of all interpretations: society is sufficiently complex and social processes are sufficiently random, accidental, unpredictable, and disorderly to make us wary of citing even "major" causes. It also seems likely that our disposition toward transitive statements, as in my earlier stricture that an explanation for a decline must also be included in the explanation for a rise, is a requirement of our own passion for order but is not necessarily to be found in reality. All explanations are fanciful reconstructions— fictions—designed to (1) reassure us that there is some logic to history, no matter how dreadful; (2) further our entrepreneurial career aims; and (3) affirm political positions that we hold and espouse. The "progress" in social science inquiry is to make these fictions and espousals more wilt-resistant, attractive, and sophisticated. But all theory must be revisionist, because it serves those three ends, and new careers and politics require new assertions of order and logic to history. But that will be the subject of a forthcoming volume, *A Society of Organizations*.

ENDNOTES

1. There is no one work that makes all these points, of course. The general outline can be found in Perrow, *The Radical Attack On Business* (1972), for those not familiar with such arguments; those familiar with them will have their own superior sources. For example, on the fiscal crisis of the state, James O'Connor (1973); on manipulation and legitimacy, Herbert

Marcuse (1964) and Jurgen Habermas (1975). The papers of the Kapitalistate collective are often striking.

Project members are exploring some of these issues, though not in the extreme viewpoint presented here.

Strategies for Investigating Violence and Social Change: Illustrations from Analyses of Racial Disorders and Implications for Mobilization Research

David Snyder and William R. Kelly

INTRODUCTION

Racial Disorders in the 1960s:
Unprecedented Magnitude and Reaction

Although both the occurrence and analysis of violent action are long standing, investigations of collective violence—perhaps stimulated by an apparent increase in such phenomena—have proliferated considerably over the past few years.[1] In the United States, the urban racial disorders that occurred during the 1960s constitute the most recent and compelling evidence of this "everyday" quality of collective violence. But, despite at least some incidence of racial violence throughout U.S. history, the extent of race-related civil disturbances in American cities during the 1960s was unprecedented.[2] Moreover, these disorders generated exceptional awareness and concern in American society, as political officials (Johnson, 1971, pp. 167–68; National Advisory Commission, 1968; Governor's Select Commission, 1968) and the public at large (Blumenthal et al., 1972, pp. 19–21) recognized that the disturbances signaled a racial crisis in America. And, not surprisingly, academic attention concentrated heavily on the preconditions, causes, dynamics, efforts to control, and political significance of disorder.[3]

National Institutes of Mental Health Small Grant #MH 29817–01 provided financial support of portions of our work. We are also grateful to Paula M. Hudis and Anthony M. Orum for comments on an earlier version. The authors retain full responsibility for all statements of fact and interpretation.

Neglect of the Consequences of Disorder:
Broader Implications

Despite these substantial official, public, and academic reactions to racial violence, virtually none of the resultant attention and analysis has focused on "social changes" (or their absence) in urban America that may be attributable to the 1960s disorders. "Social changes" —we also use the terms "consequences" and "outcomes" interchangeably—refer neither to immediate strategies of control or eventual termination of disorder (which are preferably conceptualized as part of the process of violence itself: see Marx, 1970; Snyder and Tilly, 1972; Tilly, 1975), nor to the largely symbolic establishment of riot commissions (Lipsky and Olson, 1973) and reassurances of political officials (Mueller, 1975).[4] Instead, we take "social change," "outcome," and so on to signify *objective, nontransitory* shifts in (1) the resources of groups involved in violence (black Americans) and (2) the larger-scale "systems" in which violence occurs (in this case, urban areas).[5] Although there have been a few sketchy attempts to study such "structural" outcomes, assessments of this work typically conclude that the incomplete and unsystematic evidence and analysis brought to bear on disorder consequences require much further research (Masotti, n.d.; Feagin and Hahn, 1973, pp. 199–260, which also summarizes previous findings).

Though this inattention to the consequences of racial disturbances is itself important, broader significance lies in its reflection of more general neglect of the relationship between violence and social change. Surveys of the literature on collective violence, when they address this issue at all, continue to lament the lack of research on it. For instance, Eckstein (1965, p. 136) states that "almost nothing careful and systematic has been written about the long-run social effects of internal war. . . . Little more is available on the determinants of success or failure in internal war." Focusing on analyses of revolution, Bienen (1968, p. 66) concludes: "None seem to have generalized about the effects of violence on change. In fact, once revolution is defined in terms of violence, emphasis shifts to explaining the kinds of change involved in revolution, sometimes in a circular way, but the place of violence per se seems neglected." Gamson (1975, p. 73) reaches a similar assessment: "There is no consensus on the set of conditions under which violence is a more or less effective strategy, and the issue has been seriously analyzed only in the international sphere." And finally, writing on the social movements that underlie a wider range of (not necessarily violent) collective behavior, Marx and Wood (1975, p. 403) report: "Most statements about the consequences of social movements are primarily descriptive or taxonomic. The systematic study of social movement consequences is much less developed than that of the prior conditions that give rise to movements." It therefore appears as if the status of research on racial disorder consequences is characteristic of a large gap in the analysis of various forms of collective action and violence.

Toward a Theoretical and Empirical Agenda
for Research on Violence and Social Change

We are currently undertaking a systematic empirical examination of the relationship between racial violence and dimensions of change in American cities from 1960 to 1975. We believe that there are strong warrants for such an investigation in its own right—including its plausible relevance to important public policy issues (e.g., changes in racial inequality and urban ills), the exceptional quality of data on racial violence and U.S. cities, and its potential influence on future official responses to disorder.[6] But, though we will consistently cite the case of racial disorders for illustrative purposes, our intent is not to report empirical results.

Instead, our major purpose in this paper is to specify broader theoretical, strategic, and methodological issues (including problems and tractable solutions) in the analysis of violence and social change. In particular, we explain the general neglect of this relationship in previous work; suggest theoretical complementarities between resource mobilization perspectives (versus other approaches) and the study of violence and its outcome; provide strong substantive reasons why the investigation of consequences should be incorporated into the mainstream of research on social movements, collective violence, and related forms of action; and develop an analytic model for this incorporation. Perhaps most important, we intend this model to be a *general framework* for the analysis of collective action and social change, that is, general in the sense that it can address a variety of forms of collective action, violent or otherwise. Therefore, we will treat violence as one of a range of available "tactics" rather than as a separate phenomenon of interest per se. In summary, we plan to indicate how analyses of violence and its outcome may be integrated with the central concerns of mobilization research.

However, our objectives are not limited to demonstrating importance and relevance. Conducting research on the consequences of collective action and violence requires consideration of several additional issues. Therefore, we also deal with potential conceptual pitfalls—for example, what are salient dimensions of social change? can apparently spontaneous phenomena such as racial disorders be approached with the same framework as action undertaken by clearly organized collectivities? And, because the few previous analyses of violence and change often manifest empirical difficulties, we present methodological guidelines that encompass strategies of research design and data collection. We aim toward making the analysis of outcome empirically as well as theoretically tractable.

THEORETICAL DEVELOPMENT

Violence and Social Change: Sources of Neglect

It is difficult to attribute the neglect of the relationship between violence and its consequences either to lack of importance—this issue's salience for both rebels and authorities is obvious (Russell, 1974, pp. 4–5)—or to the primary concern with "causes" of violence that is generally seen as the major reason for ignoring outcomes (Bienen, 1968; Russell, 1974). Instead, this inattention is more fundamentally related to assumptions in theories of the occurrence of violence and consequent conceptual difficulties in extending them to explanations of outcome. In this context, we briefly illustrate the (generally unrecognized) implications of three major lines of argument concerning the causes of "collective behavior" (including violent forms): (1) rapid change/social disorganization approaches (Kerr et al., 1960; Smelser, 1963; Johnson, 1966); (2) relative deprivation arguments (Davies, 1962; Gurr, 1970); and (3) resource mobilization formulations (McCarthy and Zald, 1973b; Oberschall, 1973; Tilly, 1970, 1975; Gamson, 1975). We assume readers' familiarity with these theories (see Tilly, 1975; Useem, 1975, for divisions similar to ours and detailed treatments of relevant literatures), and therefore do not explicate them here.

For our purposes of considering their implications for the study of violence and social change, the first two lines of inquiry may be linked together. Whether violent action is attributed to anomie and dislocation or to frustration and anger, the alleged participants (see Caplan, 1970; McPhail, 1971, for contrary evidence) are unassimilated and/or "marginal" individuals whose behavior tends to lack legitimacy in the established political and normative order. Therefore, violence that evolves from disorganization or frustration is usually treated as meaningless and irrational insofar as its main function is "tension release" (see Berkowitz, 1965; Currie and Skolnick, 1970). Tilly (1975, p. 493) makes the criticism that deprivation and disorganization theories exclude "purely instrumental accounts of rebellion, in which violence is simply the most efficient means available in accomplishing some collective end." And Ted Gurr, probably the most influential macropolitical frustration-aggression theorist, reaffirms such a characterization: "Frustration-instigated behavior is distinguished from goal-directed behavior by a number of characteristics: it tends to be fixed and compulsive; it is not necessarily deterred by punishment which may increase the degree of frustration; it takes the form most readily available, *little influenced by anticipated consequences"* (Gurr, 1970:34–35; emphasis added). In summary, two major approaches to the determinants of violence and related collective phenomena definitionally reject the relevance of violence to its structural consequences.[7]

Conversely, mobilization theories are in principle more applicable to investigating outcomes of violence because they stress the *instrumental* pursuit of common *goals* that are often *contested* by other groups. These are all dimensions that at least make possible (1) the specification of objective and substantively meaningful consequences of violence (via goals: cf. Gamson, 1975); (2) the location of this process squarely in the "everyday" study of politics and of social change; and (3) a rudimentary conceptual framework that implies that the results of violent (and other kinds of) action depend on the relative power and strategies of the parties involved. But, despite some recent exceptions (Gamson, 1975; Snyder and Kelly, 1976b), these complementarities have not stimulated much theoretical or empirical analysis, perhaps because of difficulties in representing "power" (or resource mobilization itself) and "strategies" in nonexperimental settings (Tilly, 1970; Marx and Wood, 1975).

Mobilization, Collective Action, and Outcome: Some Crucial Interconnections

Even in the context of mobilization theories, questions of outcome remain largely separate from efforts to isolate the "causes" of social movements, protest, and violence. However, it may be demonstrated that the two issues *must* be explicitly linked for the informed treatment of either. We have elsewhere argued that the consequences of violence cannot be properly understood or analyzed without reference to its determinants, and urged an approach that specifies "the preconditions, occurrence and consequences of violence as a temporal process in which consequences depend on the preconditions as well as the violence itself" (Snyder and Kelly, 1976b, p. 134).

However, we are now prepared to venture considerably beyond that earlier argument for interrelated analyses of violence and its outcome: specifically, we also maintain that *the investigation of consequences is critically important for understanding the determinants of changes in the extent and form of (sometimes violent) collective action, including how resources are mobilized and applied.* Our discussion of the rationale underlying this statement will be aided if we initially make two distinctions: first, between social movements and social movement organizations, or SMOs (see Zald and Ash, 1966); and second, between these SMOs (which we consider to be the units of analysis for present purposes) and collective protest or violence (which we treat as "events" conceptually discrete from but involving SMOs).[8] Consider a simple sequence specified by mobilization perspectives and bearing strong resemblance to the "life histories" of the groups studied by Gamson (1975): Movement organizations (1) "emerge" (i.e., come into being with certain goals); (2) mobilize resources to varying degrees; (3) apply those resources in some form(s) of collective action, the magnitude of which should vary (net of other factors such as the responses of authorities) positively with the level of resources controlled;[9] and (4) differentially experience success or failure on certain objective criteria (usually those goals articulated by the organization at its outset).

Beginning with this linear process suggests at least three ways in which such group-specific outcomes or goals [10] are immediately relevant to (or "feed back" on) the current core concerns of mobilization research (i.e., steps 1, 2, and 3 above):

1. *The type and extent of outcome (achievement of goals) will affect the level of resources mobilized by the collectivity.* For example, failure or even success in attaining limited objectives may result in demobilization (Zald and Ash, 1966; Tilly, 1970), often to the point of group collapse (see Gamson, 1975, pp. 145–53). Conversely, certain types of tactics resulting in successful outcomes will increase collective control over resources in either of two ways: (1) via a concentrated flow from a *centralized* source, such as a new political party tapping into the federal election campaign funds; or (2) via an *aggregation* of resources extracted from a number of smaller units. Probably the most typical case in point is the recruitment of additional members after a successful outcome—for example, the possibility of workers joining unions after successful strikes. This importance of outcomes to subsequent mobilization levels is also consistent with "risk-reward" models of movement recruitment or participation (Oberschall, 1973). Although such models may not faithfully represent recruitment processes in all movements, it seems reasonable to suppose that the previous outcome of group action constitutes a large component of the more or less rational calculations attributed to potential members.[11]

2. *The type and extent of outcome (achievement of goals) will affect the forms of collective action ("strategies") that groups undertake.* Assuming that "ultimate" goals have not been achieved, the acquisition of resources generated by a successful outcome (see above) ought to increase a group's *capacity* for collective action and permit more "expensive" strategies than were previously possible.[12] Consequences may also affect forms of action because success or failure can produce a qualitative shift in the organization itself (Zald and Ash, 1966). For example, Marx and Wood (1975, p. 394) note that "Sects become churches. Successful revolutionaries can become the old guard." But

whereas they invoke such changes in organizations over time as *impedi-ments* to generalizations about movement dynamics, we view such shifts as both an opportunity and a warrant to bring outcomes into theory construction concerning why such changes in collectivities and their actions occur.

3. *The type and extent of outcome will affect not only the level of resources and the form of collective action, but also the relationship between them.* For example, Tilly's (1970, 1975) arguments concerning the importance of groups' national political positions indicate that (1) among "contenders for power" there should be a positive relationship between resource mobilization and their degrees of involvement in collective violence, but (2) once groups have achieved "polity membership" they should disappear from the ranks of the unruly (regardless of their resource level), because alternative means of influence are then open to them. Snyder's (1975) studies of fluctuations in a different form of collective action (industrial strike activity), particularly in the United States, provide empirical evidence of such a shift in the very relationship between mobilization (measured by union membership) and strikes. Alterations in the position of the American labor movement around World War II result in a change from a strong positive relationship between unionization and strikes before the war to the absence of any association in the postwar period. The general point is that researchers analyzing the effects of mobilization on either violence or strike activity would be confused by such results if they were unaware of the discontinuous impact of outcome on the relationship between these two central variables.

Although all the foregoing points are at least implicit in writing on social movements and related phenomena, their relevance to the central issues of mobilization research has not, to our knowledge, been so explicitly recognized. However, we wish to proceed further in our claims for the importance of outcome—and not incidentally, to develop a more appealing analytic model—by relaxing a widely employed but largely mistaken assumption in the above (and others') treatment of these issues. We have considered the feedback effects of success or failure in achieving goals on "earlier" steps (e.g., mobilization, collective action) as if there is only a single outcome in the sequence for any group (or at best a series of goals that shift only at long intervals). This "single-outcome-as-goal" model also characterizes all quantitative studies of the consequences of protest or violence (e.g., Gamson, 1975; Russell, 1974; Shorter and Tilly, 1971; Snyder and Kelly, 1976b). But such a model for analyzing consequences merely reflects the limitation that outcome data tend to be available at only one time, usually in terms of the group's articulated goals. This single-outcome-as-goal model is generally not the result of any theoretical considerations (with the exception of Gamson,

1975) and will be highly misleading for attempts to incorporate consequences into analyses of social movement dynamics. The relevant outcomes of collective action are *not* only those long-range objectives that are articulated by groups and perceived by their members and constituents. In fact, movement organizations (as do all groups) routinely experience relative success or failure on various dimensions as a consequence of their everyday activities. For example, most organizations will rarely articulate increases in size or wealth as goals for the organization itself (though they may indicate that benefits for their individual members are desired objectives). Yet success in acquiring collective control over members (loyalties), money, and less tangible resources should be critically important for the organization's capacity to pursue and achieve its longer-run goals.[13]

Our treatment therefore specifies "outcome" as a general category, of which group goals (which are necessarily articulated, perceived, and usually longer run) are a conceptually distinct and restricted type (though "goals" and "outcomes" may converge empirically in particular instances). In light of this distinction, we outline an analytic framework for incorporating the study of violence and its consequences directly into research on social movements and other forms of collective action.

An Analytic Model

Social movements and their organizations do not necessarily, or even typically, move through a (nearly) linear sequence in which there is a single outcome (or at most a few). Instead, they are entities that persist through time,[14] during which they *continually mobilize resources, apply them in various forms of collective action or "tactics," and experience the consequences of those strategies in a fully interrelated process that also affects subsequent "rounds" of mobilization, action, and outcome.*[15] Figure 1 presents a heuristic diagram of this fully interrelated model and contrasts it with the linear sequence of single-outcome model (i.e., outcomes as goals) usually employed. The circled letters designate linkages in the process in order to facilitate discussion: *A* indicates the emergence of an SMO to the point where we can identify it as such. Such identification necessarily means an original nonzero accumulation of resources (Tilly, 1970). *B* merely represents an already elaborated point, that the range and magnitude of a group's collective actions are constrained by (among other factors) its prior resource mobilization. *D* indicates that the repertoire of actions utilized will generate objective outcomes, and *C* that such outcomes depend on the potential "strength" of a group as well as on its actions (e.g., the same threat will more likely be effective if made by a group able to carry it through). *E* represents the effect of prior outcome(s) on the subsequent level of resource mobili-

Figure 1 *Heuristic Diagrams of Models That Incorporate Outcomes of (Sometimes Violent) into the Analysis of Mobilization Processes*

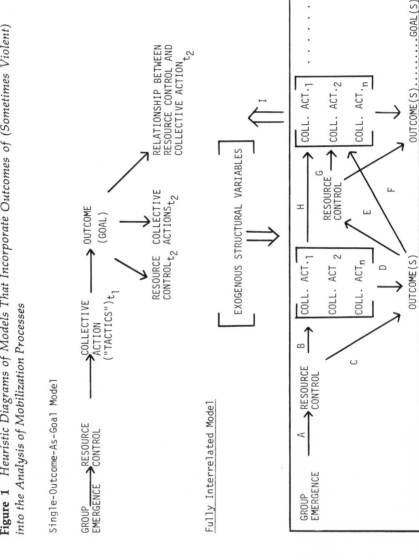

Single-Outcome-As-Goal Model

Fully Interrelated Model

zation by the group. *Note the important point that collective actions or strategies affect subsequent resource levels only through their success (or failure) in generating favorable consequences.* Letters F, G, and H respectively indicate (1) the effects of prior outcomes on subsequent collective actions (e.g., the hypotheses that previous failures will produce change in tactics, and successes either a continuation of similar strategies or escalation to more expensive ones); (2) the same argument made above for B;[16] and (3) that, net of "learning" from previous outcomes and the current level of resource control, the current range of collective actions depends in part on prior tactics. Thus, the H linkage allows the possibility that changes in tactics, even when they are "objectively" warranted, may not occur, because leaders blindly commit themselves to certain strategies or because such changes may be organizationally costly to institute. This model specifies continued interaction of all these factors until "ultimate" goals are achieved and/or the organization ceases to exist. It also permits possible "structural" changes as consequences of collective actions (I); we later develop further this distinction between "systemic" consequences and the group-specific outcomes. Finally, we recognize that structural factors exogenous to groups themselves will affect all components and linkages in the model we have described. Included among such variables would be governmental repression, aggregate economic fluctuations, and so on. Despite their importance, we give these variables only token mention because their influence is hardly at issue and space limitations preclude more detailed consideration here.

An Extension: Collective Action and Outcomes Independent of Movement Organizations

Our analytic model has been developed thus far on the assumption that collective actions are always at least minimally coordinated by some identifiable movement organization. In many instances—for example, the case of labor movements and workers' collective actions—this assumption is not open to dispute. But in others—racial disorders constitute a prime example—there is no clear organizational basis for the collective action (e.g., National Advisory Commission, 1968). That such apparently spontaneous events imply difficulties for applying our model should not be surprising—our treatment derives from "classical" mobilization theories, which have not themselves been particularly successful in explaining racial disorders or similar events. But, as we have argued for the general utility of our model, we indicate how apparently spontaneous collective action can, with some modification, be incorporated in our framework.

Current mobilization theories were developed in part to account for what has since been designated "the assembling process" (McPhail and Miller, 1973; Weller and Quarantelli, 1973)—that is, how individuals come together in time and space to participate collectively in often large-scale events. Mobilization arguments imply a "centralized" type of assembling process: a formal organization instructs its members to participate in a particular collective action (e.g., a demonstration) at a given time and place. But assembling also occurs via a different mechanism (e.g., in racial disorders). McPhail and Miller (1973) plausibly argue that certain episodes themselves (hostile police-citizen encounters, in this case) constitute nonverbal cues or "instructions" to assemble for individuals in visual or aural proximity. Participants are also "mobilized" indirectly, through verbal instructions transmitted via informal networks (person A telephones B, who in turn contacts C, D, and E). Events based on this type of "situational assembling" process do not require organizational capacity (in the conventional sense) for collective action. Instead, they depend on a combination of precipitating episodes and, more importantly, the distribution of persons and activities across time and space in a given ecological unit (cf. McPhail and Miller, 1973).

These considerations indicate that our framework should encompass two discrete levels of analysis: (1) the movement organizations that generate certain forms of collective action, and (2) the ecological units that underlie other ("spontaneous") forms of action. In the latter case, some modification of the variables in the model presented in figure 1 is required to conform to the ecological level analysis: "group emergence" is replaced by "existing ecological units"; "resources controlled" (by groups) must be reconceptualized as the "conduciveness" of the ecological unit for collective action (in terms of communication patterns among members, the "density" of individuals with certain preferences for change, and probably the individual resources of members of the population). We are therefore arguing that the characteristics of ecological units are analogous to the control of resources by organized groups insofar as both determine (in conjunction with structural variables) the probability of collective action. Finally, "outcomes" must be formulated to refer to aggregate success or failure of certain social categories (e.g., blacks) in this context of "exclusive" membership rather than the "inclusive" type that is more characteristic of movement organizations (cf. Olson, 1965). But, despite the necessity of modifying the *variables* in the model to conform to ecological units of analysis, we maintain that the important linkages or *relationships* need not be altered to investigate these processes in the case of spontaneous collective action.

Substantive Advantages

The most general benefit of our model is that it locates the analysis of violence and its consequences in a wider concern with the relationship of collective action to social change. It suggests a movement away from questions such as, Is violence effective? and toward those inquiring, Under what conditions are various tactics of collective action relatively more or less effective in generating the outcomes that aid or hinder groups in accomplishing their collective goals?

More specifically, this framework should also be useful for addressing issues concerning the waxing and (especially) waning of particular forms of collective action. In studies of violence, little attention has been given to why it terminates; in the case of racial disorders, there has been no adequate explanation of the "riot wind-down" (Masotti, n.d.) that occurred after 1969 (or 1968, if we consider large magnitude and intensity to be defining criteria). Among several possibilities (see Masotti, n.d., for a more complete range of alternatives) are recognition by blacks that violence was not an efficacious strategy or (conversely) some attainment of collective goals and resultant shift to other (nonviolent) tactics. In either case, knowledge of the outcome of violence would be necessary to explain the termination of disorder.

Another application (this one at the level of the movement organization) is in understanding different "career patterns" of organizations: for example, immediate collapse; dramatic expansion from an originally small resource base, as a function of "pyramiding" a sequence of highly successful strategies into large amounts of resource control; oscillation in resource acquisition (within limiting boundaries of "ultimate" success or collapse) as series of successful tactics are followed by strategic blunders, and so on.

We are of course aware of the major limitation of our proposed approach: the appropriate longitudinal data for empirical specification are not in most cases available. But we have proceeded on the grounds that this situation is preferable to that in which we would be limited in our arguments by the types of information that are easily gathered. Moreover, our later treatment suggests feasible (if labor-intensive) methods for collecting the requisite information, and one possibility for employing currently available data.

STRATEGIC ISSUES

Establishing the importance of studying collective action and social change and developing an analytic model do not themselves deal with conceptual/methodological issues or problems that characterize past research and will arise in the future investigations we hope to stimulate. We identify several such issues, discuss their implications for analyses of outcome, and offer strategies for resolving difficulties.

Dimensions of Social Change or Outcome

Lack of agreement on and indiscriminate use of the term "social change," both generally and in conjunction with collective action/ violence, poses two problems for research in this area: (1) specifying what *types* of change are under investigation, and (2) selecting substantively important indicators from a potentially much broader set of data. In the extreme, some analysts fail to consider the occurrence and consequences of violence as conceptually distinct variables (e.g., note confounding of the two in definitions of revolution in Brinton, 1938, and by revolutionaries themselves: see Bienen, 1968; Tilly, 1975, for discussion). For purposes of designating types of change to be examined, the cross-classification of the outcome versus goal and group-specific versus systemic distinctions we have mentioned specifies four dimensions.[17] Group-specific outcomes apply to movement organizations or to a broader constituency associated with a movement (e.g., all workers or all blacks). For example, in our study of racial disorder consequences, changes in the economic, housing, and political resources (or "status") of blacks are group-specific. Systemic outcomes are shifts in the characteristics of the broader units of social organization within which collective action/violence occurs (in our study, U.S. urban areas; e.g., to what extent is "white flight" from cities attributable to violence?). Gamson's (1975) challengers all provide examples of group-specific goals; though systemic goals (especially changes in them) are more difficult to identify, the shift in objectives of the Japanese political elite after the Meiji Restoration is a case in point.

We stress that the foregoing classification is merely a crude heuristic device to distinguish relevant types of change. Certain consequences fall in more than a single category; for example, changes in black political representation (measured by the percentage of all elected officials) are both group-specific and systemic. Despite the crudeness of the categorization, we make these distinctions in order to emphasize that "social change" is multidimensional and that assessments of the effects of violence on outcomes and/or goals—particularly when the latter are defined in terms of "success" or "failure"—necessitate examination of multiple dimensions. Conclusions of "no change" may well be mistaken if they are based on a highly restricted set of outcomes. To take a hypothetical example from the analysis of racial disorder consequences (but one that loosely conforms to some of our preliminary empirical results), it might appear as if the disorders had no effect on the resources (or "status") of blacks, as measured by such conventional economic indicators as income or unemployment. Conversely, investigation of less obvious "second order" linkages—running from greater "white flight" to increased central city political representation in disorder cities—might produce an opposite conclusion, particularly if in the slightly longer run blacks will also experience increased economic welfare in those cities where they have stronger political bases.

Despite this rationale for investigating multidimensional outcomes of violence, analyses of this issue continue to employ single or highly restricted measures of consequences. We have also been guilty on this count (Snyder and Kelly, 1976b), and we recognize that such difficulties are often due strictly to the unavailability of requisite information. But we suspect that, at least sometimes, limited data are employed precisely because researchers tend to conceptualize outcome in unidimensional terms.[18] And we view this issue of outcome multidimensionality as particularly important because we suspect that the divergent results of the few empirical studies of violence and its consequences are partly caused by differences in the types of outcome considered.[19]

Determining Relevant Goals and Outcomes

Recognizing the multidimensionality of change does not directly deal with the related issue of choosing substantively meaningful indicators of goals and outcomes. The severity of the problems associated with determining goals varies considerably according to the context within which collective action takes place. For example, Gamson's (1975) analysis concerns the relation between violence and change for groups involved in an ongoing process of political contention. The conceptual advantage in Gamson's analysis is that the goals of the group are known *a priori* and, in fact, constitute the reason for the group's existence in the first place. A similar advantage is evident in many analyses of events; for example, the outcomes of labor-management disputes (the success, compromise, or failure of workers' stated demands) are regularly recorded (Snyder and Kelly, 1976b). In general, it appears that identifying goals from groups' articulated aims is straightforward when an organizational base underlies collective action. However, because such action does not necessarily occur in the context of a formal organizational structure, we must isolate strategies for determining relevant goals in apparently spontaneous situations.

Because inferences concerning the intentions of participants in violence are subject to various sources of contamination (e.g., observer bias, post facto rationalization, or politicization of violence), other means of determining goals must be established. A first possibility is that, in some cases, knowledge of the "causes" can provide clues to relevant goals of collective action. That is, if the causes of a particular event or series of episodes were found to be "economic," then economic variables could be justified as measures of those actions' goals.[20] Of course, not all analyses of collective action generate substantive explanations that are similar enough to specify relevant goals in clear fashion. For example, the only consistent findings concerning the causes of racial disorders in the 1960s are the influence of nonwhite population size and the differential probability of occurrence by region, which suggest that a different strategy is necessary in such cases.[21]

A final method of ascertaining goals, which relies on empirical findings that tend to be less ambiguous than analyses of causes, has two aspects. One involves attempts to determine grievances as indicators of community goals, either via post-riot surveys (e.g., National Advisory Commission, 1968) or, preferably, using fortuitously available evidence of grievances for the population at risk *prior* to the occurrence of protest or violence (see Morgan and Clark, 1973, for a cogent example).[22] The other strategy would base interpretations of events and consequent inferences concerning goals on examinations of riot processes. For example, analyses of the form of racial disorders, such as the selective and restrained patterns of violence, supports the conclusion that they were political protests aimed at redressing grievances rather than emotional outbursts (e.g., Fogelson, 1971; Olson, 1971; Berk and Aldrich, 1972). Because such conclusions can be evaluated with objective data, they are probably more valid than the official interpretations that reflected "vested interests" (Lipsky and Olson, 1969).[23]

Obviously, none of these types of data or methods for isolating group goals in the context of ecological analyses will be available in all instances, or definitive in most. But cases such as racial disorders, which generate convergent research on causes, grievances, and form, will at least provide certain indications of goals for ecological analyses of the consequences of collective action.

In principle, specification of group-specific outcomes (as distinct from goals) of collective action is subject to fewer ambiguities and strategies because it involves only a single conceptual mandate. Researchers need "only" compile an exhaustive list of resources such that success or failure in acquiring them has consequences for the capacity (of organizations or ecological units) to undertake further collective action. In practice, these procedures are fraught with difficulties, as mobilization researchers well know. We could, of course, present a list of successful outcomes, but it would be seriously incomplete and biased toward those standard items (increases in money or members) that are more tangible and easier to measure. The major burden of further delineating group-specific outcomes falls back on mobilization theory itself, which is sorely in need of more coherent substantive mapping of "resources" and greater attention to measurement issues.

Finally, relevant "systemic" outcomes are probably most difficult to identify because (with the exception of official organizational responses) there is little theoretical guidance to indicate what is typically important or how it is affected by collective action or violence. In this sense, such systemic consequences are conceptualized as "by-products" of collective action and are likely to be selected on ad hoc bases. For example, Masotti (n.d.) notes that the rate of migration out from U.S. cities increased dramatically between 1966 and 1968 (the years of especially frequent and severe racial violence), a finding that focuses attention on these and related (e.g., commercial outflows) demographic processes. Though such consequences may be important for understanding U.S. urban ills in the 1960s and 1970s, this method hardly constitutes a systematic or rigorous approach to systemic outcomes.

Dimensions of Collective Action: Differential Effects on Consequences

The conceptualization and measurement of collective action (specifically protest and violent conflict) ranges from simple frequency (e.g., Gamson, 1975; Spilerman, 1970) to more complex indexes of severity or intensity (e.g., Spilerman, 1976; Morgan and Clark, 1973) to analyses of the "form" of violence (e.g., Snyder and Kelly, 1976b, which considers differential consequences according to the targets of industrial violence). Although this multidimensionality is often recognized in principle, with few exceptions it is ignored in studies of violence and its outcome. We particularly urge more attention to "form," which has been severely neglected in previous work. Form of violence, as we consider it here, goes beyond the distinction of targets (Snyder and Kelly, 1976b) and encompasses the strategies or tactics employed (e.g., for racial violence, form would include sniping, looting, vandalism, personal versus property damage, etc.).

There are several reasons for distinguishing among the effects of these dimensions. First, a major assumption (or untested hypothesis) underlying the use of simple frequency is that all events meeting some operational definition are homogeneous in their effects. This assumption is limiting to the degree that events of varying magnitude or severity are treated as equivalent. In empirical analyses, the heterogeneity of events (as well as their distribution) could be expected to have important influences on variations in outcome. For example, a plausible expectation is that cities experiencing larger, more severe disorders would also experience greater rates of "white flight" than cities with smaller, more contained riots, holding frequency constant.

Second, many analyses that employ severity (e.g., Spilerman, 1976; Wanderer, 1968) as a dimension of collective action include (weighted) qualitative variables (i.e., presence or absence of sniping, looting, vandalism, etc.) that might reflect the form (as noted above) of action, rather than severity.[24] The differential effect of form and severity is an empirical question; however, differences on theoretical grounds could again be expected. For example, disorders that were essentially expressive outbursts might stimulate reactions such as "white flight," whereas more selective, economically oriented riots might tend to result in local economic reform programs. In general, such considerations strongly suggest simultaneous examination of these conceptually and empirically discrete dimensions of violence (frequency, severity, and form) with respect to the outcomes under investigation.

Proper Specification of Empirical Models

Here we identify two major sources of (and strategic solutions for) specification errors—that is, those caused by omission of relevant variables—which may result in spurious conclusions in empirical analyses of collective action and social change. Although this issue may be obvious, we emphasize it because (primarily bivariate) cross-tabular analyses dominate previous work (Gamson, 1975; Shorter and Tilly, 1971; Russell, 1974).

One common source of such error is implied in our conceptualization of the determinants, outbreak, and consequences of violence as an interrelated process. Thus, to the degree that the determinants and consequences of collective action are themselves empirically related, omission of the determinants in models that estimate the effect of collective action on outcome will result in an overstatement or understatement (depending on particular conditions; Theil, 1971, p. 393) of the relationship between collective action and social change. The obvious strategy is to control for the determinants of collective action when estimating such empirical models, although this procedure is often difficult because it presupposes knowledge of such determinants.

A second source of specification error involves omission of exogenous determinants of social change.[25] Once again, the only tractable solution is to find well-specified models of the causes of such changes and to include them in the analysis. Although such models occasionally exist (e.g., in the case of racial violence consequences, there has been a great deal of work—though for other purposes—on sources of change in American cities), in most cases they will not be readily available. However, such difficulties cannot be ignored. Until both sources of error are adequately addressed, they will continue to vitiate the results and conclusions of analyses of the effects of collective action on outcome.

DESIGNING RESEARCH ON COLLECTIVE ACTION AND ITS OUTCOME

We now consider some strategic essentials for designing and conducting research on these issues, separately for the organizational and ecological analyses specified earlier. Before doing so, we want to dismiss a third unit of analysis—the individual event (Snyder and Kelly, 1976b; Shorter and Tilly, 1971)—on two grounds. First, the use of events is extremely limited because it permits assessment only of immediate, group-specific consequences. Examination of (often substantively more important) longer-run and/or systemic outcomes are necessarily precluded. A second problem with this event strategy is that collective action is treated as a necessary component of the process of change; that is, one is unable to study situations where change occurs but collective action does not (see Bienen, 1968, p. 104, which cautions against making change contingent on violence). Although analogous errors are possible with other units of analysis—for example, studying outcomes only in riot cities, as the National Advisory Commission (1968) did—such errors are avoidable if other units are employed (e.g., comparing outcomes in cities that experienced disorders with those in cities that did not). Consequently, events are far less appropriate for analyzing outcomes of collective action than are organizational or ecological units.

Studying Outcomes of Movement Organizations

Gamson's (1975) study represents a strategic advance that need only be modified in certain respects for compatibility with our analytic model. Gamson collects information on an unbiased sample of all collectivities in the United States, from 1800 through 1945, which meet his operational definition of a challenging group.[26] His procedures include reading a variety of historical accounts to generate a list of protest groups; sampling from that list; excluding groups if they do not qualify as challengers; and using the accounts for information on group characteristics (e.g., size, goals, involvement in violence) and the outcome of the political challenge.

Gamson's strategy would, for purposes of using our analytic framework, be ideal except for one considerable drawback—information on each group is culled exclusively from historical accounts. These accounts are quite sketchy, as they are likely to be for any random sample of groups. Therefore, use of such secondary sources will not provide data on most resources. More important, the temporal dimension is attenuated because information on resource mobilization, collective action, and outcomes (as distinct from goals) is not available at regular period-to-period intervals, and regularity is a necessity for implementing our model in empirical research.

This assessment indicates that modifications of Gamson's strategy must proceed in directions that will develop far richer detail of information while preserving the essential design of following groups over time. Such information can be gathered only by relying on internally generated data sources of the groups under study—for example, membership lists, financial statements, and related types of records [27]—and on such sources as newspapers for evidence of collective actions. This strategy will require "samples of convenience," that is, explicitly choosing groups for which the appropriate information is either known or likely to exist over a relatively long time span.

The obvious cost of this modification, as Gamson (1975, pp. 22–23) notes, is that well-documented groups are more likely to be highly mobilized and successful (or in some cases, "interesting failures"). Although the importance of detailed information for our purposes arguably outweighs the need for representativeness, it would (with enormous effort) be possible to incorporate both benefits in a "mixed" research design: the presence of sampling bias per se is not problematic; difficulties arise in the (usual) circumstance that the direction and extent of the bias are unknown. With a known bias, observations on the sampled units (groups) can be weighted in analyses, according to each unit's true proportion in the population. With these considerations in mind, researchers could implement Gamson's methods to define the entire population of groups and make some rough assessments (from secondary accounts) of characteristics such as size, success, and so on for a sample of them. Data would then be collected for a second sample of well-documented groups, as suggested here. Analyses of the latter would be weighted according to differences in comparable characteristics of the biased and unbiased samples.

By no means do we claim that these procedures will be anything but labor-intensive and costly. Nevertheless, they are feasible. In fact, one crude but tractable empirical specification of our general model for groups with available data might come from time-series analyses of industrial strike activity (see Shorter and Tilly, 1974; Hibbs, 1974; Snyder, 1975, for reviews of relevant literatures, data, and technical procedures). Using union membership as a rough indicator of resource mobilization and strikes as a measure of collective action and information on the success of industrial conflict, researchers could begin to construct and estimate models of the form proposed here. Moreover, several studies identify exogenous sources of variation in these factors, so that the dangers of model misspecification we have discussed would be minimized. Despite these possibilities, we suspect that such studies at the organizational level will be outweighed in the foreseeable future by ecological analyses because of the far greater availability of data for the latter.

Studying Outcomes by Employing Ecological Units: Contemporary American Racial Violence as an Exemplary Case

The potential difficulties in ecological analyses of apparently spontaneous collective action and social change (e.g., necessarily indirect assessments of relevant goals) are offset by certain strategic opportunities. These are particularly advantageous in the case of racial violence outcomes, as we indicate in the context of outlining general procedures for conducting areal research on collective action and social change. However, the research design we propose is not intended to "test" all aspects of the model developed earlier. For example, we assume that the mechanisms that facilitate assembling for collective action, as well as preferences for change, operate as described (see McPhail and Miller, 1973, for empirical support). Because ecological analyses are undertaken at rather high levels of aggregation, they necessarily involve assumptions about underlying processes.

SPECIFIC UNIT OF ANALYSIS. The two greatest advantages of employing ecological units are that (1) data are more readily available for them than for groups, and (2) researchers are able to compare a large number of cases with wide variation in both collective action and dimensions of change. The choice of a specific unit of analysis in ecological studies should take into account these practical advantages, as well as certain conceptual considerations—such as what areal units define the "population at risk" for having participated in collective action or violence. For example, our study of racial disorder consequences examines the universe of cities in the United States that had a minimum population of twenty-five thousand in 1960 (cf. Spilerman, 1970). Several of the factors cited above dictate the choice of cities (defined by political boundaries) rather than some larger unit, such as Standard Metropolitan Statistical Areas (SMSAs). The latter are composed of many discrete, heterogeneous social, economic, and political units (Hill, 1974a), and their use would preclude analysis of whether *local* characteristics affect the violence-change relationship (e.g., how do local governments respond to disorder?). Additionally, because the probability of disorder is positively related to nonwhite, and thus total, population (Spilerman, 1970), SMSAs would tend to oversample large, more severe disorders, thereby restricting the variation in violence. Finally, given the continued concentration of blacks in central cities, these areas are more appropriate boundaries for the population at risk for having participated in violence. Consequently, studies of disorder probability (Spilerman, 1970) are undertaken on a city basis and provide strong (though not necessarily substantively interesting) empirical models of structural determinants for inclusion in analyses of outcome.

DATA. The requisite data for ecological analyses are (1) measures of outcome at a minimum of two time points (in order to assess change) for the included areas; (2) information concerning the form(s) of action under investigation; and (3) measures of the determinants of variation in the form of action and in the outcomes of interest. Of course, indicators of collective action should intervene temporarily between "baseline" and "later" measures of outcome.

Measures of relevant changes (and control variables) are generally available in standard statistical yearbooks (for example, the *County and City Data Book, Municipal Yearbook,* and decennial censuses compile a wide variety of city characteristics). The particular advantage of analyzing racial violence consequences in this setting is that previous empirical studies of changes in American cities have specified the determinants of many of the group-specific and systemic outcomes of interest (e.g., Hill, 1974b, on racial differences in income; Hodge, 1973, on unemployment differentials). Information on collective action will (typically) be derived from standard newspaper and related sources, and needs no extended discussion. However, we do point out that racial disorder data meet the two important criteria for use in this type of analysis: detail (to assess impacts of different dimensions of violence) and validity (see Snyder and Kelly, 1977a, for more complete treatment of this issue).

ANALYTIC TECHNIQUES. In most cases, the availability of data on outcome at only two (or at most a few widely spaced) points in time will dictate the use of a panel analysis of areas in which the difference between the measures of outcome (as an indicator of change) is assessed as a function of collective action occurring in the interval. However, where the requisite data exist (as they occasionally do in the case of racial disorder outcomes), a pooled cross-sectional/time-series design (i.e., where the city-year is the unit of analysis) is optimal. More confidence can be placed in causal relationships inferred between violence and its consequences concerning the timing of change in a pooled analysis.[28] Moreover, a cross-sectional/time-series framework avoids one possible source of accepting the null hypothesis (that violence has no effect on outcome) that is inherent in a simple panel design. In the latter, no empirical effects of violence on outcome could mean either that (1) violence is indeed unimportant in generating change, or that (2) violence is important, but its effects are distributed uniformly across the ecological units (cf. Spilerman, 1970, for a related conclusion on the structural determinants of disorder). Incorporating year-to-year fluctuations in the analysis would permit researchers to test such a hypothesis and, in addition, would obviously facilitate examination of temporal lags in the relationship between violence and its consequences. We do not maintain that detailed enough data will always be available to support such analyses, or that these procedures will in any way substitute for careful theoretical statements on the impacts of collective action and violence. However, the strategies outlined here will at least allow researchers to begin to approach these long-neglected issues in appropriate fashion.

SUMMARY AND CONCLUSIONS

Because we have traversed a good deal of ground, we will reiterate our major conclusions for added emphasis:

1. The relationship between violence (more broadly, collective action) and social change or outcome has been neglected, though not for the "obvious" reasons of primary concern with the "causes" of these phenomena.
2. Resource mobilization theories lend themselves (more so than alternative perspectives on collective action) to the analysis of violence and its outcome.
3. The analysis of outcome is not a peripheral issue but is centrally important to current core concerns of theories of resource mobilization and collective action. We have drawn on some of these interrelationships to develop a general analytic framework for the investigation of processes of mobilization, collective action, and consequences.
4. Empirical analyses of these issues must recognize and incorporate the multidimensionality of collective action and social change and take more care in specifying appropriate quantitative models of these processes.
5. Determining relevant goals and outcomes of collective action will be difficult. Part of the burden for further progress in this area lies with mobilization research itself; in particular, more attention to complete theoretical specification of "resources" and measurement issues is needed.
6. Finally, we have provided two exemplary designs for empirical research on collective action and outcome, separately for the movement organizations and ecological units of analysis that most appropriately address the issues of substantive interest.

However, we do not claim to have considered all relevant aspects of the analysis of collective action and social change. For example, we have avoided formulating concrete hypotheses concerning the conditions under which particular dimensions of collective action will generate specific types of change. In our assessment, further theoretical and empirical work is necessary before these hypotheses can be specified with any confidence; we expect that the conceptual and methodological guidelines we have provided will facilitate such efforts. We are obviously proceeding along these lines, but we hope that others will join us in attempting to make the analysis of violence and social change more tractable.

ENDNOTES

1. Evidence indicates that for "collective violence in general" such increases may be only apparent (Kirkham, Levy, and Crotty, 1970; Snyder and Tilly, 1972, p. 523; Tilly, 1969), though this is not necessarily the case for any given form of violence (e.g., the racial disturbances discussed below).

2. We base our conclusion concerning the peak levels of the 1960s violence on comparisons of our own data (Snyder and Kelly, 1977a) and those of Spilerman (1970, 1976) for this period with reports of studies of earlier times. The conclusion holds for each dimension *except* violence to persons (number killed). Disorders during the 1960s were, relative to earlier episodes, characterized by damage to property far more than to persons, a fact reflected in Janowitz's (1969) labeling of these events as "commodity riots."

3. Empirical investigations that attempt to address these issues are variously reported in survey analyses of attitudes and demographic characteristics of participants (see Caplan, 1970, and McPhail, 1971, for comprehensive summaries of this line of inquiry and its findings); city-level studies of the structural characteristics associated with disorder proneness (Spilerman, 1970, 1976; Morgan and Clark, 1973); and "natural histories" of riot processes (McPhail and Miller, 1973; Stark et al., 1974).

4. The latter types of response *may* signify *attempts* at change—although available evidence (Lipsky, 1968; Lipsky and Olson, 1973) indicates that commissions and official promises are more often strategic efforts to subvert implementation of reform policies.

5. We consider that these specifications of relevant consequences raise issues of greater substantive importance—that is, whether collective violence effectively facilitates various forms of "structural" change—than those concerned solely with symbolic responses. Therefore, our current treatment explicitly excludes (in addition to these symbolic actions) two types of outcome: (1) very temporary consequences, for example Quarantelli and Dynes's (1968) conceptualization of "looting as an index of social change" (though looting increased some blacks' consumer goods in the

very short run, this is a trivial form of economic change); and (2) psychological or attitudinal shifts of blacks and whites. The latter are important both theoretically (Coser, 1956) and in their direct relevance to American race relations (Myrdal, 1944). However, for present purposes we ignore the impact of disorder on these subjective dimensions because of practical limitations on scope and greater methodological problems in assessing such changes.

6. See Snyder and Kelly (1976a) for detailed discussion of these points. Briefly, the relevance of disorder to racial inequality, white flight from central cities, and so on is suggested by a gross temporal correlation between substantial changes in these factors (Farley and Hermalin, 1972; Urban America, Inc., 1969) and the onset of racial violence in the mid-1960s. Though this correspondence by no means proves causation, it does indicate a need for appropriate causal analyses. On the influence of academic findings on official policy in dealing with disorder, Skolnick (1969, p. 342) argues that social control rather than reform responses are partly due to social science characterizations of violence as "emotional outbursts." However, our confidence in this rationale for studying consequences of racial violence is admittedly not so great as in the others.

7. More precisely, we should point out that these assessments refer only to what we have designated "group-specific" consequences of violence. There are no assumptions in either of these arguments that necessarily preclude the study of "systemic" outcomes. We are grateful to Larry Isaac for raising this issue.

8. We temporarily ignore the issue of whether our arguments also apply in the case of "events" (collective actions) that have no clear organizational basis. We later address this question, but first we want to present our central arguments without pausing to make detailed qualifications.

9. "Resource mobilization" generally designates an *increase* in some unit's collective control over resources (Etzioni, 1968, pp. 388–89; Tilly, 1970). Our use of the phrases "level of mobilized resources" and "resource control" refers to the absolute *amount* of collectively controlled resources *at a single point in time*, but can be easily adjusted to the standard definition by considering differences in the level of mobilized resources over any given time interval.

10. We will subsequently make a very important distinction between outcomes as a general category of consequences and "goals" (groups' articulated objectives) as a specific class of outcomes. In the discussion immediately below we consider outcome only in relation to goal achievement, because this is the sense in which it is generally treated in the limited literature on the consequences of violence.

11. The foregoing examples all suggest that successful collective action *directly* results in an increase in the group's resource control level. Such processes sometimes occur *indirectly*—for example, a successful strike raises the wages of workers and thereby increases the resources "at risk" for mobilization by the organization (union) itself.

12. For example, labor organization A controls few resources and can undertake little collective action. It applies these resources toward a limited goal

(say, organizing the workers at plant Y) by handing out printed leaflets at the gates. If this tactic is successful (workers at plant Y join the union), the group then has the capacity to undertake qualitatively different types of action (e.g., a strike at plant Y).

13. Lipsky (1968) provides an example of the distinction we are making. Although mobilization of external support is not a goal of the powerless groups undertaking public protests, Lipsky points out that success in gaining third-party support and media attention is a necessary (but far from sufficient) condition for such groups to achieve their goals. Also, whereas Lipsky considers protest to be a political "resource," our treatment will make it clear that protest can be conceptualized only as a collective action or tactic (dependent on the resource of members' loyalties).

14. Many organizations exist—that is, we can identify them as being the "same" one—only over a limited period of time, and our treatment refers to them only during this "life span."

15. Although we prefer to think of this as a continuous process, our model and discussion (as well as any empirical analyses that might follow) are presented in discrete-time frames.

16. As we have indicated, we also expect that outcomes will affect the relationship between resource control and subsequent collective action. However, as we do not have any simple way to represent this "interaction effect" pictorially, it is not shown in figure 1.

17. These types of change can of course be further classified along other dimensions, such as material/objective versus psychological/symbolic. We do not do so because our concern with the latter here is at best peripheral.

18. Racial disorders in urban America in the 1960s provide a compelling example of this point. Although there is an abundance of high-quality data on a variety of outcomes (Snyder and Kelly, 1976a), the sketchy analyses that have previously been reported tend to rely on extremely limited subsets of indicators (Feagin and Hahn, 1973, pp. 199–260).

19. For an overview of empirical findings on this issue, see Snyder and Kelly (1976b). We hasten to add that "structural" differences and methodological errors in some analyses are two other plausible sources of discrepant findings.

20. We recognize that not all events have such "causes." In this context, see Marx (1972) on "issueless riots."

21. Despite the consistency of findings, there is no consensus on their proper interpretation, particularly in the case of nonwhite population size. The effects of this measure are variously attributed to national-level influences on individual blacks (Spilerman), to greater local levels of black mobilization or alienation, and so on.

22. Surveys of grievances might be thought susceptible to the same contamination that affects attempts to determine intentions. However, grievances are probably less subject to short-run change and, in any case, can be partially subjected to independent tests of validity by evaluating the objective condition (e.g., housing conditions, unemployment) that corresponds to a given grievance dimension.

23. In this case, survey evidence (cf. Caplan, 1970, for a summary of relevant findings) may also be used to validate the "political" aspects of racial disorders inferred from evidence on the selectivity of targets and so on.

24. Severity, as the underlying construct of a multiple-indicator measurement model, is supposed to tap the magnitude and intensity of collective action. Form, as we propose it, should be used to measure the tactics or strategies employed by participants (independent of severity).

25. For present purposes, we focus on only one type of specification error, the omission of relevant variables. Other forms, such as ignoring nonlinearity in relationships, may also be important. For example, it is substantively plausible that violence has "threshold effects" on certain types of outcome—that is, no impact until some "critical level" of violence is reached.

26. For theoretical and strategic reasons, Gamson (1975, pp. 16–17) restricts challenging groups to those that seek to mobilize an unmobilized constituency and have an antagonist outside their own constituency (e.g., the national government). Gamson notes that this definition thereby excludes groups with an already mobilized constituency, which would of course be of theoretical interest to the issues addressed in this paper.

27. Without undertaking a detailed verification, we will assert that data will be available for a sufficient number of groups to make this type of analysis feasible (labor unions are one obvious example). After all, until recently it would have appeared impossible to follow individuals over time, although procedures for doing so have now developed (Thernstrom, 1973).

28. If, instead, a panel model that measures change over a relatively long time span (say, 1960 to 1970) must be employed, there is a greater possibility that results will be artifactual. For example, if a positive effect of violence on change is observed, it may be partly caused by the occurrence of change prior to the outbreak of any violence (in this case, until 1967 for most cities that experienced racial disorders).

EPILOGUE: AN AGENDA FOR RESEARCH

Understanding how people and resources are aggregated in order to pursue social change is the central task of social movement analysis. The preceding essays have considered a wide variety of factors that encourage or constrain the likelihood that mobilization will begin and continue around social change goals. The availability of appropriate tactics in the experience of participants, the responses of authorities and target groups, the availability of material resources, the availability of leadership cadres, the nature and extent of preexisting social networks, the way in which movements are portrayed or ignored by the mass media, and the experience of prior movements are a few of the factors that have been discussed.

Let us conclude by briefly noting several issues raised by the resource mobilization perspective that we believe require additional attention. We shall discuss these questions under two general headings: (1) the importance of the fabric of preexisting social relations, and (2) the interaction between social movement organizations (SMOs) and various other more or less formally organized segments of a society. Both of these emphases recognize how the possibilities of mobilization and the behavior of social movements are crucially shaped by the structure of the society within which the pursuit of change goals is attempted.

SOCIAL RELATIONS

The social fabric of a society, the structured social relations between individuals and groups, provides the backdrop to any attempts at collection action. Substantial attention has been paid, recently, to how the preexisting social relations of those who are sympathizers to a particular cause either encourage or discourage the possibilities of mobilizing those sympathizers for collective action. The structured preexisting social relations that characterize sympathizers are, in our view, also of crucial importance in understanding the recruitment strategies available to SMOs that find their sympathizers scattered prior to initial mobilization attempts, beyond the observation that such sympathizers are less mobilizable. As well, such social relations are important in understanding the operation of social control mechanisms.

Recruitment

Oberschall (1973), Freeman (1973), Fireman and Gamson in this volume, and many others have stressed the point that the more closely sympathizers to any social change goal approximate a solidary group, the more easily mobilizable they are. But SMOs may find potential constituents isolated from one another. The sympathizers may exhibit patterns of preexisting social relations that range from perfect bloc structure, where all sympathizers are structured into groups that are homogeneous in sympathy for the social change goals, to perfect isolated structure, where no sympathizers are structured into interaction with other sympathizers. Although, of course, the perfect cases are empirically unlikely, the mobilization strategies available to SMOs with sympathizers who approximate an isolated structure are quite different from the strategies available when bloc structures exist. Wilson and Orum (1976) suggest that broad social trends may create mobilization opportunities by increasing the "blocedness" of sympathizers. But many modern social movement leaders have been unwilling to await such opportunities and have, rather, attempted to recruit constituents who are isolated. Recruiting from blocs typically operates through the social relations that exist; the recruitment of isolates takes rather different forms. The two primary strategies of recruitment when confronted with isolated structures seem to be direct contact with the isolates and attempts to aggregate sympathizers to make recruitment attempts more efficient. Though mass mailing seems to be the most widespread technique of attempting to contact isolated, or presumed isolated, constituents, in the modern United States newspaper advertising, telephone canvassing, and door-to-door canvassing have also been used. The targeting of markets that are potentially dense with sympathizers can make such contact more efficient.

On the other hand, social movement leaders may target assemblies that have occurred for other reasons or produce their own assemblies in order to aggregate sympathizers for recruitment attempts. Parades, entertainments, sports events, and even certain street corners may draw high proportions of sympathizers, depending upon the social change goals considered. The production of assemblies, especially when combined with side benefits such as food and entertainment, makes recruitment attempts more efficiently pursued.

We know very little systematically about these aggregation techniques and the conditions under which they are more or less successful in constituent recruitment (but see Snow, 1977, for an excellent review and synthesis of material on this issue). It seems plausible to hypothesize that small friendship groups may provide the building blocks of aggregation when the mobilization of isolated constituents is successful. The less formally structured social relations of sympathizers, then, may mean that though they are isolated from face-to-face contact with the SMO with which they sympathize, they may not be isolated from other sympathizers. We have argued elsewhere (1973b, 1977) that mass mail constituencies are an increasingly important segment of the constituencies of many SMOs. Understanding the recruitment mechanisms that succeed in gathering such constituents into SMOs and the way in which preexisting social relations shape the operation of these mechanisms is necessary to a full understanding of the modern social movement sector.

Social Control

Social control processes have been seriously neglected in the study of social movements. When social control is considered, and the papers by Marx and Tilly in this volume are important additions to our understanding of it, the emphasis has been heavily upon direct social control of partisans by authorities. There is a wide variety of less formal social control mechanisms that are quite important to the functioning of social movements, however. Though these mechanisms may not be independent, totally, from the behavior of authorities, they cannot be described and understood by an exclusive focus on how authorities attempt to bring pressure to bear upon social movement participants. The concept of structured social relations provides access to an understanding of these processes.

It is obvious that individuals and organizations other than authorities may desire social control of social movements. In the same way that structured social relations may provide opportunities for mobilization, they may provide opportunities for social control. Crucial to such opportunities are structured socioeconomic relationships. Private organizations and individuals may sanction social movement participants, for instance, as a result of their social movement activities. The recent exchange between Sigmund Diamond and McGeorge Bundy over Harvard's reaction to former CP membership illustrates the operation of such a sanction (see Von Hoffman, 1977). Oberschall's (1973) observation that southern black ministers operated with a greater degree of freedom in civil rights activities as a result of their separateness from white economic institutions illustrates the other side of this mechanism. The more economically dependent social movement participants are upon individuals and organizations who desire the frustration of the pursuit of certain social change goals, the more vulnerable to sanction they will be. In context, as well, sometimes few sanctions are necessary—it is the possibility of their operation that inhibits social movement activity (Lazarsfeld and Thielens, 1958). In his study of the Southern Farmers' Alliance, Michael Schwartz (1976) illustrates this point quite nicely by showing how the tactics of the SMOs were frustrated by the economic dependence of tenant and yeoman farmers upon the entire credit system and cotton marketing system. Though authorities cooperated in social control attempts upon the alliance, the structured socioeconomic relations made farmers particularly vulnerable to social control by nonauthorities.

The general concept of social control fallout (Hancock, 1975) is useful here. Social control fallout consists of sanctions brought by nonauthorities that result from the direct social control efforts of authorities. Social control fallout is facilitated by the unwillingness of authorities to exercise social control upon those private citizens and organizations that engage in illegitimate social control themselves. By action and words, authorities may make clear to the opposition to various movements that control will be unlikely upon those who attempt to constrain the actions of social movement participants.

We are arguing here for a reintroduction of a broader, Durkheimian definition of social control (see Janowitz, 1975) in order fully to comprehend the operation of social control upon social movements. Structured social relations may inhibit social movement mobilization because of the cross-cutting allegiances of potential recruits—an old idea that was incorporated into the mass society thesis. The way in which social movement opponents are structured into ongoing social relations will make it more or less likely that they will, if they so desire, be able to influence the course of a social movement. In the same way that there are mobilization opportunities for sympathizers, there ought to be mobilization opportunities for opponents. Social control by nonauthorities ought to be maximized when preexisting blocs are homogeneous in opposition to the social change goals under consideration; when they operate with the belief that authorities will not sanction their behavior and, in fact, may approve of it; and when they are structured into economic relations with movement participants in ways that allow direct sanctions. The operation of these less formal social control mechanisms may occur short of any formal social control efforts by authorities. The exclusive focus upon authorities, then, will obscure understandings of how social control affects the course of SMOs.

SOCIAL MOVEMENT ORGANIZATIONS AND SOCIETY

The fabric of social relations of a society exists within a fabric of relations between organizations. Once in operation, SMOs must interact with a wide variety of more or less organized segments of a society. This is true for both national and local organizations, where laws governing operation, other SMOs pursuing similar and different goals, government agencies, private organizations, and powerful individuals form the environment in which goals are pursued. The nature of the environment may make goal pursuit and mobilization more or less possible. The leaders of SMOs typically attempt to exploit this environment for their own purposes and occasionally attempt to alter it for their own benefits. A number of connections between SMOs and their environments are particularly worth additional attention: the connection with other SMOs, the connection with governmental apparatus, and the connection with elites.

Cooperation and Competition among
Social Movement Organizations

All of those organizations that attempt to pursue a particular change goal can be called a social movement industry (McCarthy and Zald, 1977). Though it might seem obvious that the organizations in such an industry ought to cooperate in order to bring about commonly shared goals, a resource mobilization perspective highlights the fact that similar organizations are in competition over the mobilization of resources. We find, however, examples within the same social movement industry ranging from close cooperation to bitter conflict. The conditions under which cooperation and conflict are facilitated among SMOs have received very little attention from social movement analysts.

Although a social movement industry may consist of a single organization, it typically consists of numerous organizations pursuing similar goals. In many industries domain agreements are worked out over time concerning the strategies for pursuing change and rights to segments of sympathizers, in much the same way that social service agencies, for instance, develop working agreements in locales. The recent work of Robert Stallings (1977) describing an emergent coalition of SMOs illustrates one example of this process. Stallings examines the plethora of organizations involved in a conservation issue in a small city, finding over one hundred interlinked organizations. A domain consensus is rarely formal in social movement industries, and competition for symbolic leadership of movement industries appears. The position of being the leading organization in an industry should aid in the recruitment of constituents, as well as in providing better access to institutional resources of foundations, for instance.

In some industries extensive cooperation occurs among organizations, and facilities, mailing lists, volunteers, and the like are shared. Ad hoc coalitions for the mounting of pressure for specific changes are not unusual in many industries. Organizational mergers, though rare, are possible. Factions separating from the parent organization are common.

The range of possibilities of interorganizational relations is quite broad, then. The sum of such relationships for any organization ought to be quite important in determining its ability to mobilize resources. Interorganizational competition ought to divert resources from the pursuit of change. Industries can be characterized according to the general level of conflict inherent among organizations, and we would expect this level to affect the total impact of the industry on the broader society. It is our impression that the modern environmental movement is far less conflict-ridden than, for instance, the earlier socialist movement in the United States. Gamson (1975) shows that movement organizations with internal factionalization are less likely to succeed in producing change than those without such conflict. Though we would expect this same pattern to hold generally for industries, some differences can be expected. Conflict among organizations over change strategies can serve to provide legitimacy and the sound of moderation to certain organizations within an industry (Killian, 1972).

Continuity and Institutionalization: Government against Itself

In the early stages, many modern movement organizations in the United States draw upon the resources of the government, both federal and local. Typically, such aid develops either through preexisting social relations between government functionaries and movement participants or through formal programs designed to benefit or develop information concerning some segment of the population that the social movement participants claim to represent. Sympathetic functionaries may provide information, access, and even direct organizing skills that can be of use to struggling movement organizers. The modern governmental apparatus is so large and diverse that individuals within it may use resources to aid social movements unbeknownst to their superiors. One of the editors of this volume encountered, for instance, during John Mitchell's tenure as attorney general, two Justice Department attorneys who were on a nationwide trip to organize public housing tenants into pressure groups. They admitted that the attorney general would not approve of their activities if he had known of them, but he did not. A federal system seems to multiply the interstices from which movement sympathizers can aid a fledgling movement organization (see Zald and McCarthy, 1975).

If SMOs are thought to mobilize constituencies that have been on the periphery of the formally organized political system, sometimes that mobilization is successful in integrating such constituencies by broadening existing channels and creating new ones for allowing the pursuit of social movement goals within the formal political system. As Lowi (1971) and others have argued, many governmental agencies are the result of successful social movements. The bureaucratic and policy outcomes of social movement pressures upon government certainly affect the continuity of movement organizations and social movement industries. An expanded Civil Rights Division in the Justice Department, the Equal Employment Opportunity Commission, the U.S. Commission on Civil Rights, and various sections and officers in other governmental agencies at the federal level certainly have the effect of shifting the ground and tactics of contention for organizations and individuals interested in pursuing civil rights change goals. Shifting from the use of unorthodox tactics designed to pressure authorities into taking legislative and executive action to the use of pressure upon authority segments that have been mandated to pursue similar change goals must have important effects upon the required structure and personnel in previously effective movement organizations. Organizations effective in mounting mass demonstrations and local community contention may be particularly unsuited for bureaucratic bargaining. Organizational adaptation in such a changing environment may alter the relations between organization and constituencies and thereby alter the resource mobilization task.

This issue of the institutionalization of social movement goals in the formal political process has not, we believe, received the attention it deserves concerning its impacts upon movement organizations. Though political scientists have, in the past, focused upon the workings of such institutions, with few exceptions (see particularly Freeman, 1975) little attention has been paid to their impacts upon social movements.

Elites and Elite Mobilization

A resource mobilization perspective highlights the importance of elite involvement in social movement success, but, as Perrow's criticism of some statements of such a perspective points out, the conditions under which elites become involved in movements that pursue change goals need illumination if we are to understand fully cycles of movement success and failure. It is obvious that whether or not elites are sympathetic to social movements is crucial to their possibilities of resource mobilization, because elites control large resource pools. Sympathy, as well, ought to encourage mass involvement. Though increased surpluses of wealth may provide the conditions favorable to social movement growth, Perrow is correct in his essay in this volume that this observation does not inform us which issues will receive elite backing. A perspective on the long-term development of elite divisions in modern welfare states, as well as an understanding of elite relations with governmental apparatus, seems necessary to provide the theoretical backdrop to an understanding of modern social movements.

Jenkins and Perrow (1977) and McAdam (1977) document through their analysis of *New York Times* reports steadily increasing elite support for change in farm worker and civil rights issues through the 1950s and 1960s. Assuredly, the rise of movements related to these issues reflected the normal political processes of American society. But what is the logic of elite divisions that produces substantial support from segments of the elite? Does an electoral politics perspective stressing the growth of new segments of the electorate (i.e., Piven and Cloward, 1971) explain the trends we have seen? Does a perspective that focuses upon divisions between old northeastern money and manufacturing and new sunbelt fortunes (i.e., Sale, 1976) explain them? Does a neo-Marxist perspective stressing systemic contradictions and manipulative elites buying time with symbolic cooptation explain them? Does Schumpeter's (1947) assessment of the common interests of entrepreneurs and dissidents explain them? Or do we need a newer analytic perspective on the modern welfare state, stressing the interpenetration of government and corporate institutions, to explain these trends?

In any case, the posing of questions of this sort illustrates clearly how the study of social movements must be nested within broader perspectives upon politicohistorical processes. The modern study of social movements has evolved beyond a recent narrowness—with a flavor of "Ripley's Believe It or Not"—toward a view that stresses how crucial the political and economic trends in the environment of the broader society are to the success or failure of specific movements. This evolution brings the study of social movements back into the mainstream of political sociology.

Bibliography

AGEE, P. (1974) Inside the Company. Harmondsworth, England: Penguin.

ALINSKY, S. (1971) Rules for Radicals. New York: Random House.

ALTHEIDE, D. L. (1976) Creating Reality: How TV News Distorts Events. Beverly Hills: Sage.

ANDERSON, W. A., and R. R. DYNES (1973) "Organizational and political transformation of a social movement." Social Forces (March): 330–41.

BENET, J., A. DANIELS, and G. TUCHMAN (eds.) (Forthcoming) Home and Hearth: Images of Women in the Mass Media. New York: Oxford University Press.

BERK, R. A., and H. A. ALDRICH (1972) "Patterns of vandalism during civil disorders as an indicator of selection of targets." American Sociological Review 37 (October): 533–46.

BERKOWITZ, L. (1965) "The concept of aggressive drive." In L. Berkowitz (ed.) Advances in Experimental Social Psychology. Vol. 2. New York: Academic.

BERMAN, J., and M. HALPERIN (eds.) (1975) The Abuses of Intelligence Agencies. Washington: Center for National Security Studies.

BERNSTEIN, I. (1960) The Lean Years: A History of the American Worker, 1920–1933. Boston: Houghton Mifflin.

BETHELL, T. N. (1969) "Conspiracy on coal." Washington Monthly (March): 16–23, 63–72.

BIENEN, H. (1968) Violence and Social Change: A Review of the Current Literature. Chicago: University of Chicago Press.

BLACK, E. C. (1963) The Association: British Extraparliamentary Political Organization, 1769–1793. Cambridge, Mass.: Harvard University Press.

BLACK LUNG ASSOCIATION (n.d.) "Memo: what we're here for."

BLAU, P. (1965) "The comparative study of organizations." Industrial and Labor Relations Review 18:323–38.

BLUMENTHAL, M. D., R. L. KAHN, F. M. ANDREWS, and K. B. HEAD (1972) Justifying Violence: Attitudes of American Men. Ann Arbor: Institute for Social Research.

BLUMER, H. (1969) "Collective behavior." In A. M. Lee (ed.) Principles of Sociology. 3rd ed., pp. 65–122. New York: Barnes and Noble.

BOHSTEDT, J. (1972) "Riots in England, 1790–1810, with special reference to Devonshire." Ph.D. dissertation. Harvard University.

BOOKIN, H. (1973–76) Private notes and personal conversations.

BOSTON GLOBE (1975) 19 November.

BOULDING, K. (1963) Conflict and Defense. New York: Harper Torchbooks.

BREED, W. (1955) "Social control in the newsroom." Social Forces 33:326–35.

BRINTON, C. (1938) The Anatomy of Revolution. New York: Vintage.

BROWN, R. M. (1975) Strain of Violence: Historical Studies of American Violence and Vigilantism. New York: Oxford University Press.

——— (1963) The South Carolina Regulators. Cambridge, Mass.: Belknap Press of Harvard University.

BROWN, R. (1965) Social Psychology. Glencoe, Ill.: Free Press.

BURLINGHAM, B. (1977) "Community union." Working Papers for a New Society 4 (Winter): 20–22.

CANNON, J. (1973) Parliamentary Reform, 1640–1832. Cambridge: Cambridge University Press.

CAPLAN, N. (1970) "The new ghetto man: a review of recent empirical studies." Journal of Social Issues 26 (Winter): 59–73.

CARDEN, M. (1974) The New Feminist Movement. New York: Russell Sage.

CECIL, R. (1963) "Oligarchy and mob-rule in the American revolution." History Today 13:197–204.

COLEMAN, B. (1977) "The response of women's magazines to the feminist movement." M.A. thesis. University of California, Santa Barbara.

COMMISSION ON CIA ACTIVITIES WITHIN THE UNITED STATES (1975) Report to the President. Washington, D.C.: U.S. Government Printing Office.

COSER, LEWIS A. (1956) The Functions of Social Conflict. New York: Free Press.

COUNTRYMAN, E. (1976) "Out of the bounds of the law: northern land rioters in the eighteenth century." In A. F. Young (ed.) The American Revolution. DeKalb: Northern Illinois University Press.

CURRIE, E., and J. SKOLNICK (1970) "A critical note on conceptions of collective behavior." Annals of the American Academy of Political and Social Science 391 (September): 34–35.

CURTIS, R. L., JR., and L. ZURCHER (1974) "Social movements: an analytical exploration of organizational forms." Social Problems 21, 3:356–70.

DAVIES, J. C. (1962) "Toward a theory of revolution." American Sociological Review 27 (February): 5–19.

DONNER, F. (1976) "Let him wear a wolf's head: what the FBI did to William Albertson." Civil Liberties Review (April/May).

DONOVAN, J. C. (1970) The Politics of Poverty. New York: Pegasus.

DOWNS, A. (1972) "Up and down with ecology—the 'issue-attention cycle.'" Public Interest 28 (Summer): 39–50.

DURKHEIM, E. (1958) Rules of the Sociological Method. Glencoe, Ill.: Free Press.

DYNES, R. R., and E. L. QUARANTELLI (1968) "Group behavior under stress: a required convergence of organizational and collective behavior perspectives." Sociology and Social Research 52 (July): 416–29.

ECKSTEIN, H. (1965) "On the etiology of internal wars." History and Theory 4:133–63.

ERIKSON, K. (1966) The Wayward Puritans. New York: Wiley.

ESTEP, R., and P. LAUDERDALE (1977) "News blackout: the bicentennial protest." Unpublished paper, University of Minnesota.

ETZIONI, A. (1968) The Active Society. New York: Free Press.

FARLEY, R., and A. HERMALIN (1972) "The 1960s: a decade of progress for blacks?" Demography 9 (August): 353–70.

FEAGIN, J. R., and H. HAHN (1973) Ghetto Revolts: The Politics of Violence in American Cities. New York: Macmillan.

FISHMAN, M. (Forthcoming) "Manufacturing the news: the social organization of media newswork." Ph.D. dissertation. University of California, Santa Barbara.

FLACKS, R. (1976) "Making history vs. making life: dilemmas of an American left." Social Inquiry 46, 3–4, 263–80.

——— (1967) "The liberated generation: an exploration of the roots of student protest." Journal of Social Issues 23 (July): 52–75.

FOGELSON, R. M. (1971) Violence as Protest. Garden City, N.Y.: Doubleday.

FREEMAN, J. (1977) "Networks and strategy in the women's liberation movement." Paper presented at this conference.

——— (1975) The Politics of Women's Liberation. New York: McKay.

——— (1973) "Tyranny of structurelessness." Ms. (July).

FROLICH, N., J. A. OPPENHEIMER, and O. R. YOUNG (1971) Political Leadership and Collective Goods. Princeton: Princeton University Press.

GAMSON, W. A. (1975) Strategy of Social Protest. Homewood, Ill.: Dorsey.

——— (1968) Power and Discontent. Homewood, Ill.: Dorsey.

GERLACH, L. P. (1971) "Movements of revolutionary change: some structural characteristics." American Behavioral Scientist 14, 6 (July/August): 812–36.

——— (1970) "Corporate groups and movement networks in urban America." Anthropological Quarterly 43, 3 (July): 123–45.

———, and V. H. HINE (1970) People, Power and Change: Movements of Social Transformation. New York: Bobbs-Merrill.

GITLIN, T. (Forthcoming) "Spotlights and shadows: explorations in the political meaning of mass communications." Ph.D. dissertation. University of California, Berkeley.

——— (1977) "Spotlights and shadows: television and the culture of politics." College English.

GOULDEN, J. (1971) The Money Givers. New York: Random House.

GOVERNOR'S SELECT COMMISSION ON CIVIL DISORDER (1968) Report for Action. State of New Jersey.

GRABER, E. (1976) "Politics' undercover agents." In Police Roles in the Seventies (Forthcoming).

GURR, T. R. (1970) Why Men Rebel. Princeton: Princeton University Press.

HABERMAS, JURGEN (1975) Legitimation Crisis. Boston: Beacon.

HALPERIN, M., and R. BOROSAGE (1976) The Lawless State. Baltimore: Penguin.

HAMILTON, R. (1972) Class and Politics in the United States. New York: Wiley.

HANCOCK, R. K. (1975) "From innocence to boredom: revolution in the west." Ph.D. dissertation. Vanderbilt University.

HARDIN, R. (1976) "The contractarian provision of group goods." Presented at the Conference of the Peace Science Society, Ann Arbor (November).

HARRINGTON, M. (1973) Fragments of a Century. New York: Dutton.

—— (1968) Toward a Democratic Left: A Radical Program for a New Majority. New York: Macmillan.

HAY, D., P. LINEBAUGH, J. RULE, E. P. THOMPSON, and C. WINSLOW (1975) Albion's Fatal Tree. Crime and Society in Eighteenth-Century England. New York: Pantheon.

HEATH, A. (1976) Rational Choice and Social Change. New York: Cambridge University Press.

HEBERLE, R. (1951) Social Movements: An Introduction to Political Sociology. New York: Appleton.

HIBBS, D. (1975) "Industrial conflict in advanced industrial societies." American Political Science Review.

—— (1974) Industrial Conflict in Advanced Industrial Societies. Cambridge, Mass.: M.I.T. Press.

HILL, R. C. (1974a) "Separate and unequal: governmental inequality in the metropolis." American Political Science Review 68 (December): 1157–68.

—— (1974b) "Unionization and racial income inequality in the metropolis." American Sociological Review 39 (August): 507–22.

HINDUS, M. S. (1971) "A city of mobocrats and tyrants: mob violence in Boston, 1741–1863." Issues in Criminology 6:55–83.

HIRSCHMAN, A. O. (1970) Exit, Voice, and Loyalty. Cambridge, Mass.: Harvard University Press.

HODGE, R. W. (1973) "Toward a theory of racial differences in employment." Social Forces 52 (September): 16–30.

HOERDER, D. (1977) Crowd Action in a Revolutionary Society: Massachusetts, 1765–1780. New York: Academic.

—— (1976) "Boston leaders and Boston crowds, 1765–1776." In Alfred F. Young (ed.) The American Revolution. DeKalb: Northern Illinois University Press.

—— (1971) People and Mobs: Crowd Action in Massachusetts during the American Revolution, 1765–1780. Berlin: Privately printed.

HOLE, J., and E. LEVINE (1971) Rebirth of Feminism. New York: Quadrangle.

HUBBARD, H. (1968) "Five long hot summers and how they grew." Public Interest 12:3–24.

HYMAN, H. H. (1942) "The psychology of status." Archives of Psychology, no. 269. New York.

JACOBS, H. (ed.) (1971) Weatherman. San Francisco: Ramparts.

JANOWITZ, M. (1975) "Sociological theory and social control." American Journal of Sociology 81 (July): 82–108.

—— (1969) "Patterns of collective racial violence." In H. D. Graham and T. R. Gurr (eds.) Violence in America: Historical and Comparative Perspectives. New York: Signet.

JENKINS, J. C., and C. PERROW (1977) "Insurgency of the powerless: farm worker movements, 1946–1972." American Sociological Review, 42 (April): 249–68.

JOHNSON, C. (1966) Revolutionary Change. Boston: Little, Brown.

JOHNSON, L. B. (1971) The Vantage Point. New York: Holt.

JOHNSTONE, J. W. C., E. J. SLAWSKI, and W. W. BOWMAN (1976) The News People: A Sociological Portrait of American Journalists and Their Work. Urbana: University of Illinois Press.

JONES, D. (1973) Before Rebecca: Popular Protests in Wales, 1793–1835. London: Allen Lane.

KAHN, S. (1970) How People Get Power: Organizing Oppressed Communities for Action. New York: McGraw-Hill.

KAY, M. L. (1976) "The North Carolina regulation, 1766–1776: a class conflict." In A. F. Young (ed.) The American Revolution. DeKalb: Northern Illinois University Press.

KENISTON, K. (1968) The Young Radicals. New York: Harcourt.

KERR, C., J. T. DUNLOP, F. HARBISON, and C. A. MYERS (1960) Industrialism and Industrial Man. Cambridge, Mass.: Harvard University Press.

KILBOURG, B. (1976) Personal interview, August.

KILLIAN, L. (1972) "The significance of extremism in the black revolution." Social Problems 20 (Summer): 41–48.

KIRKHAM, J. F., S. LEVY, and W. CROTTY (1970) Assassination and Political Violence. Washington: U.S. Government Printing Office.

KNIPE, E. E., and H. M. LEWIS (1969) "The impact of coal mining on the traditional mountain subculture: a case of peasantry gained and peasantry lost." Paper presented at Southern Anthropological Society, New Orleans, 14 March 1969.

KNOLLENBERG, B. (1965) Origin of the American Revolution: 1759–1766. rev. ed. New York: Free Press.

KOPKIND, A. (1977) "Fair share's ballot box blues." Working Papers for a New Society 4 (Winter): 26–32.

KRAMER, D. C. (1972) Participatory Democracy: Developing Ideals of the Political Left. Cambridge, Mass.: Schenkman.

KREISBERG, L. (ed.) (1977) Research in Social Movements, Conflict and Change. Greenwich, Conn.: JAI.

LAZARSFELD, P. F., and W. THIELENS, JR. (1958) The Academic Mind. New York: Free Press.

LEBON, GUSTAVE (1879) The Crowd: A Study of the Popular Mind. London: T. F. Unwin.

LEITES, N., and C. WOLF, JR. (1970) Rebellion and Authority. Chicago: Markham.

LEMISCH, J. (1968) "The American revolution seen from the bottom up." In B. J. Bernstein (ed.) Towards a New Past. New York: Vintage.

——— and J. K. ALEXANDER (1972) "The white oaks, jack tar, and the concept of the 'inarticulate.'" William and Mary Quarterly 29:109–42.

LENIN, V. I. (1967) V. I. Lenin: Selected Works. New York: International Publishers.

LESTER, MARILYN (1971) "Airing dirty linen publicly: toward a sociology of public events." M.A. thesis. University of California, Santa Barbara.

LEWIS, L., and S. BAIDEME (1972) "The women's liberation movement." In L. T. Sargent (ed.) New Left Thought: An Introduction. Homewood, Ill.: Dorsey.

LIPSKY, M. (1970) Protest in City Politics. Chicago: Rand McNally.

—— (1968) "Protest as a political resource." American Political Science Review 62:1144–58.

——, and D. J. OLSON (1973) "Civil disorders and the American political process: the meaning of recent urban riots." In H. Hirsch and D. Perry (eds.) Violence as Politics: A Series of Original Essays. New York: Harper.

—— (1969) "Riot commission politics." Trans-Action 6, 8 (July/August): 21.

LOCKRIDGE, K. A. (1973) "Social change and the meaning of the American revolution." Journal of Social History 6:403–39.

LOFLAND, J. (1977a) "The boom and bust of a millenarian movement." Preface, Doomsday Cult. New York: Irvington.

—— (1977b) "Becoming a world-saver revisited." American Behavioral Scientist (August).

—— (1966) Doomsday Cult. Englewood Cliffs, N.J.: Prentice-Hall.

LOWI, T. J. (1971) The Politics of Disorder. New York: Basic Books.

McADAM, D. (1977) "Political process and the civil rights movement, 1948–1962." Unpublished manuscript, State University of New York, Stony Brook.

McCANN, T. (1976) An American Company: The Tragedy of United Fruit. New York: Crown.

McCARTHY, J. D., and M. N. ZALD (1977) "Resource mobilization and social movements: a partial theory." American Journal of Sociology 82 (May): 1212–1239.

—— (1974) "Tactical considerations in social movement organizations." Paper presented at the 69th Annual Meeting of the American Sociological Association, 26–29 August 1974.

—— (1973a) "Toward a resource mobilization theory of social movement organizations." Paper presented at Southern Sociological Society, 12 April 1973.

—— (1973b) The Trend of Social Movements in America: Professionalization and Resource Mobilization. Morristown, N.J.: General Learning Corporation.

McCOY, A. (1972) The Politics of Heroin in Southeast Asia. New York: Harper.

McPHAIL, C. (1971) "Civil disorder participation: a critical examination of recent research." American Sociological Review 36 (December): 1058–73.

——, and D. L. MILLER (1973) "The assembling process: a theoretical and empirical examination." American Sociological Review 38 (December): 721–35.

MAIER, P. T. (1972) From Resistance to Revolution: Colonial Radicals and the Development of American Opposition to Britain, 1765–1776. New York: Random House.

MAIROWITZ, D. Z. (1974) The Radical Soap Opera. London: Wildwood.

MARCHETTI, V., and J. MARKS (1974) CIA and the Cult of Intelligence. New York: Knopf.

MARCUSE, H. (1964) One-Dimensional Man. Boston: Beacon Press.

MARTIN, J. F. (1971) "Confessions of a non bra-burner." Chicago Journalism Review 4:11.

MARX, G. T. (1974) "Thoughts on a neglected category of social movement participant: the agent provocateur and the informant." American Journal of Sociology 80:402–42.

———— (1972) "Issueless riots." In J. F. Short, Jr., and M. E. Wolfgang (eds.) Collective Violence. Chicago: Aldine-Atherton.

———— (1971) Racial Conflict: Tension and Change in American Society. Boston: Little, Brown.

———— (1970) "Civil disorder and the agents of social control." Journal of Social Issues 26 (Winter): 19–57.

————, and M. USEEM (1971) "Majority involvement in minority movements: civil rights, abolition, untouchability." Journal of Social Issues 27 (January): 81–104.

MARX, G. T., and J. L. WOOD (1975) "Strands of theory and research in collective behavior." In A. Inkeles (ed.) Annual Review of Sociology. Vol. 1. Palo Alto: Annual Reviews.

MASOTTI, L. H. (n.d.) "Riots and change: a hindsight view of urban disorder in the sixties." Mimeographed, Northwestern University.

MEINHOUSEN, D. (1969) "The changeling: the story of a HUAC spy in the student movement." Hard Times 46 (6 October).

MOLOTCH, H. (1976) "The city as a growth machine." American Journal of Sociology 82, 2:309–32.

———— (1970) "Oil in Santa Barbara and power in America." Sociological Inquiry 40:131–44.

———— (1967) Managed Integration: Dilemmas of Doing Good in the City. Berkeley: University of California Press.

————, and M. LESTER (1975) "Accidental news: the great oil spill as local occurrence and national event." American Journal of Sociology 81, 2:235–60.

———— (1974) "News as purposive behavior: on the strategic use of routine events, accidents and scandals." American Sociological Review 39, 1:101–12.

MORGAN, R. (1970) "Goodbye to all that." In L. Tanner (ed.) Voices from Women's Liberation. New York: New American Library.

MORGAN, W. R., and T. N. CLARK (1973) "The causes of racial disorders: a grievance-level explanation." American Sociological Review 38 (October): 611–24.

MORRIS, B. (1977) " 'We the people of the United States': the bicentennial of a people's revolution." American Historical Review 82:1–19.

MORRIS, M. (1973) "The public definition of a social movement: women's liberation." Sociology and Social Research 57:526–43.

MOYNIHAN, D. P. (1968) Maximum Feasible Misunderstanding. New York: Free Press.

———— (1965) "The professionalization of reform." Public Interest (Fall).

MUELLER, C. (1975) "The potential of riot violence as a political resource." Paper presented at annual meeting of the American Sociological Association, San Francisco.

MYRDAL, G. (1944) An American Dilemma. New York: Harper and Row.

NASH, G. B. (1976) "Social change and the growth of prerevolutionary urban radicalism." In A. F. Young (ed.) The American Revolution. DeKalb: Northern Illinois University Press.

NATIONAL ADVISORY COMMISSION ON CIVIL DISORDERS (1968) Report. New York: Bantam.

NEWTON, H. (1973) Revolutionary Suicide. New York: Harcourt.

NEW YORK TIMES (1976) 4 February; 11 July.

―――― (1975) 22 April.

―――― (1973) 2 May.

―――― (1972) 16 March.

OBERSCHALL, A. (1977) "The decline of the 1960's social movements." In L. Kriesberg (ed.) Research in Social Movements, Conflict and Change. Greenwich, Conn.: JAI.

―――― (1973) Social Conflict and Social Movements. Englewood Cliffs, N.J.: Prentice-Hall.

O'CONNOR, J. (1973) The Fiscal Crisis of the State. New York: St. Martin's.

OLSON, D. J. (1971) "Black violence as political protest." In E. S. Greenburg, N. Milner, and D. J. Olson (eds.) Black Politics: The Inevitability of Conflict. New York: Holt.

OLSON, M. (1968) The Logic of Collective Action. New York: Schocken.

―――― (1965) The Logic of Collective Action: Public Goods and the Theory of Groups. Cambridge, Mass.: Harvard University Press.

O. M. Collective (1971) The Organizer's Manual. New York: Bantam.

PALMER, R. R. (1977) "The fading dream: how European revolutionaries have seen the American revolution." In B. Lackner and K. R. Philp (eds.) The Walter Prescott Webb Memorial Lectures: Essays on Modern European Revolutionary History. Austin: University of Texas Press.

PERROW, C. (1972) The Radical Attack on Business. New York: Harcourt.

PIERCY, M. (1970) "The grand coolie damn." In R. Morgan (ed.) Sisterhood Is Powerful. New York: Random House.

PIVEN, F. F., and R. A. CLOWARD (1971) Regulating the Poor. New York: Pantheon.

QUARANTELLI, E. L., and R. DYNES (1968) "Looting in civil disorders: an index of social change." In L. H. Masotti and D. R. Bowen (eds.) Riots and Rebellion. Beverly Hills: Sage.

RADZINOWICZ, L. (1968) A History of English Criminal Law and Its Administration from 1750. Vol. 4: Grappling for Control. London: Stevens.

REICH, C. (1970) The Greening of America. New York: Random House.

ROBERTS, R. E., and R. M. KLOSS (1974) Social Movements: Between the Balcony and the Barricade. St. Louis: Mosby.

ROGERS, A. (1974) Empire and Liberty: American Resistance to British Authority, 1755–1763. Berkeley: University of California Press.

ROSS, D. K. (1973) A Public Citizen's Action Manual. New York: Grossman.

RUDE, G. (1971) Hanoverian London, 1714–1808. London: Secker and Warburg.

———— (1964) The Crowd in History. New York: Wiley.

———— (1962) Wilkes and Liberty. Oxford: Clarendon Press.

Rudolph, L. I. (1959) "The 18th century mob in America and Europe." American Quarterly 11:447–69.

Rush, G. B., and R. S. Denisoff (1971) Social and Political Movements. New York: Appleton.

Russell, D. E. H. (1974) Rebellion, Revolution and Armed Force. New York: Academic.

Ryder, N. (1974) In J. Coleman et al., Youth: Transition to Adulthood. Chicago: University of Chicago Press.

Ryerson, R. A. (1974) "Political mobilization and the American Revolution: the resistance movement in Philadelphia, 1765 to 1776." William and Mary Quarterly 31:565–88.

Sale, K. (1976) Power Shift. New York: Random House.

———— (1973) SDS. New York: Random House.

Sarachild, K. (1975) "Consciousness-raising: a radical weapon." In Redstockings (ed.) Feminist Revolution, p. 131. New York: Redstockings.

Schattschneider, E. E. (1960) The Semi-Sovereign People. New York: Holt.

Schelling, T. (1963) The Strategy of Conflict. New York: Oxford University Press.

Schumpeter, J. A. (1947) Capitalism, Socialism and Democracy. New York: Harper.

Schwartz, M. (1976) Radical Protest and Social Structure. New York: Academic.

Select Committee to Study Governmental Operations with Respect to Intelligence Final Report (1976) Bks. 1–6; Hearings. Vols. 1–7. Washington, D.C.: U.S. Government Printing Office.

Shelly, M. (1970) "Subversion in the women's movement: what is to be done." Off Our Backs (8 November): 7.

Shelton, W. J. (1973) English Hunger and Industrial Disorders: A Study of Social Conflict during the First Decade of George III's Reign. London: Macmillan.

Shorter, E., and C. Tilly (1974) Strikes in France, 1830–1968. Cambridge: Cambridge University Press.

———— (1971) "Le déclin de la grève violente en France de 1890 à 1935." Le Mouvement Social 79 (July/September): 95–118.

Skolnick, J. H. (1969) The Politics of Protest. New York: Ballantine.

Smelser, N. J. (1963) Theory of Collective Behavior. New York: Free Press.

Smith, J. (1977) "The complex effects of simple collective things." Proceedings of the Society for General Systems Research: 405–11.

———— (1976) "Communities, associations, and the supply of collective goods." American Journal of Sociology 82, 2: 291–307.

Smith, W. A. (1965) Anglo-Colonial Society and the Mob, 1740–1775. Ph.D. dissertation. Claremont Graduate School.

Snow, D. A. (1977) "Social networks and social movements: toward a microstructural theory of differential recruitment." Unpublished manuscript, Department of Sociology, University of Texas, Austin.

SNYDER, D. (1975) "Institutional setting and industrial conflict: comparative analyses of France, Italy and the United States." American Sociological Review 40 (June): 259–78.

SNYDER, D., and W. R. KELLY (1977a) "Conflict intensity, media sensitivity and the validity of newspaper data." American Sociological Review 42 (February): 105–23.

———— (1977b) "Strategies for investigating violence and social change: illustrations from analysis of racial disorders and implications for mobilization research." Paper presented at this conference.

———— (1976a) "Racial violence and social change: U.S. cities, 1960–75." Research grant application submitted to the National Institutes of Mental Health.

———— (1976b) "Industrial violence in Italy, 1878–1903." American Journal of Sociology 82 (July): 131–62.

SNYDER, D., and C. TILLY (1972) "Hardship and collective violence in France, 1830 to 1960." American Sociological Review 37 (October): 520–32.

SOLOMON, L. (1977) "Putting the campaign in print—Michelle deMilly." Advocate 222, 24 (August): 9, 10.

SPILERMAN, S. (1970) "The causes of racial disturbances: a comparison of alternative explanations." American Sociological Review 35, 4: 627–49.

———— (1976) "Structural characteristics of cities and the severity of racial disorders." American Sociological Review 41, 5: 771–93.

STALLINGS, R. A. (1977) "Social movements as emergent coalitions: an interorganizational approach." Working Paper No. 14, The Public Policy Institute, University of Southern California, Los Angeles.

———— (1974) "Toward the further convergence of collective behavior and social organization: interorganizational models for the study of social movements." Paper presented at the 69th Annual Meeting of the American Sociological Association, 26–29 August 1974.

STARK, M. J. A., W. J. RAINE, S. L. BURBECK, and K. K. DAVIDSON (1974) "Some empirical patterns in a riot process." American Sociological Review 39 (December): 365–76.

STEVENSON, J. (1974) "Food riots in England, 1792–1818." In J. Stevenson and R. Quinalt (eds.) Popular Protest and Public Order: Six studies in British History, 1790–1920. London: Allen and Unwin.

STINCHCOMBE, A. L. (1975) "Social structure and politics." In F. I. Greenstein and N. W. Polsby (eds.) Handbook of Political Science. Vol. 3. Reading, Mass.: Addison-Wesley.

STRICKLAND, D. A., and R. E. JOHNSTON (1970) "Issue elasticity in political systems." Journal of Political Economy. 78:1069–92.

TEODORI, M. (1969) New Left: A Documentary History. New York: Bobbs Merrill.

THEIL, H. (1971) Principles of Econometrics. New York: Wiley.

THERNSTROM, S. (1973) The Other Bostonians: Poverty and Progress in the American Metropolis, 1830–1970. Cambridge, Mass.: Harvard University Press.

THOMPSON, E. P. (1975) Whigs and Hunters: The Origin of the Black Act. New York: Pantheon.

—— (1963) The Making of the English Working Class. London: Gollancz.

TILLY, C. (1978) From Mobilization to Revolution. Reading, Mass.: Addison-Wesley.

—— (1975) "Revolutions and collective violence." In F. I. Greenstein and N. W. Polsby (eds.) Handbook of Political Science. Vol. 3, pp. 483–555. Reading, Mass.: Addison-Wesley.

—— (1973) "Does modernization breed revolution?" Comparative Politics 5 (April): 425–47.

—— (1970) "From mobilization to political conflict." Unpublished manuscript, Department of Sociology, University of Michigan, Ann Arbor.

—— (1969) "Collective violence in European perspective." In H. D. Graham and T. R. Gurr (eds.) Violence in America: Historical and Comparative Perspectives. New York: Signet.

—— (1964) The Vendée. Cambridge, Mass.: Harvard University Press.

——, L. TILLY, and R. TILLY (1975) The Rebellious Century: 1830–60, Cambridge, Mass.: Harvard University Press.

TROTSKY, L. (1959) The Russian Revolution. F. W. Dupee (ed.) Garden City, N.Y.: Doubleday-Anchor.

TUCHMAN, G. (Forthcoming) Telling Stories: The Social Construction of News as Knowledge. New York: Free Press.

—— (1972) "Objectivity as strategic ritual." American Journal of Sociology 77, 4:660–79.

TURNER, R. H. (1972) "Determinants of social movement strategies." In T. Shibutani (ed.) Human Nature and Collective Behavior, pp. 145–64. Englewood Cliffs, N.J.: Prentice-Hall.

—— (1969) "The public perception of protest." American Sociological Review 34:815–31.

UDY, S. H., JR. (1965) "The comparative analysis of organizations." In J. G. March (ed.) Handbook of Organizations, pp. 678–709. Chicago: Rand McNally.

URBAN AMERICA, INC., AND THE URBAN COALITION (1969) One Year Later. New York: Praeger.

USEEM, M. (1975) Protest Movements in America. Indianapolis: Bobbs-Merrill.

—— (1973) Conscription, Protest, and Social Conflict. New York: John Wiley.

VIORST, M. (1976) "FBI mayhem." New York Review of Books 22 (18 March).

VON HOFFMAN, N. (1977) Washington Post (8 August).

WALL, R. (1972) "Special agent for the FBI." New York Review of Books (27 January).

WALSH, R. (1959) Charleston's Sons of Liberty. Columbia: University of South Carolina Press.

WANDERER, J. J. (1968) "1967 riots: a test of the congruity of events." Social Problems 16 (Fall): 193–98.

WASHINGTON POST (1975) 19 November.

WELLER, J. M., and E. L. QUARANTELLI (1973) "Neglected characteristics of collective behavior." American Journal of Sociology 79 (November): 665–85.

WERNETTE, D. R. (1977) "Collective action and collective goods." Unpublished manuscript, Department of Sociology, Kean College of New Jersey.

WHITE, L. (1976) "Rational theories of participation." Journal of Conflict Resolution 20, 2:255–77.

WILSNACK, R. (1977) "Information control: a conceptual framework for sociological analysis." Paper presented at 1977 American Sociological Association Meeting.

WILSON, J. (1977) "Social protest and social control." Social Problems 24 (April): 469–481.

———— (1973) Introduction to Social Movements. New York: Basic Books.

WILSON, J. Q. (1973) Political Organizations. New York: Basic Books.

———— (1961) "The strategy of protest: problems of Negro civic action." Journal of Conflict Resolution 5:291–303.

WILSON, K. L., and A. ORUM (1976) "Mobilizing people for collective political action." Journal of Political and Military Sociology 4 (Fall): 187–202.

WISE, D. (1976) The American Police State. New York: Random House.

————, and T. ROSS (1974) The Invisible Government. New York: Random House.

WOOD, G. S. (1966) "A note on mobs in the American revolution." William and Mary Quarterly, 3d ser. 23:635–42.

YOUNG, A. F. (1973) "Pope's day, tar and feathers, and 'cornet joyce, jun.' from ritual to rebellion in Boston, 1745–1775." Paper presented to the Anglo-American Labor Historians' Conference, Rutgers University.

———— (1976) "Afterword." In A. F. Young (ed.) The American Revolution. DeKalb: Northern Illinois University Press.

ZALD, M. N., and J. D. McCARTHY (1975) "Organizational intellectuals and the criticism of society." Social Service Review 49 (September): 344–62.

————, and R. ASH (1966) "Social movement organizations: growth, decay and change." Social Forces 44 (March): 327–41.

————, and P. DENTON (1963) "From evangelism to general service: on the transformation of the YMCA." Administrative Science Quarterly 82 (September): 214–34.

Notes on Contributing Authors

Bruce Fireman is a sociologist at the Center for Research on Social Organization of the University of Michigan. He is currently working on an experimental study of rebellion in small group encounters with evil authorities and on a study of reform movements in Massachusetts from 1815 to 1860.

Jo Freeman is spending the year as a Brookings Staff Associate in Employment Policy, where she will be working on a research and development strategy to increase the employment opportunities of women. She is the author of *The Politics of Women's Liberation: A Case Study of an Emerging Social Movement and Its Relation to the Policy Process* (McKay, 1975), which won a prize given by the American Political Science Association, and the editor of *Women: A Feminist Perspective* (Mayfield, 1975).

William A. Gamson is Professor of Sociology at the University of Michigan and a staff member of the Center for Research on Social Organization. His most recent book is *The Strategy of Social Protest*, a study of the careers of a sample of challenging groups in American society from 1800 to 1945. He is currently engaged in research on micro-mobilization episodes.

William R. Kelly is Assistant Professor of Sociology in the Department of Sociology, University of Texas at Austin. Current research interests include the consequences of collective violence and the relation between modernization and population change. Recent publications appear in the *American Journal of Sociology, American Sociological Review, Demography,* and *Comparative Studies in Sociology,* ed. R. Tomasson.

John Lofland is Professor of Sociology at the University of California, Davis, and founding editor of *Urban Life: A Journal of Ethnographic Research.* His most recent publications include *Doing Social Life, State Executions* (with H. Bleackley), *Social Strategies* (editor), and an enlarged edition of *Doomsday Cult.* He is currently researching demonstrations at the California State Capitol.

John D. McCarthy is Associate Professor of Sociology and research associate, Boys Town Center for the Study of Youth Development, at the Catholic University of America in Washington, D.C. His research interests include the development of modern social movement organizations and the comparative study of self-esteem and behavior among ethnic youth.

Gary T. Marx, Professor of Sociology at MIT, spent 1977–78 teaching at the University of California, San Diego, in the departments of sociology and political science. His paper is one of a series of essays focusing on the interdependence between those who enforce the law and those who break it. The most recent of these essays is "The New Police Undercover Work," *Civil Liberties Review,* July/August 1977.

Harvey Molotch is Professor of Sociology at the University of California at Santa Barbara, where he carries out research on mass media, population change, and community power. His most recent work includes *The Effects of Urban Growth* (Praeger, 1977).

Anthony Oberschall, Professor at Vanderbilt University, has also taught at Harvard, Columbia, UCLA, and Yale. He was a Guggenheim fellow in 1975–76. He continues researching and writing about social movements, conflict, and conflict regulation and has also been studying social change in Subsaharan Africa, in particular Uganda, Zambia, and Zaire.

Charles Perrow is Professor of Sociology, State University of New York at Stony Brook. He received his Ph.D. from Berkeley and has taught at the universities of Michigan, Pittsburgh, and Wisconsin and held visiting appointments at Berkeley and London Business School. He is the author of numerous articles and four books on organizations. In addition to directing a study of insurgency in the United States since 1950, he is planning a volume titled "A Society of Organizations."

David Snyder is Associate Professor of Sociology at Indiana University. He has recently written or coauthored articles on industrial strike activity, collective violence, and the measurement of conflict data, which have appeared in the *American Sociological Review, American Journal of Sociology,* and other journals.

Charles Tilly is Professor of Sociology, Professor of History, and Director of the Center for Research on Social Organization, University of Michigan, as well as Directeur d'Etudes Associe, Ecole des Hautes Etudes en Sciences Sociales (Paris). His research deals mainly with urbanization, industrialization, and political change. His most recent books are *An Urban World* (1974), *Strikes in France* (with Edward Shorter, 1974), *The Formation of National States in Western Europe* (editor and coauthor, 1975), *The Rebellious Century* (with Louise Tilly and Richard Tilly, 1975), *From Mobilization to Revolution* (1977), and *Historical Studies of Changing Fertility* (editor and coauthor, 1977).

Mayer N. Zald is Professor of Sociology and Social Work at the University of Michigan. His publications include *Social Welfare Institutions: A Sociological Reader, Organizational Change: The Political Economy of the YMCA,* and numerous books and articles on political sociology, social control of institutions, and organizations.

Index

A

Action, group
  analysis, 225
  broad constituency of, 224
  ecology, build-up in, 222
  incentives needed for, 11
  mobilization of, 18
  repertoire of, 132
  systematic goals of, 224
Activists. *See also* American Revolution
  tion
  concrete goals, need for, 73
  FBI accusations of, 103
  full-time, 67
  government harassment of, 99–103
  mass media, use of, 72, 77
  names for, 117
  protest, methods of, 127
Actors
  action, commitment to, 17
  advertisement of selective incentives, 12
  authorities, interplay with, 135
  collective action, 42, 134
  collective good, 18, 43
  as decision makers, 19
  in conflict with solidarity, 25
  definition of, 11
  effective mobilization of, 16
  effect of group gain on, 15
  as free riders, 15
  group assessment by, 18
  influence demonstrated, 24, 30
  and mobilization, 13, 18, 25
  news media, use of, 74

participation, basis of, 19
repertoire, change in, 134
self-interest of, 11
training of, 165
trust, loss of, 28, 29
utilitarian approach of, 21
Advertisers
  influence on news media, 83
  as resource, 201
Affluence, 206
Agnew, Spiro, 97
Agreement
  concessions to, 50
  conciliation, goal of, 8
Albertson, William. *See* Communist party
Alinsky, S., 22–30, 226
American Civil Liberties Union (ACLU), 59, 175
American Indian Movement, 194
American Revolution
  armed forces, seizure of ships, 128
  authority, respect for, 141
  Boston Tea Party, 127
  British as advocate of, 146
  British government, 127
  collective action in, 128–30, 139–40
  colonists, 128
  demonstrations, use of, 129–31
  effigies, use of, 129, 130
  gatherings, 140, 141
  government, beginnings of, 127
  growth of, 140
  Guy Fawkes' Day, 129
  protest, changing forms of, 137, 138
  recruitment of personnel, 129

American Revolution (*cont.*)
  repertoire of action, effect on, 136
  town meetings, 128
American trade, tariff, 142
Amnesty, IRA, 55
Antagonists, in nonconventional con-
    flict, 47
Ash, Roberta, 183, 217
Authorities
  actors, interplay with, 135
  and collective welfare, 63
  constitutional constraint of, 58
  power, decline of, 32
  pressure of nonconventional con-
    flict, 47
  privileged target, protect by, 47
  as problem in mobilization, 28
  social control policy of, 10
  undermining of trust in, 29

B

Backlash, black, white, 208
Bargaining
  in American Revolution, 130
  beginnings of, 134
  bureaucracy in, 244
  challengers of authority, 67
  negotiation by, 46
  by organizers, 24
  threat to, 29
Barker, Bernard, 105
Bay of Pigs, 109
Beneficiaries, political, 174
Berk, Richard A., 226
Berkowitz, Leonard, 215
Berman, J., 100, 101, 104
Bienen, Henry, 213, 214, 229
Bill of Rights, 95
Black, Eugene, 146
Black Muslims, 104
Black Panthers
  factors in success of, 121
  FBI discreditation of, 98
  FBI involvement in, 104
  influence of media on, 81
  self-defense of, 82

Blacks. *See also* Civil rights movement
  backlash to movement, 66
  gains of, 66
  power demands of, 208
  presidential election, role in, 208
  race consciousness of, 65
  riots, analysis of, 65
  violence of, 213
  and whites, 46
Blue collar worker, 207
Blumenthal, M. D., 212
Blumer, H., 159
Bookin, H., 161
Boston, 140
Boston Gazette, 137, 138
Boston Tea Party. *See* American Rev-
    olution
Boycott
  of bus, 170, 202
  and decision making, 170
  free riders in, 17
  revolt, as method of, 128
  strategy of, 170, 186
Britain, government
  French and Indian War, 138
  history of social protest, 144
  Stamp Act, 138, 139
Brown, Roger, 64
Bundy, McGeorge, 241
Bureaucracy, 244
Business firms, 8, 14
Bystander, public, 187, 188

C

Cambodia, 163
Camden draft board raid, 118
Campus protest, 199
Capitalism, 201, 208
Caplan, Nathan, 215
Carter, Jimmy, 91
Castell, Manuel, 207
Catholics, 46
Central Intelligence Agency (CIA)
  DPs, funding of, 161
  manipulation of media, 98
  personnel after retirement, 116

Central Intelligence Agency (*cont.*)
  social movements, aid to, 197
Challenger
  choice of confrontation by, 52
  coercion tactics of, 46, 60
  collective good, as producers of, 56
  conciliation, danger to, 51
  costs and benefits of, 48, 52–54, 59
  effect of prolonged conflict on, 50,
    67
  exchange unlikely, 46
  funding, 57
  in informal organizations, 64
  mechanics of, 48
  nuisance power of, 60
  organization of, 62
  resources of, 58
  size, effect on, 59, 60
  social control, effect on, 50
  support, outside, 60
  tactics of, 131
  target groups, repression by, 47
Chang, Rev. Soon Sun, 158
Change, social
  determinants of, 216
  multidimensionality of, 225, 234
  racial violence in, 213–16, 233
  youth culture in, 197
Churches, 204
Civil rights movement
  antagonism toward women's move-
    ment, 180, 181
  beginnings of, 194
  blacks in, 202, 208
  and black youth, 65
  bus boycott by, 202
  churches, mobilization of, 202
  coercive pressure, decline of, 66
  conciliation of, 62
  federal legislation in, 205
  government organization of, 244
  institutions, mobilization of, 175,
    202
  job discrimination, 175
  King, Jr., Martin L., 65
  as loose organization, 63
  old guard, engulfment of, 203
  philanthropy in, 204

political realignment in, 202
public bystander as supporter of,
  188
reasons for joining, 14
rioting, decline of, 66
role of personal experiences in, 180
scope of, 62
sit-ins, 170, 175
southern black as primary beneficiary, 64
spread of, 180
success of, 120
tactics of, 62, 181
violence pattern in, 201, 226
and war, 199
and younger women's movement,
  108, 184
Clark, Terry N., 226
COINTELL
  approval by Hoover, 115
  creation, reasons for, 112
  FBI, actions in, 119
  social movement, facilitation of, 106
Collective action
  in American Revolution, 128–31,
    139–40
  and anti-Catholicism, 146
  assembling workers, 222
  authority, petitioning through, 141
  bargaining power of, 59
  blocking of, 25
  challenger, size of, 59, 60
  changes in, 152
  and constituents, 32
  coordination of, 221
  costs and gains of, 33, 65, 135
  courses of action, alternatives to, 29
  credibility of, 30, 31
  culture, influence on, 32
  ecological analysis of, 222, 226
  events, as determinant of outcome,
    30, 229
  factors leading to, 14
  flexibility in, 132
  free riders, 17
  French and Indian War, during, 137
  funding of, 58
  goals, determination of, 226

Collective action (*cont.*)
  group repertoire, effect on, 135
  history of in Britain, 135
  informal organization in, 19
  inventory, importance of, 136
  intervention, use of misinformation, 105
  measurement, types of, 227
  mobilization in, 45
  necessity of, 29
  news media as source of information, 232
  nonparticipation in, 18
  opposition to, 25
  organization of, 23, 225
  parallel, British and American, 153, 154
  popular ideas concerning, 131
  public occasions, use of, 141
  repertoire of, 131
  repression, influence on, 135
  research, methods of, 231
  resource building of, 217, 218
  riots in, 65, 145
  scab workers, and, 35
  Stamp Act, effect on, 131, 138–39
  street theater in Britain, 145
  time element in, 28, 41, 64
  violence in, 214
  waning of, 223
Collective good
  actors, mobilization facilitated by, 18
  benefits of, 53
  conciliation, cost of, 51
  constituents' interest in, 28
  definition of, 26
  as entitlement, 26
  mobilization by groups for, 13
  and selective incentives, 33
  winning of, 23
College enrollment, 197, 198
Colby, William, 98
Communes, 187
Communication, 201
Communist party
  Albertson, William, 103
  factors in success of, 121

FBI pressure on, 77, 98
  Hoover's assessment of, 114, 115
  and news media, 83
Conciliation
  benefits and costs of, 50, 59
  in collective action, 60
  defined, 48
  difficulties from prolonged conflict, 50, 51
  in informal groups, 64
  need for mutual trust, 51
  outside support, effect on, 60
Conflict
  nonconventional, 46, 51, 66
  protracted, problems of, 50, 51
  support, outside of, 60
Confrontation
  civil rights movement, 62
  costs of, 46, 57
  in group conflict, 45
Congress, 62
Constituency
  conscience of, 174
  free riding, handled by, 18
  as a solidarity group, 21, 23
  structure of, 24
Constituent
  actor, estimate of, 17, 30
  collective bad and good, 17, 18
  common interests of, 24
  mobilization dedicated to, 28, 157
  potential resources of, 10
Control, social
  agencies of, 58, 105–13
  challenger, effect on, 50
  dimensions of, 58
  as embarrassment, 48
  nonauthoritarian, 7
Congress of Racial Equality (CORE), 175
Corporations, 114
County and City Data Book, 232
Cuba, 108, 203
Culture
  change in, 197
  as factor in mobilization, 32
  responsibility instilled by, 32
Currie, Elliott, 215

D

Davis, Angela, 85
Davies, James C., 21
Decision making
  actors, 11
  challengers, 48
  "Get Oil Out" activists, 72
  group ability in, 207
  organizations, 11, 19
  strategy of, 170
  target groups, 48
  women's liberation organization, 169
Dellinger, Dave, 81
Democratic party
  and black power, 208
  effect on civil rights movement, 196
Demography, 196
Demonstrations
  in American Revolution, 129, 130
  antiwar, 16, 105
  civil rights, 186
  free riders to, 16
  mass, decline of, 111
  nonconventional conflict, use in, 47
  Wilkite group in England, 146
  women's liberation movement, 178
Diamond, Sigmund, 241
Donner, F., 104
Donovan, J. C., 99
Downs, Anthony, 193
DPs
  Chang, Soon Sun, leader, 160
  commitment, full time to, 160
  decline of in U.S.A., 164
  early movement in U.S.A., 158
  evangelists of, 160
  funding, 161
  goals of, 158
  missionaries, Japanese, 160
  organization, methods of, 150
  peak of, 164
  productivity tactics of, 161
  rallies of, 158
  recruitment of, 162, 163
Draft, 199

Dugway proving grounds, 84
Durkheim, E., 117

E

Economics
  and American Revolution, 128
  and capitalism, 207
  conceptual imagery of, 8
  in early U.S.A., 142
  input-output in, 200
  and resource mobilization, 201
  resources, theory of, 20
Eckstein, Harry, 213
Effigies, 130
Eisenhower, Dwight D., 205
Ellsberg, Daniel, 105
Employers
  as problem in mobilization, 28
  stand toward unions, 12
Entrepreneurs
  as organizers of collective action, 19
  in social movement organizations, 245
Environment, 209
Equality in women's movement, 178
Erickson, K., 117

F

Farm workers, 209, 210
Federal Bureau of Investigation (FBI)
  changing role of, 111–13
  COINTELL, actions in, 119
  Communist party, discreditation by, 97, 98
  definition of self, 113
  growth of, 114
  influence on media, 97, 98
  Operation Hoodwink, 104
  personnel, retirement of, 116
  as social movement deterrent, 99–104
Feagin, Joe R., 213
Fishman, Mark, 76

Flacks, Richard, 197, 205
Fogelson, Robert M., 191, 226
Fonda, Jane, 98, 201
Ford Foundation, 100
Ford, Gerald, 173
Foundations, 204
Fraternal orders, 34
Freeman, J., 120, 194, 238, 244
Free riders
    in collective action struggle, 17
    in informal organization, 19
    and mobilization, 39
    norms, violation of, 17
    as problem for organizers, 16
    protests, loosely structured, 63
    tolerance of, 17
    and utilitarian approach, 15
Freedom of Information Act, 107
"Freedom Ride," 186
French and Indian War, 137–38
Freud, Sigmund, 201
Frohlich, N. J., 19
Funding
    by collective action, 58
    decline in, 204
    free riders in, 15
    institutional philanthropy in, 204
    mobilization for, 165
    peddling by individual DPs, 161
    persuasion, types of, 19
    of social movements, 158
    strategic interaction with, 57

G

Gamson, W. A., 17, 187, 196, 200,
    239, 243
Gatherings
    changes in, 136, 137
    decline of, 150
    as means of protest, 136
    purpose, 140
Gay rights movement, 186
Gerlach, L. P., 181, 187
Goals
    achieve as recruiting tool, 217
    attainability of, 30

centralized movement in, 183
conflict, nonconventional form of,
    46
determination of, 225, 226
government, changing aid to, 244
interaction, 22
of organized bargaining, 24
resource mobilization in, 217
short and long term, 219
women's movement organization,
    young and old, 184
Government
    as cooperative institution, 175
    extensions of, 95
    foreign, 108
    intervention, 110, 118, 120
    policy change, 10
    social control, 123
    social movement, aid to, 105–107
    support, reasons for, 106–108
    U.S.A., birth of, 140
Goulden, J., 100
Graber, E., 114
Graham, Billy, 105
Great Britain, 147
Grievances
    manufacture of, 200
    shared, redress of, 10
Group
    actors' assessment of, 15
    common identity of, 21
    interests, subjective of, 24
    solidarity, 22, 23, 24, 25, 36,
        170
Gurr, T. R., 187, 215
Guy Fawkes' Day, 129

H

Hahn, Harlin, 213
Halperin, M., 100, 101, 104, 115
Hancock, R. R., 241
Hardy, Robert, 118
Hibbs, Douglas A., 230
Hierarchy
    DPs, organizational power of, 160
    in social movement, 169

Hierarchy (*cont.*)
  in women's liberation movement, 177
Hill, Richard C., 237, 238
Hine, V. W., 187
Hirschman, A. O., 32
Hodge, Robert W., 232
Hoerder, Dick, 127
Hoover, J. Edgar
  actions by, 110
  assessment of Communist party, 114, 115
  attack and praise of, 109, 110
  COINTELL, approval of, 115
  power, desire for, 114, 115
  protest, plan of action against, 105, 106
  and social movements, 104
Human rights, 145
Huston Plan, 112
Hutchinson, Governor, 127

I

Ideology
  affluence, effect on, 206
  in collective action, 16
  and organizational structure change, 184
  strategy, determined by, 1, 2
  youth, protest by, 199
Incentives
  collective good, common stake in, 19
  cost of collective action, 33
  definition of, 10
  entrepreneurs, political, 18
  groups, antiwar, 33
  material and nonmaterial, 21
  mobilization, as explanation of, 34
  money as, 20
  resources, 19, 22
  utilitarian theory of, 21
Individual action
  cost of, 53, 54
  difficulty in pooling resources, 9
  gain in loosely structured movement, 66
  and ideological analysis, 27
Individual interests, relationship with actors, 16
Individual rights, protection of, 58
Indochina, 53
Industry, and social movement, 242
Inflation
  ineffectiveness of individual against, 16
  in U.S.A., 204
Influence, as resource, 173
Institutions, as mobilization resource, 174
Insurgency
  control of movements of, 207
  prediction of, 210
Interests
  as aids in mobilizing, 14
  common consciousness of, 9
  group action of, 8
  objectives, change in, 10
  protection of, 29
Internal Revenue Service, 111
IRA
  benefits, problems of attaining, 54
  conflict, benefits from, 55
  individual incentives of, 54, 55
  organizational structure of, 63
  revival of, 50
  tactics, change in, 55

J

Janowitz, M., 241
Jenkins, J. Craig, 193, 245
Job market, student movement in, 208
John Birch Society, 110
Johnson, Chalmers, 215
Johnson, Lyndon
  determination to link social movements, 114
  intervention in social affairs, 115, 116
  use of labeling by, 86, 97

K

Kelly, William R., 215, 216, 225, 232
Keniston, Kenneth, 202, 205
Kent State, 163
Kerr, Clark, 215
King, Jr., Martin L. *See also* Civil
   rights movement
   assassination of, 65
   decline of movement, 90
   discredit, campaign to, 102
   media coverage of, 97
   northern support, loss of, 90
Korean War, 199
Ku Klux Klan
   factors in success of, 121
   FBI and, 101, 119, 120
   police aid to, 107

L

Labor
   analysis of disputes, 225
   mobilization by business firms, 14
   strikes, use of, 186
Law
   discriminatory practices of, 182
   social control, as means of, 44, 58
Lazersfeld, P. F., 241
Leadership
   action of, 24
   in civil rights movement, 202
   in women's liberation movement,
     178
Leap frogging, as means of funding,
   162
Lee, Yoon Sook, 158
Lenin, Joseph, 202
Liberty tree, in American Revolution,
   127, 128
Lipsky, Michael, 212, 226
Lobbies
   mobilization of, 8
   pay to, 17
   strategy of NOW, 179, 184
London, 145, 150, 151
Long, Huey, 122
Lowi, T. J., 244

M

Maier, Pauline, 130
Malcolm X, 104
Marcuse, Herbert, 85
Mass society theory, 25
Marx, Gary, 54, 195, 213–17, 240
Marx, Karl, 202
Masotti, Louis H., 213, 223, 227
McAdam, Douglas, 202
McCarthyism
   government aid to, 107
   social movement, pressure on, 100
McCarthy, John, 8, 9, 11, 94, 117,
   157, 174, 200, 215, 242, 244
McCarthy, Joseph, 194
McPhail, Clark, 215, 222, 231
Media, mass
   and black rioting, 65
   control of, 75
   ruling class, 76
   and social movement, 71, 238
   use of in recruitment, 239
Media, news
   advertisers, influence of, 83
   bias of, 87
   civil rights movement, 89
   DPs, unfavorable to, 164
   government use of, 96–97
   journalistic responsibility of, 85, 86
   as morale booster, 77
   newsmen's own interest in, 76, 84
   protest, importance in, 142
   as social force, 58, 75, 205
   war, use in, 137, 138
Meetings, as means of protest, 144
Meiji restoration, 224
Militancy
   of social movement organizations,
     194
   of teachers, 199
Millenarian movement, 158
Miller, David L., 222, 231
Milling, 64
Mitchell, John, 243
Mobilization
   benefits to potental constituents, 9
   conflict dynamics of, 45

Mobilization (*cont.*)
  costs of, 57
  DPs in U.S.A. *See* DPs
  host society of, 157
  of opponents, 241
  organizational structure, limited by, 169
  of participants, 222
  passim, 14–15
  research study of, 219, 227
  social movement goals, 238
Montagu, Admiral, 125
Moon, Reverend, 108, 123
Morgan, William R., 226
Moslems, 46
Movement, mass
  benefits, pyramidal, 34
  churches, involvement in, 204
Movement, social
  decision making in, 207
  decruitment of, 99–102
  discontent of 1970s, 163
  FBI, harassment by, 105
  government in, 95, 55–103, 106, 110–13, 116–18, 123
  hierarchy of, 169
  internal conflict in, 103
  internal forces of, 94
  leaders, 202
  mobilization, early problems of, 34
  news coverage of, 77
  prosperity, effect on, 204
  radicals in, 207
  research of, 10
  resources, 157
  strategy, 186
  strikes, 105
  timing of, 165
  trends of, 200
  violence in, 213
  Vietnam war, 199
Movement, student
  beginnings of, 194
  counterculture, 208
  demise, reasons for, 196
  followers, role of, 198
  old guard, engulfment of, 203
  philanthropy in, 204

Vietnam war, 198
Moynihan, Daniel, 14
Mueller, Carol, 212

N

Nader, Ralph, 107, 186
Namath, Joe, 201
National Advisory Committee, 226, 229
National Association for the Advancement of Colored People (NAACP), 121, 175
National Liberation Front, South Vietnam, 51, 63
National Organization of Women (NOW). *See* Women's movement
Nee, George, 23
Negotiation
  problems of, 50, 51
  by target group, 47
Neighborhoods, 64
New Left, 113
Newton, Huey, 81, 82
New York Annual Index, 193
New York Times, 101, 118
Niles' Register, 142
Nixon administration, 209
Nixon, Richard
  intervention in social affairs, 115, 116
  labeling by, 96, 97
  protests of 1960s, 206

O

Oberschall, A., 8, 9, 195, 200, 206, 215, 217, 222, 226, 238, 241
Office of Economic Opportunity, 99
Olson, Mancur, 8, 9, 11–22, 132
O. M. Collective, 30
Operation Hoodwink, 104
Organization
  as actor, 19
  benefits, use of common, 34
  change, internal, 153

Organization (*cont.*)
collective good, struggle for, 11
communal, 10
competition, 12
decision making, 11
ideology, 167
interactions of, 242
loose structure, black riots as, 64
members, social control of, 19
power of, 16, 146
program, concrete, 24
resources of, 18, 62, 182
strategy of, 30
Organizational structure
changes in, 183
classic model of, 183
and collective action, 225
communications in, 169
in literature, 182
political action of, 186
social groups, strength of, 121
of women's liberation movement,
168
Organizers
collective actors, 11
passim, 18–33
strategy of, 10

P

Paine, Thomas, 146
Palestine Liberation Front, 51
Palestinians, 56
Perrow, Charles, 193, 244, 245
Philanthropy, 204
Planters' Protective Association, 17
Political action
lack of opportunity for, 18
redefinement of, 186
women's movement organization,
183
Political economy, 33
Political freedom, 20
Political science, 163
Politics
and collective change, 225

effects of discontent, 164
protest, type of, 200
religion, disguised as, 164
resource limitations of, 201
role in social movement organizations, 218, 244
violence in, 216
Politicians, as resourceful actors, 18
Pope's Day. *See* Guy Fawkes' Day
Population
determinant of collective action, 135
importance of youth, 196, 197
Power
of the challenger, 59
constituent, gain of, 32
development of, 30
methods of increasing, 50
news media, 76
resource, 200, 219
structure, change in, 142
third party support, 62
women's liberation organization,
169
Propaganda
as means of advertising movements,
12
news media, acceptance of, 78
Protestants, 46
Protests
American Revolution, 126, 127
antiwar, 104–105
costs of loosely organized structure,
64
diversity of issues, 194
of farm workers, 194, 199
internal forces behind, 153
London as center of, 150
as political process, 200
resources of, 200
restrictions by police, 105
social movement organizations, 217
strategy, effective, 186
student involvement in, 170
Public bystander, as third party, 187
Publicity
DP movement, 159
resource, 170

Q

Quarantelli, E. L., 222

R

Race. *See also* King, Jr., Martin L.
  crisis, reaction to, 211
  disorder, 226, 231, 232
  violence, 214
Radicals
  funding by foundations, 209
  student, decline of, 120
  and women's organization, 180, 181
Rap group, 180, 182
Reagan, Ronald, 173
Rebellion, 215
Recession, 203, 209
Recruitment
  goal achievement of, 217
  group, 239
  in organizations, 182, 188
  success of strategy, 217
Reformers, 19, 200, 205
Reich, Charles, 205
Religion, 114, 163–65
Repression, 134–36, 209
Resources
  changing uses of, 219
  collective action, 218
  economics of, 200
  government power as, 200, 243, 244
  influence as, 173
  institutions as, 174
  from older movements, 172
  participants as, 173, 195
  political factors of, 201
  professional mobilization of, 170, 200
  strategies of, 27
  time as, 186
  youth movement as approach to, 193
Revere, Paul, 128
Revolution
  American, 127

attainment, means of, 182
  collective action in, 131
  definitions of, 224
  goals, 167
  problems of, 18
  tactics, 131, 180
  violence, change to, 213
  women's movement, desire for, 181
Rhodesia
  1976 Geneva Conference, 50
  whites, 57
Riots
  analyses of, 65
  black, 64, 65
  cost of, 65, 66
  food, in Britain, 144
  political action, as form of, 186
  process of, 226
Roosevelt, Franklin, 115, 116
Ross, D. K., *quoted*, 30
ROTC, 206
Roszak, Theodore, 197
Russell, D. E., 214, 218, 228
Russian trade unions, 108
Rustin, Bayard, 202
Ryder, Norman, 196, 197

S

Sale, Kirkpatrick, 196, 245
Santa Barbara Oil Spill, 84
Schattschneider, E. E., 31, 185
Schelling, T., 50
Schumpeter, J. A., 245
Select Committee, 110, 113
Scab labor
  and unions, 12
  utilitarian logic of, 35
Shorter, Edward, 230
Sit-ins, 175, 202
Skolnick, Jerome, 215
Smelser, Neil, 215
Smith, Ian, 50
Smith, W. A., 145
Snow, D. A., 240

Snyder, David, 213, 216, 219, 226, 228, 230, 232
Social clubs, 34
Socialist Workers party
    goals of, 167
    recruitment of, 104
    repression of by FBI, 115, 119
Social movement organizations, 194–98, 217–19
    challenges, scope of, 62
    collective action in, 222
    control of, 240
    costs, reduction of, 33
    decision making in, 170
    entrepreneurs in, 245
    environment, role of, 242
    framework, analysis of, 222
    free riders, handled by, 18
    goals of women's liberation, 184
    news media, use of, 91, 92
    opposition, importance of, 181
    political position of, 186, 218
    power, use of, 35, 219, 241
    pressure, outside, 221
    pyramidal effect of, 176
    relations of interorganizations, 243
    and societal structure, 238
    strategy of, 185
    and urban areas, 212, 213
    Vietnam, impact on, 194
    youth involvement in, 176, 192, 197
Solidarity, among underprivileged groups, 63
Sons of Liberty, 128, 141
South Carolina Gazette, 137–39
Southshore, Chicago integration blockage, 72
Southern Christian Leadership Conference (SCLC), 172
Southern Farmers' Alliance, 241
Soviets, and social control, 58, 59
Spilerman, Seymour, 65, 227, 231, 233
Stallings, Robert, 242
Stamp Act, 138, 139
Strategy
    bystander public, use in, 188
    in collective action research, 228, 229

cost of, 221
determination of, 167
impact of, 196
of recruitment, 217
results of, 217
of social movement organizations, 185, 216, 238
use of resources, 182
use of sympathy, 245
violence in, 213
Street theater, 143–45
Strikes
    authorities, position of, 134–35
    beginnings of, 150
    changing tactics of, 219
    free riders in, 17
    history of, 134
    protest as legal form, 134–35
    as strategy, 186
Students for Democratic Society (SDS). See Movement, student
Swartz, Michael, 241

T

Target group
    attack by challengers, 46, 59
    cost of conciliation, 48, 59, 64
    gain and loss, 48, 57
    in informal structure, 64
    and outside support, 62
    pressure on, 46
    resources of, 58
    sabotage of, 104–106
    social control, effect on, 50
    strategy interaction in success of, 57
    women's liberation movement, older groups, 182
Tariff, economics of, 142
Theil, H., 228
Third party, 31
Thompson, E. P., 144
Tilly, C., 8, 169, 200, 212, 215, 220, 228, 230, 241
Time, as resource, 173
Times Index, 194

Tinkertown, 160
Tobacco night riders, 14
Town meetings, 137
Transportation, 201
Trotsky, L., 31

U

Uglow, David, 202
Underground press, 178
Unemployment, 14
Unions
  farm workers, 210
  as mobilizing agent, 17
  scab labor, 12
  social movement involvement, 204
  struggles to establish, 12
  work week reduction, effect on, 34
  World War II, effect on, 21
United Fruit Company, 108
United States
  collective action, changes in, 144
  ground troops in Indochina, 53
Urban areas, 213
Useem, Michael, 215
Utilitarian approach
  free rider, 16
  solidarity in, 21

V

Vietnam war
  coed protest of, 199
  college deferment in, 199
  denunciation of by Martin L. King,
    90
  opposition to, 101
  rise of militancy during, 194
Violence
  in American Revolution, 130, 140
  analysis of, 216, 232
  collective goals of, 222, 223
  demography of, 227
  disorganization in, 215
  French and Indian War, 137
  frustration as factor in, 215, 216

grievances as cause of, 226
individuals in, 215
news media bias of, 225, 226
outcome of, 215, 216, 227
racial disorder in cities, 212, 232
research model of, 219
resource mobilization theory, 213,
  233
and social change, 233
as tactic, 196, 214
termination of, 213, 223
Vigilantes
  in American colonies, 130, 138
  and collective action, 131
Viorst, M., 104

W

Wallace, George, 66
Wanderer, Jules J., 228
War
  French and Indian, 137–38
  internal effects of, 195, 213
  on poverty, 106, 176, 205, 208
  protest, effect on, 199
  World War II, 202
Watergate, 111, 116
Weatherman
  beginning of, 179, 196
  "days of rage," 179
  revolutionary vanguard, 167
  tactics of, 179
Welfare, 204
Weller, Jack M., 222
Wernette, D. R., 27
White collar workers, 207
Wilkes, John, 145–46
Wilson, John, 240
Wise, D., 98, 102, 104
Witch hex, 178
Women's Equality Action League
  (WEAL), 168, 178, 180, 185
Women's liberation movement
  branches, diversified backgrounds
    of, 177
  decision making in, 169
  equality as goal, 177, 178

Women's liberation movement (*cont.*)
  generation gap in, 168
  hierarchy, lack of, 177
  history of, 168
  mass demonstration experience, 178
  offshoot of radical movements, 209
  organizational structure of, 160
  professional women in, 168
  two branches, comparison of, 176, 177
Women's movement
  beginnings of, 208
  continuation of, 206
  differences in younger and older groups, 183, 184
  government pressure on, 179
  lobbying of, 184
  National Women's Political Caucus, 184
  organizational structure of, 178
  political alignment of, 202
  rap group in, 182
  rights, 181, 208
  strategy of, 179
  target groups of, 182

  younger, 168, 169, 178, 180, 182, 184, 188
Wood, James L., 212, 213, 217

Y

Yippies, 27
Young, Andrew, 81
Youth culture
  demise of, 198, 199
  and social change, 163, 197, 199

Z

Zap action, 178
Zeitlin, Maurice, 85, 86
Zemurray, Samuel, 108
Zald, M. N., 8, 9, 94, 100, 117, 174, 175, 183, 200, 213, 242, 243